The Truth about Water Policies and Social Issues

The Truth about Water Policies and Social Issues

Maryam Noor
Amir Ansari

CYBER TECH PUBLICATIONS
4264/3, Ansari Road, Daryaganj, New Delhi-110002 (India)
Ph.: 011-23244078, 011-43559448 Fax: 011-23280028
E-Mail: cyberpublicationsdelhi@yahoo.com
Website: www.cybertechpublications.com

THE TRUTH ABOUT WATER POLICIES AND SOCIAL ISSUES

Maryam Noor
Amir Ansari

First Edition 2010

Asian Offset Printers

Published by :

G.S. Rawat for **Cyber Tech Publications**
4264/3, Ansari Road, Daryaganj, New Delhi-110002 (India)
Ph.: 011-23244078, 011-43559448 Fax: 011-23280028
E-Mail: cyberpublicationsdelhi@yahoo.com
Website: www.cybertechpublications.com

Preface

Urbanization is a reality of our changing world. In developing countries, the lack of job opportunities in rural areas, decline in subsistence economies, and hope of a better life have given rise to the modern megalopolis. Unfortunately, urban infrastructure, institutions, and the natural resource base are often inadequate to support these burgeoning populations. A central question worldwide is, "how can our cities be sustained under these circumstances?" Water, like air, is a vital resource without substitute. Its supply, allocation, and disposal present numerous challenges, all of which must be met to support these growing metropolitan regions.

Certainly there is no dearth of scientific research or policy initiatives in the fields of marine ecology, or human population, as independent fields of study. Yet while a significant body of knowledge exists on these subjects individually, little scientific research has been undertaken on them in relation to one another, as one discipline.

This requires factoring in land-use, social and economic aspects, especially in developing countries. Another conclusion is that complex problems can and must be posed and negotiated with the help of models, mapping techniques and science-based facts. However complex these may be, there are ways to translate them to easily interpretable and visualisations of alternative scenarios and courses of action. This book provides numerous examples of the potential of such approaches to draft environmental programmes solve transboundary disputes and reduce the economic consequences of droughts and climate instability.

—Author

Preface

CONTENTS

1

Introduction

Today, India ranks second worldwide in farm output. Agriculture and allied sectors like forestry, logging and fishing accounted for 16.6% of the GDP in 2007, employed 60% of the total workforce and despite a steady decline of its share in the GDP, is still the largest economic sector and plays a significant role in the overall socio-economic development of India.

India is the largest producer in the world of milk, cashew nuts, coconuts, tea, ginger, turmeric and black pepper. It also has the world's largest cattle population (193 million). It is the second largest producer of wheat, rice, sugar, groundnut and inland fish. It is the third largest producer of tobacco. India accounts for 10% of the world fruit production with first rank in the production of banana and sapota.

India has many farm insurance companies that insure wheat, fruit, rice and rubber farmers in the event of natural disasters or catastrophic crop failure, under the supervision of the Ministry of Agriculture. One notable company that provides all of these insurance policies is agriculture insurance company of india and it alone insures almost 20 million farmers.

India's population is growing faster than its ability to produce rice and wheat. The most important structural reform for self-sufficiency is the ITC Limited plan to connect 20,000 villages to the Internet by 2013.

This will provide farmers with up to date crop prices for the first time, which should minimise losses incurred from neighbouring producers selling early and in turn facilitate investment in rural areas.

OVERVIEW

India ranks second worldwide in farm output. Agriculture and allied sectors like forestry, logging and fishing accounted for 18% of the GDP in 2007, employed 60% of the total workforce and despite a steady decline of its share in the GDP, is still the largest economic sector and plays a significant role in the overall socio-economic development of India. Yields per unit area of all crops have grown since 1950, due to the special emphasis placed on agriculture in the five-year plans and steady improvements in irrigation, technology, application of modern agricultural practices and provision of agricultural credit and subsidies since Green revolution in India. However, international comparisons reveal that the average yield in India is generally 30% to 50% of the highest average yield in the world.

Indian Punjab is called the "Granary of India" or "India's bread-basket." It produces 14% of India's cotton, 20% of India's wheat, and 9% of India's rice.

Insurance

India has many farm insurance companies that insure wheat, fruit, rice and rubber farmers in the event of natural disasters or catastrophic crop failure, under the supervision of the Ministry of Agriculture. One notable company that provides all of these insurance policies is agriculture insurance company of india and it alone insures almost 20 million farmers.

INITIATIVES

The required level of investment for the development of marketing, storage and cold storage infrastructure is estimated to be huge. The government has implemented various schemes to raise investment in marketing infrastructure. Among these schemes are *Construction of Rural Go downs*, *Market Research and Information Network*, and *Development / Strengthening of Agricultural Marketing Infrastructure, Grading and Standardization*.

The Indian Agricultural Research Institute (IARI), established in 1905, was responsible for the research leading to the "Indian Green Revolution" of the 1970s. The Indian Council of Agricultural

Research (ICAR) is the apex body in agriculture and related allied fields, including research and education. The Union Minister of Agriculture is the President of the ICAR.

The Indian Agricultural Statistics Research Institute develops new techniques for the design of agricultural experiments, analyses data in agriculture, and specializes in statistical techniques for animal and plant breeding. Prof. M.S. Swaminathan is known as "Father of the Green Revolution" and heads the MS Swaminathan Research Foundation. He is known for his advocacy of environmentally sustainable agriculture and sustainable food security.

Problems

Slow agricultural growth is a concern for policymakers as some two-thirds of India's people depend on rural employment for a living. Current agricultural practices are neither economically nor environmentally sustainable and India's yields for many agricultural commodities are low. Poorly maintained irrigation systems and almost universal lack of good extension services are among the factors responsible. Farmers' access to markets is hampered by poor roads, rudimentary market infrastructure, and excessive regulation. —*World Bank: "India Country Overview 2008"*

The low productivity in India is a result of the following factors:

- According to World Bank's "India: Priorities for Agriculture and Rural Development", India's large agricultural subsidies are hampering productivity-enhancing investment. Overregulation of agriculture has increased costs, price risks and uncertainty. Government intervenes in labor, land, and credit markets. India has inadequate infrastructure and services. World Bank also says that the allocation of water is inefficient, unsustainable and inequitable. The irrigation infrastructure is deteriorating.
- Illiteracy, general socio-economic backwardness, slow progress in implementing land reforms and inadequate or inefficient finance and marketing services for farm produce.

- The average size of land holdings is very small (less than 20,000 m^2) and is subject to fragmentation, due to land ceiling acts and in some cases, family disputes. Such small holdings are often over-manned, resulting in disguised unemployment and low productivity of labour.
- Adoption of modern agricultural practices and use of technology is inadequate, hampered by ignorance of such practices, high costs and impracticality in the case of small land holdings.
- Irrigation facilities are inadequate, as revealed by the fact that only 52.6% of the land was irrigated in 2003–04, which result in farmers still being dependent on rainfall, specifically the Monsoon season. A good monsoon results in a robust growth for the economy as a whole, while a poor monsoon leads to a sluggish growth. Farm credit is regulated by NABARD, which is the statutory apex agent for rural development in the subcontinent.

HISTORY

Indian agriculture began by 9000 BCE as a result of early cultivation of plants, and domestication of crops and animals. Settled life soon followed with implements and techniques being developed for agriculture. Double monsoons led to two harvests being reaped in one year. Indian products soon reached the world via existing trading networks and foreign crops were introduced to India. Plants and animals—considered essential to their survival by the Indians—came to be worshiped and venerated. The middle ages saw irrigation channels reach a new level of sophistication in India and Indian crops affecting the economies of other regions of the world under Islamic patronage. Land and water management systems were developed with an aim of providing uniform growth. Despite some stagnation during the later modern era the independent Republic of India was able to develop a comprehensive agricultural program.

FORESTRY IN INDIA

Forestry is a major government enterprise in India which faces the challenges of dwindling forest cover area due to overpopulation, farming and environmental factors.

HISTORY

Some 500,000 square kilometres, about 17 percent of India's land area, were regarded as Forest Area in the early 1990s. In FY 1987, however, actual forest cover was 640,000 square kilometres. However, because more than 50 percent of this land was barren or bushland, the area under productive forest was actually less than 350,000 square kilometres, or approximately 10 percent of the country's land area. The growing population's high demand for forest resources continued the destruction and degradation of forests through the 1980s, taking a heavy toll on the soil. An estimated 6 billion tons of topsoil were lost annually. However, India's 0.6 percent average annual rate of deforestation for agricultural and non-lumbering land uses in the decade beginning in 1981 was one of the lowest in the world and on a par with Brazil. Sir Dietrich Brandis was a German forester who worked in India. He is considered the *Father of tropical forestry*.

Distribution

Many forests in the mid-1990s are found in high-rainfall, high-altitude regions, areas to which access is difficult. About 20 percent of total forestland is in Madhya Pradesh; other states with significant forests are Orissa, Maharashtra, and Andhra Pradesh (each with about 9 percent of the national total); Arunachal Pradesh (7 percent); and Uttar Pradesh (6 percent). The variety of forest vegetation is large: there are 600 species of hardwoods, sal (*Shorea robusta*) and teak being the principal economic species.

Strategy to Increase Cover

India's long-term strategy for forestry development reflects three major objectives: to reduce soil erosion and flooding; to supply the growing needs of the domestic wood products industries; and to supply the needs of the rural population for fuelwood, fodder, small timber, and miscellaneous forest produce. To achieve these objectives, the National Commission on Agriculture in 1976 recommended the reorganization of state forestry departments and advocated the concept of social forestry. The commission itself worked on the first two objectives, emphasizing traditional forestry and wildlife activities; in pursuit of the third objective, the commission recommended the establishment of a new kind of unit to develop community forests. Following the leads of Gujarat and Uttar Pradesh, a number of other states also established community-based forestry agencies that emphasized programs on farm forestry, timber management, extension forestry, reforestation of degraded forests, and use of forests for recreational purposes.

Such socially responsible forestry was encouraged by state community forestry agencies. They emphasized such projects as planting wood lots on denuded communal cattle-grazing grounds to make villages self-sufficient in fuelwood, to supply timber needed for the construction of village houses, and to provide the wood needed for the repair of farm implements. Both individual farmers and tribal communities were also encouraged to grow trees for profit. For example, in Gujarat, one of the more aggressive states in developing programs of socioeconomic importance, the forestry department distributed 200 million tree seedlings in 1983. The fast-growing eucalyptus is the main species being planted nationwide, followed by pine and poplar.

Conservation

The role of forests in the national economy and in ecology was further emphasized in the 1988 National Forest Policy, which focused on ensuring environmental stability, restoring the ecological balance, and preserving the remaining forests. Other objectives of the policy were meeting the need for fuelwood, fodder, and small timber for rural and tribal people while recognizing the need to actively involve local people in the management of forest resources.

Also in 1988, the Forest Conservation Act of 1980 was amended to facilitate stricter conservation measures. A new target was to increase the forest cover to 33 percent of India's land area from the then-official estimate of 23 percent. In June 1990, the central government adopted resolutions that combined forest science with social forestry, that is, taking the sociocultural traditions of the local people into consideration.

Conservation has been an avowed goal of government policy since independence. Afforestation increased from a negligible amount in the first plan to nearly 89,000 square kilometres in the seventh plan. The cumulative area afforested during the 1951-91 period was nearly 179,000 square kilometres. However, despite large-scale tree planting programs, forestry is one arena in which India has actually regressed since independence. Annual fellings at about four times the growth rate are a major cause. Widespread pilfering by villagers for firewood and fodder also represents a major decrement. In addition, the forested area has been shrinking as a result of land cleared for farming, inundations for irrigation and hydroelectric power projects, and construction of new urban areas, industrial plants, roads, power lines, and schools.

CHIPKO MOVEMENT

Since the early 1970s, as they realized that deforestation threatened not only the ecology but their livelihood in a variety of ways, people have become more interested and involved in conservation. The best known popular activist movement is the Chipko Movement, in which local women under the leadership of sunderlal bahuguna decided to fight the government and the vested interests to save trees.

The women of Chamoli District, Uttar Pradesh, declared that they would embrace—literally "to stick to" (chipkna in Hindi)—trees if a sporting goods manufacturer attempted to cut down ash trees in their district. Since initial activism in 1973, the movement has spread and become an ecological movement leading to similar actions in other forest areas. The movement has slowed down the process of deforestation, exposed vested interests, increased ecological awareness, and demonstrated the viability of people power.

Timber mafia

Protected forest areas in several parts of India, such as Jammu and Kashmir, Himachal Pradesh, Karnataka and Jharkhand, are vulnerable to illegal logging by timber mafias that have coopted or intimidated forestry officials, local politicians, businesses and citizenry. Clear-cutting is sometimes covered-up by conniving officials who report fictitious forest fires.

SOCIAL FORESTRY IN INDIA

The term 'Social forestry' first used in 1976 by The National Commission on Agriculture, Government of India. It was then that India embarked upon a social forestry project with the aim of taking the pressure off the forests and making use of all *unused and fallow land.*

Social Forestry Programme

Government forest areas that are close to human settlement and have been degraded over the years due to human activities needed to be afforested. Trees were to be planted in and around agricultural fields. Plantation of trees along railway lines and roadsides, and river and canal banks were carried out. They were planted in village common land, Government wasteland and Panchayat land.

Involvement of Common People

Social forestry also aims at raising plantations by the common man so as to meet the growing demand for timber, fuel wood, fodder, etc, thereby reducing the pressure on the traditional forest area. This concept of village forests to meet the needs of the rural people is not new. It has existed through the centuries all over the country but it was now given a new character. With the introduction of this scheme the government formally recognised the local communities' rights to forest resources, and is now encouraging rural participation in the management of natural resources. Through the social forestry scheme, the government has involved community participation, as part of a drive towards afforestation, and rehabilitating the degraded forest and common lands.

Need of Social Forestry

This need for a social forestry scheme was felt as India has a dominant rural population that still depends largely on fuelwood and other biomass for their cooking and heating. This demand for fuel wood will not come down but the area under forest will reduce further due to the growing population and increasing human activities. Yet the government managed the projects for five years then gave them over to the village panchayats (village council) to manage for themselves and generate products or revenue as they saw fit.

Social Forestry Scheme can be Categorized into Groups

Farm forestry, community forestry, extension forestry and agro-forestry.

Farm Forestry

At present in almost all the countries where social forestry programmes have been taken up, both commercial and non commercial farm forestry is being promoted in one form or the other. Individual farmers are being encouraged to plant trees on their own farmland to meet the domestic needs of the family. In many areas this tradition of growing trees on the farmland already exists. Non-commercial farm forestry is the main thrust of most of the social forestry projects in the country today. It is not always necessary that the farmer grows trees for fuelwood, but very often they are interested in growing trees without any economic motive. They may want it to provide shade for the agricultural crops; as wind shelters; soil conservation or to use wasteland.

Community Forestry

Another scheme taken up under the social forestry programme, is the raising of trees on community land and not on private land as in farm forestry. All these programmes aim to provide for the entire community and not for any individual. The government has the responsibility of providing seedlings, fertilizer but the community has to take responsibility of protecting the trees.

Some communities manage the plantations sensibly and in a sustainable manner so that the village continues to benefit. Some others took advantage and sold the timber for a short-term individual profit. Common land being everyone's land is very easy to exploit. Over the last 20 years, large-scale planting of Eucalyptus, as a fast growing exotic, has occurred in India, making it a part of the drive to reforest the subcontinent, and create an adequate supply of timber for rural communities under the augur of 'social forestry'.

Extension Forestry

Planting of trees on the sides of roads, canals and railways, along with planting on wastelands is known as 'extension' forestry, increasing the boundaries of forests. Under this project there has been creation a of wood lots in the village common lands, government wastelands and panchayat lands.

Schemes for afforesting degraded government forests that are close to villages are being carried out all over the country.

Agro-forestry

In agroforestry silvicultural practices are combined with agricultural crops like leguminous crop, along with orchard farming and live stock ranching on the same piece of land. In a lay man language agroforestry could be understood as growing of forest tree along with agriculture crop on the same piece of land.

In a more scientific way agroforestry may be defined as a sustainable land use system that maintains or increases the total yield by combing food crop together with forest tree and live stock ranching on the same unit of land,using management practices that takes care of the social and culture characteristic of the local people and the economic and ecological condition of the local area.

Objectives of Social Forestry and Environment Wing

Social forestry, schemes that have been started all over the country have made a considerable difference in overall forest cover in a short time. Afforestation outside the conventional forest area for the benefit of rural and urban communities. The main objective is to :-

1. Improve the environment for protecting agriculture from adverse climatic factors,
2. Increase the supply of fuel wood for domestic use, small timber for rural housing, fodder for livestock, and minor forest produce for local industries,
3. Increase the natural beauty of the landscape; create recreational forests for the benefit of rural and urban population,

4. Provide jobs for unskilled workers and
5. Reclaim wastelands.
6. Finally, its object is to raise the standard of living and quality of life of the rural and urban people.

Mission

- To carry out a need based and time bound programme of afforestation with special emphasis on fuel wood and fodder development on all degraded and denuded lands/ forests.
- Afforestation of abandoned jhum lands and mined areas.
- Linear strip plantation of fast growing species on sides of public roads, rivers, streams and irrigation canals.
- Afforestation on unutilized lands under State/Corporate, institutional or private ownership.
- Green belts in urban/industrial areas.
- Shelter belt (generally more extensive than the wind breaks) for the purpose of shelter from wind and sun covering areas larger than a single farm on a planned pattern.
- Farm forestry in the form of raising rows of trees on bund or boundaries of fields and individual trees in private agricultural land as well as creation of wind breaks round a farm or orchard by raising one or two lines of trees.
- Raise flowering trees and shrubs mainly to serve as recreation forests for the urban and rural population.
- Elicit people's participation involving women and young people in conservation of forests, wildlife and environment.
- Environmental awareness generation and celebration of vanamahotsava, environment day, wildlife week etc.

FORESTRY

Forestry is the art and science of managing forests, tree plantations, and related natural resources. Silviculture, a related science, involves the growing and tending of trees and forests. Modern forestry generally concerns itself with: assisting forests to provide timber as raw material for wood products; wildlife habitat; natural water quality management; recreation; landscape and community protection; employment; aesthetically appealing landscapes; biodiversity management; watershed management; erosion control; and a 'sink' for atmospheric carbon dioxide. A practitioner of forestry is known as a forester. Note that the word "forestry" can also refer to a forest itself.

Forest ecosystems have come to be seen as one of the most important components of the biosphere, and forestry has emerged as a vital field of science, applied art, and technology.

Activities

Foresters may be employed by the Forestry Commission (in Britain) industry, government agencies, conservation groups, local authorities, urban parks boards, citizens' associations, or private landowners. Industrial foresters are predominantly involved in planning the forest regeneration process that starts with careful harvesting. Other foresters have specific jobs which include a broad array of responsibilities. For example, urban foresters work within town and city environments to manage teh trees in urban greenspace. Some foresters work in tree nurseries growing seedlings for woodland creation or regeneration projects. Others are involved with tree genetics or developing new building systems as forest engineers. The profession has expanded to include a wide diversity of jobs, typically requiring an honours degree or college bachelor's degree up to the PhD level for highly specialised areas of work.

Traditionally, professional foresters develop and implement "forest management plans". These plans rely on tree inventories showing an area's topographical features as well as its distribution of trees (by species) and other plant cover. They also include roads, culverts, proximity to human habitation, hydrological conditions, and soil reports ecological sensitive areas. Finally, forest management plans include the projected use of the land and a timetable for that use.

In Britain, the Public Forest Estate cared for by the Forestry Commission, is also managed for social objectives, including public access and recreation (including the very popular forest concert venues), habitat conservation, biodiversity,

Plans for harvest and subsequent site treatment are influenced by the objectives of the land's owner or leaseholder (for instance, a timber company that holds cutting rights to a given tract of land, or the government in the case of state-owned forests). It is a feature of "good forestry practice" in Britain that plans must always consider the needs of other stakeholders (e.g., nearby communities or neighbourhoods, or rural residents living within or adjacent to the woodland area). Plans are developed with the tree felling and environmental legislation in mind. They ultimately result in a prescription for the sustinable harvesting and replacement of trees, and will indicate whether road building or other forest engineering operations are required.

Traditional forest management plans are chiefly aimed at providing logs as raw material for timber, veneer, plywood, paper, wood fuel or other industries. Hence, considerations of product quality and quantity, employment, and profit have been of central, though not always exclusive, importance.

Foresters also frequently develop post-harvest site plans. These may call for reforestation (tree planting by species), weed control, fertilization, or the spacing of young trees (thinning of trees that are crowding one another). While other duties of foresters may include preventing and combatting insect infestation, disease, forest and grassland fires, there is an increasing movement towards allowing these natural aspects of forest ecosystems to run their course, where possible, usually excepting epidemics or risk of life or property. Foresters are specialists in measuring and modelling the growth of forests (forest mensuration). Increasingly, foresters may be involved in wildlife conservation planning and watershed protection.

The use and management of forest resources has a long history in China, dating from the Han Dynasty and taking place under the landowning gentry. It was also later written of by the Ming Dynasty Chinese scholar Xu Guangqi (1562-1633). In the Western world, formal forestry practices developed during the Middle Ages, when land was largely under the control of kings and barons. Control of the land included hunting rights, and though peasants in many places were permitted to gather firewood and building timber and to graze animals, hunting rights were retained by the members of the nobility. Systematic management of forests for a sustainable yield of timber is said to have begun in the 16th century in both the German states and Japan. Typically, a forest was divided into specific sections and mapped; the harvest of timber was planned with an eye to regeneration.

The practice of establishing tree plantations was promoted by John Evelyn; it had already acquired some popularity in the British Isles. Schools of forestry were established after 1825; most of these schools were in Germany and France. During the nineteenth and early twentieth centuries, forest preservation programs were established in the United States, Europe, and British India. Many foresters were either from continental Europe (like Sir Dietrich Brandis), or educated there (like Gifford Pinchot).

The enactment and evolution of forestry laws and binding regulations occurred in most Western nations in the 20th century in response to growing conservation concerns and the increasing technological capacity of logging companies.

Tropical forestry is a separate branch of forestry which deals mainly with equatorial forests that yield woods such as teak and mahogany. Sir Dietrich Brandis is considered the father of tropical forestry.

Today

Today a strong body of research exists regarding the management of forest ecosystems and genetic improvement of tree species and varieties. Forestry also includes the development of better methods for the planting, protecting, thinning, controlled burning, felling, extracting, and processing of timber. One of the applications of modern forestry is reforestation, in which trees are planted and tended in a given area.

In many regions the forest industry is of major ecological, economic, and social importance. Third-party certification systems that provide independent verification of sound forest stewardship and sustainable forestry have become commonplace in many areas since the 1990s. These certification systems were developed as a response to criticism of some forestry practices, particularly deforestation in less developed regions along with concerns over resource management in the developed world. Some certification systems are criticised for primarily acting as marketing tools and lacking in their claimed independence.

In topographically severe forested terrain, proper forestry is important for the prevention or minimization of serious soil erosion or even landslides. In areas with a high potential for landslides, forests can stabilize soils and prevent property damage or loss, human injury, or loss of life.

Public perception of forest management has become controversial, with growing public concern over perceived mismanagement of the forest and increasing demands that forest land be managed for uses other than pure timber production, for example, indigenous rights, recreation, watershed management, and preservation of wilderness and wildlife habitat. Sharp disagreements over the role of forest fires, logging, motorized recreation and others drives debate while the public demand for wood products continues to increase.

Education

The first dedicated forestry school was established by Georg Hartig at Dillenburg in Germany in 1787, though forestry had been taught much earlier in central Europe. The first in North America, the Biltmore Forest School was established near Asheville, North Carolina, by Carl A. Schenck in 1898 on the grounds of George W. Vanderbilt's Biltmore Estate. Another early school was the New York State College of Forestry at Cornell also established in 1898. Early North American foresters went to Germany from the nineteenth century to study forestry. Some early German foresters also emigrated to North America. In South America the first two forestry schools were established in Brazil, specifically in Viçosa, Minas Gerais, and in Curitiba, Paraná.

Today, an acceptably trained forester must be educated in general biology, botany, genetics, soil science, climatology, hydrology, economics and forest management. Education in the basics of sociology and political science is often considered an advantage. An interesting scope of work opens up for foresters interested in international politics. Organizations such as the Forest Policy Education Network (FPEN)are dedicated to facilitate the way into forest politics and to exchange information on the subject.

In India, forestry education is imparted in the agricultural universities and in Forest Research Institutes (deemed universities). Four year degree programmes are conducted in these universities at the undergraduate level. Masters and Doctorate degrees are also available in these universities Tropic Ventures Rainforest Enrichment and Sustainable Forestry Project is registered under the Auxiliary Forest Program of Puerto Rico, and is a demonstration project for students and foresters interested in the sustainable management and preservation of tropical rainforest land. In the United States of America, postsecondary forestry education leading to a Bachelor's degree or Master's degree is accredited by the Society of American Foresters.

SUSTAINABLE FOREST MANAGEMENT

Sustainable forest management (SFM) is the management of forests according to the principles of sustainable development. Sustainable forest management uses very broad social, economic and environmental goals. A range of forestry institutions now practice various forms of sustainable forest management and a broad range of methods and tools are available that have been tested over time.

The Forest Principles adopted at The United Nations Conference on Environment and Development (UNCED) in Rio de Janeiro in 1992 captured the general international understanding of sustainable forest management at that time. A number of sets of criteria and indicators have since been developed to evaluate the achievement of SFM at both the country and management unit level. These were all attempts to codify and provide for independent assessment of the degree to which the broader objectives of sustainable forest management are being achieved in practice. In 2007, the United Nations General Assembly adopted the Non-Legally Binding Instrument on All Types of Forests. The instrument is the first of its kind, and reflects the strong international commitment to promote implementation of sustainable forest management through a new approach that brings all stakeholders together.

Definition

A definition of the present day understanding of the term sustainable forest management was developed by the Ministerial Conference on the Protection of Forests in Europe MCPFE), and has since been adopted by the Food and Agriculture Organization (FAO). It defines sustainable forest management as: the stewardship and use of forests and forest lands in a way, and at a rate, that maintains their biodiversity, productivity, regeneration capacity, vitality and their potential to fulfill, now and in the future, relevant ecological, economic and social functions, at local, national, and global levels, and that does not cause damage to other ecosystems.

In simpler terms, the concept can be described as the attainment of balance-balance between society's increasing demands for forest products and benefits, and the preservation of forest health and diversity. This balance is critical to the survival of forests, and to the prosperity of forest-dependent communities.

For forest managers, sustainably managing a particular forest tract means determining, in a tangible way, how to use it today to ensure similar benefits, health and productivity in the future. Forest managers must assess and integrate a wide array of sometimes conflicting factors-commercial and non-commercial values, environmental considerations, community needs, even global impact-to produce sound forest plans. In most cases, forest managers develop their forest plans in consultation with citizens, businesses, organizations and other interested parties in and around the forest tract being managed.

Because forests and societies are in constant flux, the desired outcome of sustainable forest management is not a fixed one. What constitutes a sustainably managed forest will change over time as values held by the public change.

Criteria and Indicators

Criteria and indicators are tools which can be used to conceptualise, evaluate and implement sustainable forest management. Criteria define and characterize the essential elements, as well as a set of conditions or processes, by which sustainable forest management may be assessed. Periodically measured indicators reveal the direction of change with respect to each criterion. Criteria and indicators of sustainable forest management are widely used and many countries produce national reports that assess their progress toward sustainable forest management.

There are nine international and regional criteria and indicators initiatives, which collectively involve more than 150 countries. Three of the more advanced initiatives are those of the Working Group on Criteria and Indicators for the Conservation and Sustainable Management of Temperate and Boreal Forests (also called the Montreal Process), the Ministerial Conference for the Protection of Forests in Europe, and the International Tropical Timber Organization. Countries who are members of the same initiative usually agree to produce reports at the same time and using the same indicators. Within countries, at the management unit level, efforts have also been directed at developing local level criteria and indicators of sustainable forest management.

The Center for International Forestry Research, the International Model Forest Network and researchers at the University of British Columbia have developed a number of tools and techniques to help forest-dependent communities develop their own local level criteria and indicators. Criteria and Indicators also form the basis of the Canadian Standards Association certification standard for sustainable forest management.

There appears to be growing international consensus on the key elements of sustainable forest management. Seven common thematic areas of sustainable forest management have emerged based on the criteria of the nine ongoing regional and international criteria and indicators initiatives. The seven thematic areas are:

- Extent of forest resources
- Biological diversity
- Forest health and vitality
- Productive functions and forest resources
- Protective functions of forest resources
- Socio-economic functions
- Legal, policy and institutional framework.

This consensus on common thematic areas (or criteria) effectively provides a common, implicit definition of sustainable forest management. The seven thematic areas were acknowledged by the international forest community at the fourth session of the United Nations Forum on Forests and the 16th session of the Committee on Forestry.. These thematic areas have since been enshrined in the Non-Legally Binding Instrument on All Types of Forests as a reference framework for sustainable forest management to help achieve the purpose of the instrument.

Ecosystem Approach

The Ecosystem Approach has been prominent on the agenda of the Convention on Biological Diversity (CBD) since 1995. The CBD definition of the Ecosystem Approach and a set of principles for its application were developed at an expert meeting in Malawi in 1995, known as the Malawi Principles. The definition, 12 principles and 5 points of "operational guidance" were adopted by the fifth Conference of Parties (COP5) in 2000. The CBD definition is as follows.

The ecosystem approach is a strategy for the integrated management of land, water and living resources that promotes conservation and sustainable use in an equitable way. Application of the ecosystem approach will help to reach a balance of the three objectives of the Convention.

An ecosystem approach is based on the application of appropriate scientific methodologies focused on levels of biological organization, which encompasses the essential structures, processes, functions and interactions among organisms and their environment. It recognizes that humans, with their cultural diversity, are an integral component of many ecosystems. Sustainable forest management was recognized by parties to the Convention on Biological Diversity in 2004 (Decision VII/11 of COP7) to be a concrete means of applying the Ecosystem Approach to forest ecosystems.

The two concepts, sustainable forest management and the ecosystem approach, aim at promoting conservation and management practices which are environmentally, socially and economically sustainable, and which generate and maintain benefits for both present and future generations. In Europe, the MCPFE and the Council for the Pan-European Biological and Landscape Diversity Strategy (PEBLDS) jointly recognized sustainable forest management to be consistent with the Ecosystem Approach in 2006.

Independent Certification

Growing environmental awareness and consumer demand for more socially responsible businesses helped third-party forest certification emerge in the 1990s as a credible tool for communicating the environmental and social performance of forest operations. There are many potential users of certification, including: forest managers, investors, environmental advocates, business consumers of wood and paper, and individuals.

With forest certification, an independent organization develops standards of good forest management, and independent auditors issue certificates to forest operations that comply with those standards. This certification verifies that forests are well-managed—as defined by a particular standard—and ensures that certain wood and paper products come from responsibly managed forests. This rise of certification led to the emergence of several different systems throughout the world. As a result, there is no single accepted forest management standard worldwide, and each system takes a somewhat different approach in defining standards for sustainable forest management. Third-party forest certification is an important tool for those seeking to ensure that the paper and wood products they purchase and use come from forests that are well-managed and legally harvested.

Incorporating third-party certification into forest product procurement practices can be a centerpiece for comprehensive wood and paper policies that include factors such as the protection of sensitive forest values, thoughtful material selection and efficient use of products. There are more than 50 certification standards worldwide. Some common certification standards are:

- Canada's National Sustainable Forest Management Standard (CSA)
- Forest Stewardship Council (FSC)
- Sustainable Forestry Initiative (SFI)

- Programme for the Endorsement of Forest Certification schemes (PEFC)

The area of forest certified worldwide is growing rapidly. As of December 2006, there were over 2,440,000 square kilometres of forest certified under the CSA, FSC or SFI standards, with over 1,237,000 square kilometres certified in Canada alone. While certification is intended as a tool to enhance forest management practices throughout the world, to date most certified forestry operations are located in Europe and North America. A significant barrier for many forest managers in developing countries is that they lack the capacity to undergo a certification audit and maintain operations to a certification standard.

ANALOG FORESTRY

Analog forestry is a system of growing trees and plants that seek to establish a tree-dominated ecosystem that is analogous in architectural structure and ecological function to the original climax and sub-climax vegetation community.

Thus, analog forestry draws design input not only from traditional models but also from the natural forest successional dynamics. When an ecosystem is designed to be analogous to the indigenous climax state, the efficiency and dynamics of the natural processes can be replicated.

These quasi-natural forests are designed to mimic the structural and functional aspects of indigenous forests and are referred to as analog forests. In addition to their ecological characteristics, analog forests are also designed to provide economic benefits.

However, its is not until all the ecological requirements of the location are satisfied that economic values of species are considered. Therefore, an analog forest may be comprised of natural and exotic species in any proportion, the contribution to structure and function being the overriding factor that determines its use.

In analog forestry, conservation of biodiversity is an equally important goal as economic gain. By contrast, agroforestry sees an increase in the production of crops and income generation as the desired goal.

It arose in Sri Lanka around 1981 as an alternative to monocultures of Pinus and Eucalyptus and has spread to India, Viet Nam, Philippines, Australia, Peru, Ecuador, Colombia, Brazil, Costa Rica, Dominican Republic,Honduras,Mexico, Canada, Kenya and Zimbabwe at present.

FOREST MANAGEMENT

Forest management includes a range of human interventions that affect forest ecosystems. These activities include both conservation and economic activities, such as extraction of timber, planting and replanting of various species, cutting roads and pathways through forests, and techniques for preventing or making out breaks of fire.

In developed countries, the environment has increased public awareness of natural resource policy, including forest management. As a direct result, primary concerns regarding forest management have shifted from the extraction of timber to other forest resources including wildlife, watershed management, and recreation. This shift in public values has also caused many in the public to mistrust resource management professionals.

2

Indian Agriculture

INTRODUCTION

India has made lot of progress in agriculture since independence in terms of growth in output, yields and area under many crops. It has gone through a green revolution, a white revolution, a yellow revolution and a blue revolution. Today, India is the largest producer of milk, fruits, cashew nuts, coconuts and tea in the world, the second largest producer of wheat, vegetables, sugar and fish and the third largest producer of tobacco and rice. The per capita availability of food grains has risen in the country from 350 gm in 1951 to near about 400 gm per day now, of milk from less than 125 gm to 226 gm per day and of eggs from 5 to 30 per annum despite the increase in population from 35 crores to 95 crores. At present only 2330 per cent of the farmers are able to derive any benefits of extension services provided by various government agencies and every year about 20 per cent of the crop is lost due to mishandling, spillage, floods, droughts and pests and diseases. In fruits and vegetables the loss is around 30 per cent.

Outlook

Agriculture accounts for 22 per cent of the GDP and provides livelihoods to 58 per cent of the country's population. Over the years, the agriculture sector has not received as much attention as other sectors in services and manufacturing. The emerging areas in agriculture like horticulture, floriculture, organic farming, genetic engineering, food processing branding and packaging have high potentials of growth. Development of rural infrastructure, rural extension services, agro-based and food processing industries are essential for generating employment and reducing poverty.

Indian agriculture suffers from a mismatch between food crops and cash crops, low yields per hectare except for wheat, volatility in production and wide disparities of productivity over regions and crops. Domestic production of pulses and oilseeds are still below the domestic requirements and India imports pulses and edible oils to satisfy domestic demand. India is the second largest producer of rice and wheat in the world, first in pulses production and fourth in coarse grains. A distinct bias in agricultural price support policies in favour of rice and wheat has distorted cropping pattern and input usage. Market for farm output continues to be subject to heavy procurement interventions. A shift from minimum support price system and developing alternative product markets are essential fro crop diversification and broad based agricultural development.

In recent years there has been considerable emphasis on the development of horticulture and floriculture through the creation of critical infrastructure for cold storage, refrigerated transportation, processing, packaging and quality control. India is the largest producer of coconut, cashew nuts, ginger, turmeric and black pepper and the second largest producer of groundnut, fruits and vegetables.

India accounts for 10 per cent of the world fruit production with first rank in the production of banana, sapota and acid lime. India is also the largest producer of milk, the fifth largest producer of egg and the seventh largest producer of egg and the seventh largest producer of meat. It is necessary to improve cold storage and transportation facilities and develop efficient marketing and export networks to optimize the production and export potentialities in respect of these products.

Food management is inefficient with unsustainable level of food subsidies imposing heavy burden on Government finance. The rural economy and the private sector lack the basic infrastructure to build up sufficient buffer stocks and the country remains vulnerable to weather shocks. In recent years, the

Central Government has provided various fiscal incentives for improving rural storage facilities.

The Central Government is also providing financial assistance to the State Governments for procurement and distribution of food grains at subsidized rates, particularly to the families below the poverty line.

The enhanced availability of bank credits through priority lending to agriculture and agro based industries, favorable terms of trade, liberalized domestic and external trade for agricultural products attracted private investment in agriculture in recent years.

It is likely that with the appropriate policy initiatives, this process will accelerate in the future.

Crop Prospects 2003-04

Favourable monsoon helped in attaining a substantial increase in food grains production from 174.2 million tonnes in 2003-04, due to an increase in the production of both cereals and pulses (Table 1).

There was also a significant increase in the production of oilseeds and cotton in 2003-04 (Table 2). However, production of sugarcane experienced a fall for the second year in succession, mainly because of drought affecting the crop in the major producing areas of south Madhya Maharashtra and Karnataka (Table 2)

Table 1: Food Grains Production (Million tonnes)

Crop/Year	1996-97	1997-98	1998-99	1999-2000	2000-01	2001-02	2002-03	2003-04*
Rice	81.7	82.5	86.1	89.7	85.0	93.3	72.7	86.4
Wheat	69.4	66.4	71.3	76.4	69.7	72.8	65.1	72.7
Coarse Cereals	34.1	30.4	31.3	30.3	31.1	33.4	25.3	36.8
Pulses	14.2	13.0	14.9	13.4	11.1	13.4	11.1	14.9
Food grains								
Kharif	103.9	101.6	102.9	105.5	102.1	112.1	87.8	110.5
Rabi	95.5	90.7	100.7	104.3	94.7	100.8	86.4	100.3
Total	199.4	192.3	203.6	209.8	196.8	212.9	174.2	210.8

*Third advance estimates

Source: Ministry of Agriculture

Table 2: Commercial crop production (Million tonnes)								
Crop	1996-97	1997-98	1998-99	1999-2000	2000-01	2001-02	2002-03	2003-04@
Groundnut	8.6	7.4	9.0	5.3	6.4	7.0	4.4	8.5
Rapeseed/Mustard	6.7	4.7	5.7	5.8	4.2	5.1	3.9	5.9
Soya bean	5.4	6.5	7.1	7.1	5.3	6.0	4.6	7.6
Other oilseeds	3.7	2.7	3.0	2.5	2.5	2.6	2.2	3.0
Total nine oilseeds	24.4	21.3	24.8	20.7	18.4	20.7	15.1	25.0
Cotton*	14.2	10.9	12.3	11.5	9.5	10.0	8.7	13.5
Jute & Mesta**	11.1	11.0	9.8	10.6	10.6	11.7	11.4	11.2
Sugarcane	277.6	279.5	288.7	299.3	296.0	297.2	281.6	244.8

*Million bales of 170 kgs each; **million bales of 180 kgs each; @ Third advance estimates

Source: Ministry of Agriculture.

Growth in Agriculture

Agriculture & allied sector value added registered a growth rate of 9.1 per cent in 2003-04, reflecting the growth in physical production and remunerative prices of agricultural goods. The growth rate of the sector for 2003-04 was one of the highest in recent years, and only marginally lower than the previous high of 9.6 per cent achieved in 1996-97 (Table 3).

Table 3: Tea production, consumption and trade *(Qty: Million Kgs Value: Rs Crore)*						
Year	Production	Export		Import		Domestic Consumption
1997-98	835.64	211.26	2003.15	2.61	17.79	602
1998-99	854.78	205.86	2191.84	8.93	64.73	620
1999-00	835.35	192.44	1932.66	10.36	61.97	638
2000-01	848.36	203.55	1889.78	15.23	95.47	658
2001-02	847.25	190.00	1695.78	16.02	82.70	678
2002-03	837.60	184.40	1665.04	19.67	90.91	698
2003-04*	850.49	180.43	1552.61	8.28	50.99	719

*Estimate

Source: Ministry of Commerce and Industry.

Table 4: Area and production of major horticultural crops
(Area: Million hectares, Production: Million tonnes)

Crop	1999-2000		2000-2001		2001-2002 (Provisional)		2002-2003 (Provisional)	
	Are a	Productio n	Are a	Productio n	Are a	Productio n	Are a	Productio n
Fruits	3.80	45.50	3.89	43.14	4.00	43.00	4.18	47.68
Apple	0.23	1.05	0.24	1.23	0.24	1.16	0.25	1.47
Banana	0.49	16.81	0.47	14.14	0.47	14.21	0.68	16.82
Citrus	0.53	4.65	0.50	4.40	0.62	4.80	0.60	4.72
Grapes	0.04	1.13	0.05	1.06	0.05	1.21	0.06	1.15
Guava	0.15	1.71	0.15	1.63	0.15	1.72	0.22	1.78
Litchi	0.05	0.43	0.05	0.40	0.06	0.40	0.05	0.44
Mango	1.49	10.50	1.52	10.06	1.58	10.02	1.60	10.78
Papaya	0.06	1.67	0.07	1.79	0.07	2.59	0.08	1.85
Pineapple	0.07	1.02	0.08	1.22	0.08	1.18	0.09	1.31
Sapota	0.06	0.64	0.07	0.74	0.05	0.60	0.07	0.71
Others	0.63	5.89	0.23	6.49	0.63	5.11	0.48	6.65
Vegetables	5.59	90.83	6.25	94.00	6.20	88.62	7.59	97.50
Brinjal	0.50	8.12	0.47	7.70	0.50	8.35	0.50	7.83
Cabbage	0.26	5.91	0.25	5.51	0.26	5.68	0.28	5.80
Cauliflower	0.25	4.72	0.26	4.69	0.27	4.89	0.28	4.80
Okra	0.35	3.42	0.35	3.34	0.35	3.32	0.37	3.53
Onion	0.49	4.90	0.45	4.72	0.50	5.25	0.53	5.45
Pea	0.27	2.71	0.32	3.01	0.30	2.04	0.35	3.20
Potato	1.34	25.00	1.21	22.44	1.25	24.45	1.37	25.00
Tomato	0.46	7.43	0.46	7.24	0.46	7.46	0.54	7.60
Others	2.07	28.63	2.48	35.35	2.31	27.18	3.37	34.74
Flowers	0.09	0.52	0.10	0.56	0.11	0.54	0.15	0.70
Spices	2.50	3.02	2.50	3.02	3.22	3.77	-	-
Cashew nut	0.69	0.52	0.72	0.45	0.74	0.46	0.73	0.47
Areca nut	0.29	0.33	0.29	0.33	0.29	0.33	-	-
Coconut*	1.77	12.23	1.82	12.68	1.89	12.82	-	-
Other Horticultur al crops	NA	1.75	0.11	0.15	0.12	0.17	0.13	0.19

NA: Not available *-production in thousand million nuts
Source: Ministry of Agriculture.

India owns one of the largest livestock population in the world and has now become the largest global producer of milk. India is the sixth largest producer of fish and second largest producer of inland fish in the world. Fisheries sector is recognized as a powerful generator of income and employment. It is also a source of cheap land nutritious food besides being a major foreign exchange earner. The major thrust of the policies and programmes of the Government of India relating to livestock and fisheries is in the areas of rapid genetic up gradation of milch animals, improvement in the delivery mechanism of breeding inputs, control of animal diseases, creation of disease free zones, increased availability of nutritious feed and fodder, development of dairy activities and backyard poultry, development of processing and marketing facilities and enhancement of production and profitability of livestock and fisheries enterprises.

Table 5: Gross capital formation in agriculture at 1993-94 prices (Rs crore)

Year	Total	Public	Private	Percent share Public	Percent share Private	Investment in agriculture as per cent of GDP
1990-91	14836	4395	10441	29.6	70.4	1.9
1991-92	13389	3871	9518	28.9	71.1	1.7
1992-93	14508	4076	10432	28.1	71.9	1.8
1993-94	13523	4467	9056	33.0	67.0	1.6
1994-95	14969	4947	10022	33.0	67.0	1.6
1995-96	15690	4849	10841	30.9	69.1	1.6
1996-97	16176	4668	11508	28.9	71.1	1.5
1997-98	15942	3979	11963	25.0	75.0	1.4
1998-99	14895	3870	11025	26.0	74.0	1.3
1999-00	17304	4221	13083	24.4	75.6	1.4
2000-01	16906	3927	12979	23.2	76.8	1.3
2001-02	17328	4127	13201	23.8	76.2	1.3
2002-03*	18657	4538	14119	24.3	75.7	1.3

*Quick estimates

Source: Central Statistical Organization

Agri-Trade

Agri-exports: Agricultural exports increased from $5.9 billion in 2001-02 to $6.7 billion in 2002-03 (Table 6). However, as a percentage of total merchandise exports, the share of agri-exports declined from 13.5 per cent in 2001-02 to 12.8 per cent in 2002-03. Marine products, contributing around 20 per cent of the total agri-exports, is amongst the dominant items of the agri-exports, is amongst the dominant items of the agri-exports of the country.

The exports of food grains (rice and wheat) have picked up considerably in recent years, accounting for around 20 per cent of the agri-exports. The Government's special efforts to encourage export of food grains in recent years through grant of WTO compatible subsidies has placed India as one of the leading exporters of food grains in the international market

Exim Policy 2002-07 emphasized the importance of agricultural exports and announced the following policy measures to.

Table 6: Agricultural Exports

Crop	2001-02		2002-03		2002-03 (April-Feb.)		2003-04 (April-Feb.)	
	Million US Dollar	Percent share of agri exports	Million US Dollar	Percent share of agri exports	Million US Dollar	Percent share of agri exports	Million US Dollar	Percent share of agri exports
Tea	360.5	6.1	343.6	5.1	320.3	5.3	317.1	4.9
Coffee	229.6	3.9	205.5	3.1	180.6	3.0	201.4	3.1
Rice	665.5	11.3	1238.1	18.4	1106.0	18.2	799.7	12.3
Wheat	278.9	4.7	363.6	5.4	339.0	5.6	453.2	7.0
Sugar & Molesses	373.6	6.3	375.1	5.6	304.2	5.0	258.3	4.0
Tobacco	169.3	2.9	212.5	3.2	181.0	3.0	205.4	3.2
Spices	313.9	5.3	342.8	5.1	314.2	5.2	286.4	4.4
Cashew	375.1	6.4	424.2	6.3	396.4	6.5	331.5	5.1
Sesame and Niger Seeds	127.9	2.2	93.2	1.4	82.9	1.4	141.7	2.2
Guargum Meal	84.5	1.4	100.6	1.5	87.9	1.4	100.2	1.5
Oil meals	474.5	8.0	308.8	4.6	286.4	4.7	563.1	8.7
Fruits & Vegetables	262.8	4.5	300.2	4.5	258.2	4.2	385.1	5.9
Processed Fruits & Vegetables	107.5	1.8	118.8	1.8	109.5	1.8	66.4	1.0
Meat & Meat Preparations	250.2	4.2	284.6	4.2	263.1	4.3	310.3	4.8
Marine Products	1236.8	21.0	1431.6	21.3	1303.6	21.5	1218.8	18.7
Others	590.4	10.0	611.1	9.1	542.9	8.9	867.3	13.3
Agricultural Exports	5901.0	100.0	6734.0	100.0	6076.0	100.0	6506.0	100.0
Total Exports	43826.7		52719.4		47136.1		55716.7	
Agri Exports as per cent of Total Exports		13.5		12.8		12.9		11.7

Source: DGCI&S, Kolkata

Boost Agri-exports:

- Free exportability of all agricultural products except onion and Niger seed, export of which are canalized through approved agencies.
- Removal of procedural restrictions like requirement for registration, packaging, etc.
- Setting-up of Agri-export zones to enhance international market access and improve infrastructure facilities, and ensure better flow of credit.
- Assistance for reducing the marketing costs such as transportation, handling and processing of export of selected agricultural commodities.
- Financial assistance for improved packaging, strengthening of quality control mechanism and modernization of processing units.
- Arranging promotion campaign such as buyer-seller meets and participation in important international fairs and exhibition.

Agri-imports

The imports of agricultural products increased to $2.8 billion in 2002-03 from $2.3 billion in 2001-02. The share of agri-imports in total merchandise imports increased from 4.5 per cent to 4.6 per cent over the same period (Table 7). Edible oil, which accounts for almost two-thirds of the total agri-imports, is the single largest item of agri-imports in to the country. The dominant share of this item continued to persist even in 2003-04. Imports of pulses are also significant and accounted for 20-30 per cent of agri-imports, although its share declined to 14 per cent in 2003-04.

Agricultural Marketing

Marketing of agricultural produce is the most important activity for the farming community, particularly fro those who are small producers and have small surpluses for marketing. To protect the interests of farmers, Government promoted organized marketing of agricultural commodities through a network of regulated markets. However, studies indicate that the institutions of regulated markets have achieved limited success, as these markets restricted development of direct and free marketing, smooth raw material supplies to agro-processors, information exchange and adoption of innovative marketing systems and technologies.

To benefit the farming community from new market access opportunities, the internal agricultural marketing system in the country needs to be integrated and strengthened. In this context, an inter-Ministerial Task Force set up by the Ministry of Agriculture suggested a package of reform measures, such as amendments in the State APMC Act to encourage development of competitive agricultural markets in the private and cooperative sectors, and deregulation of marketing system to promote private investment in marketing infrastructure.

Table 7: Agricultural imports

	2001-02		2002-03		2002-03(April-Feb.)		2003-04 (April-Feb.)	
	Million US Dollar	Percent share of agri imports	Million US Dollar	Percent share of agri imports	Million US Dollar	Percent share of agri imports	Million US Dollar	Percent share of agri imports
Cereals	18.2	0.8	24.5	0.9	22.5	0.9	15.9	0.5
Pulses	662.6	28.9	565.6	20.2	529.5	20.9	449.9	13.7
Milk & Cream	1.8	0.1	2.0	0.1	1.7	0.1	19.3	0.6
Cashew Nuts	90.4	3.9	256.1	9.1	250.4	9.9	290.6	8.9
Fruits & Nuts Excl. Cashew Nuts	158.7	6.9	132.6	4.7	119.1	4.7	150.2	4.6
Sugar	6.8	0.3	6.8	0.2	6.7	0.3	9.2	0.3
Oil Seeds	0.3	0.0	2.4	0.1	2.3	0.1	2.5	0.1
Vegetable Oils Fixed (Edible)	1355.6	59.1	1814.2	64.7	1597.4	63.1	2344.7	71.4
Agricultural Imports	2294.4	100.0	2804.1	100.0	2529.6	100.0	3282.2	100.0
Total Imports	51413.3		61412.1		54877.9		69034.6	
Agri Import as per cent of total imports	4.5		4.6			4.6		4.8

Source: DGCI&S, Kolkata

3

Agriculture of Water Resource Issues

OVERVIEW

An interesting observation arising from the preparation of this year's special chapter on water and agriculture is how difficult it is to generalize about water. Almost any statement requires qualification. For example, while we can say that water is one of the most abundant resources on earth, we know that less than 1 percent of the total supply is reliably available for human consumption. Water is a liquid for the most part, but it can also be a solid and a vapour. Drinking-water is certainly essential for human survival but water-related illnesses are the most common health threat in the developing world. An estimated 25 000 people die every day as a result of water-related sicknesses.1

One statement, however, needs no qualification: human existence depends on water. The geosphere, the atmosphere and the biosphere are all linked to water. Water interacts with solar energy to determine climate and it transforms and transports the physical and chemical substances necessary for all life on earth.

In recent years, water issues have been the focus of increasing international concern and debate. From 26 to 31 January 1992, the UN system sponsored the International Conference on Water and the Environment (ICWE) in Dublin, Ireland. The ICWE called for innovative approaches to the assessment, development and management of freshwater resources. In addition, the ICWE provided policy guidance for the United Nations Conference on Environment and Development (UNCED) in Rio de Janeiro in

June 1992. UNCED highlighted the need for water sector reforms throughout the world.

In 1993, the World Bank issued a comprehensive policy paper defining its new objectives for the water sector. FAO recently established an International Action Programme on Water and Sustainable Agricultural Development (IAP-WASAD). Likewise, the UNDP, WHO, UNICEF, WMO, Unesco and UNEP are all coordinating or participating in special programmes related to water resources.

Other international, national and local organizations are becoming more active in water issues. The 1990 Montreal meeting, "NGOs Working Together", focused attention on drinking-water supply and sanitation. The Canadian International Development Agency, the French Ministry of Cooperation and Development, the German Agency for Technical Cooperation (GTZ), the United Kingdom's Overseas Development Administration and the United States Agency for International Development (USAID) have recently developed water resource strategies for foreign assistance.

The message highlighted by all these efforts is that water is an increasingly scarce and valuable resource. Of principal concern is our failure to recognize and accept that there is a finite supply of water. The consensus is that the growing water scarcity and misuse of freshwater pose serious threats to sustainable development.

Competition among agriculture, industry and cities for limited water supplies is already constraining development efforts in many countries. As populations expand and economies grow, the competition for limited supplies will intensify and so will conflicts among water users.

Despite water shortages, misuse of water is widespread. Small communities and large cities, farmers and industries, developing countries and industrialized economies are all mismanaging water resources. Surface water quality is deteriorating in key basins from urban and industrial wastes.

Groundwater is polluted from surface sources and irreversibly damaged by the intrusion of salt water. Overexploited aquifers are losing their capacity to hold water and lands are subsiding.

Cities are unable to provide adequate drinking-water and sanitation facilities. Waterlogging and salinization are diminishing the productivity of irrigated lands. Decreasing water flows are reducing hydroelectric power generation, pollution assimilation and fish and wildlife habitats.

At first glance, most of these water problems do not appear to be directly related to the agricultural sector. Yet, by far the largest demand for the world's water comes from agriculture. More than two-thirds of the water withdrawn from the earth's rivers, lakes and aquifers is used for irrigation. As competition, conflicts, shortages, waste, overuse and degradation of water resources grow, policy-makers look increasingly to agriculture as the system's safety valve.

Agriculture is not only the world's largest water user in terms of volume, it is also a relatively low-value, low-efficiency and highly subsidized water user. These facts are forcing governments and donors to rethink the economic, social and environmental implications of large publicly funded and operated irrigation projects. In the past, domestic spending for irrigation dominated agricultural budgets in countries throughout the world. For instance, since 1940, 80 percent of Mexico's public expenditures in agriculture have been for irrigation projects. In China, Indonesia and Pakistan, irrigation has absorbed more than half of agricultural investment. In India, about 30 percent of all public investment has gone into irrigation.

A significant portion of international development assistance has also been used to establish irrigation systems. Irrigation received nearly 30 percent of World Bank agricultural lending during the 1980s. Spending commitments for irrigation by all aid agencies exceeded $2 billion per year in the past decade.

Once established, irrigation projects become some of the most heavily subsidized economic activities in the world. In the mid-1980s, Repetto estimated that average subsidies to irrigation in six Asian countries covered 90 percent of the total operating and maintenance costs. Case-studies indicate that irrigation fees are, on average, less than 8 percent of the value of benefits derived from irrigation.

Despite these huge investments and subsidies, irrigation performance indicators are falling short of expectations for yield increases, area irrigated and technical efficiency in water use. As much as 60 percent of the water diverted or pumped for irrigation is wasted. Although some losses are inevitable, in too many cases this excess water seeps back into the ground, causing waterlogging and salinity. As much as one-quarter of all irrigated land in developing countries suffers from varying degrees of salinization. Moreover, stagnant water and poor irrigation drainage escalate the incidence of water-related diseases, resulting in human suffering and increased health costs.

Today, agriculture is often unable to compete economically for scarce water. Cities and industries can afford to pay more for water and earn a higher economic rate of return from a unit of water than does agriculture. (For economists, water flows uphill to money.) For the first time in many countries, agriculture is being obliged to give up water for higher-value uses in cities and industries. Irrigators in some areas are now asked to pay for the water they receive, including the full cost of water delivery. In other areas, new regulations require farmers to pay for polluting streams, lakes and aquifers.

The irony is that irrigated agriculture is expected to produce much more in the future while using less water than it uses today. At present, 2.4 billion people depend on irrigated agriculture for jobs, food and income (some 55 percent of all wheat and rice output is irrigated). Over the next 30 years, an estimated 80 percent of the additional food supplies required to feed the world will depend on irrigation.

These developments are placing enormous pressure on agricultural policy-makers and farmers. Throughout the world, governments assume the prime responsibility for ensuring food security and, because food depends increasingly on irrigation, food security is closely linked with water security. Between 30 and 40 percent of the world's food comes from the irrigated 16 percent of the total cultivated land; around one-fifth of the total value of fish production comes from freshwater aquaculture; and current global livestock drinking-water requirements are 60 billion litres per day (forecasts estimate an increase of 0.4 billion litres per year). Food security in the next century will be closely allied to success in irrigation.

Irrigation can help make yield-increasing innovations a more attractive investment proposition but it does not guarantee crop yield increases. The overall performance of many irrigation projects has been disappointing because of poor scheme conception, inadequate construction and implementation or ineffective management. The mediocre performance of the irrigation sector is also contributing to many socio-economic and environmental problems, but these problems are neither inherent in the technology nor inevitable, as is sometimes argued.

Irrigation projects can contribute greatly to increased incomes and agricultural production compared with rain-fed agriculture. In addition, irrigation is more reliable and allows for a wider and more diversified choice of cropping patterns as well as the production of higher-value crops. Irrigation's contribution to food security in China, Egypt, India, Morocco and Pakistan is widely recognized. For example, in India, 55 percent of agricultural output is from irrigated land. Moreover, average farm incomes have increased from 80 to 100 percent as a result of irrigation, while yields have doubled compared with those achieved under the former rain-fed conditions; incremental labour days used per hectare have increased by 50 to 100 percent. In Mexico, half the value of agriculture production and two-thirds of the value of agricultural exports is from the one-third of arable land that is irrigated.

Irrigation is a key component of the technical package needed to achieve productivity gains. In the future, as high levels of costly inputs are added to cropland to sustain yield increases, the security and efficiency of irrigated production will become even more important to world farming. Water will no longer be plentiful and cheap. It will be scarce, expensive to develop and maintain and valuable in use. The prospect of high-cost water may at first seem to be another problem looming for low-income economies. However, the high cost will be an incentive to use water more efficiently. The single most important factor limiting the adoption of proven irrigation and drainage technology is the low cost of water. Moreover, if farmers have opportunities for higher-value uses and can make profits, both governments and farmers will invest in irrigation.

This water dilemma-to produce more in a sustainable way with less water-points to the need for demand management mechanisms to reallocate existing supplies, encourage more efficient use and promote more equitable access. Policy-makers need to establish a structure of incentives, regulations, permits, restrictions and penalties that will help guide, influence and coordinate how people use water while encouraging innovations in water-saving technologies.

In the past, supply-side approaches dominated water resource management practices. Water itself was physically managed through technical and engineering means that captured, stored, delivered and treated water. However, the era of meeting growing demand by developing new supplies is ending. In our present-day water economy, resource management is shifting away from the goal of capturing more water towards that of designing demand- and user-focused approaches that influence behaviour.

PURPOSE AND SCOPE

This special chapter is primarily intended for agricultural policy-makers, water managers, researchers, students, development planners and agricultural project donors. It is meant to help us reflect on the way water resources are managed at present; to contribute to the discussion on sustainable water use; and to stimulate thinking, research and change. Decisions made in this decade regarding how water is used will have a profound effect on our future supplies.

This first section gives an overview of world water resources and briefly discusses the key issues: scarcity, quality and health.

The second section stresses the need to integrate the water sector with the national economy and analyses the physical, economic and social aspects of water. It then provides a conceptual foundation for understanding the circumstances under which water policies either work or fail. Section II also assesses the advantages and disadvantages of broad alternative approaches to public water policy.

Section III examines how policy analysis is applied to water resource planning, including both supply-side (physical and hydrological) and demand-side considerations. It discusses the advantages and disadvantages of various policy options for urgent water policy issues related to surface water and groundwater.

The fourth and final section reviews three specific policy issues in irrigated agriculture: declining growth and investment trends; the difficulties imposed by irrigation-induced environmental degradation; and efforts to reform managerial and administrative systems.

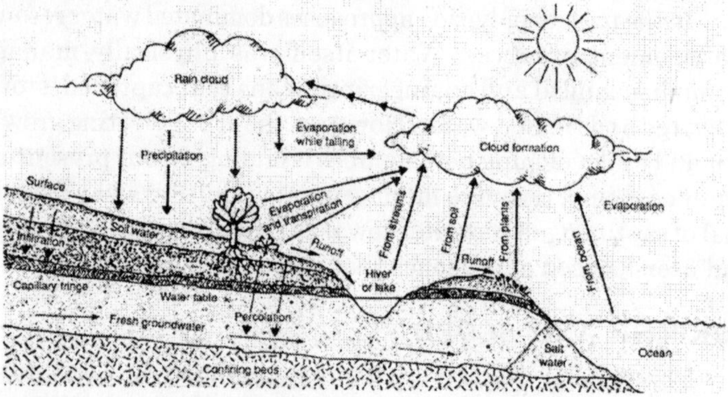

BOX : THE HYDROLOGICAL CYCLE

Water continuously circulates on the planet. The hydrological cycle has no beginning or end but we can describe it as starting with the waters of the oceans, which cover about three-quarters of the earth. Radiation from the sun and wind energy, which is itself indirectly derived from solar energy, cause evaporation of water which rises as a vapour and forms clouds. In turn, if conditions are right, these condense and fall back to earth as rain, hail or snow.

Some of this precipitation evaporates from leaves and soil, some runs over the surface and forms streams and some percolates into the soil where it may be drawn on by plants and transpired back into the atmosphere or returned to the surface by soil capillarity. Some soil moisture evaporates and some soaks down below the root zone to join the groundwater reservoir. Groundwater percolates through pores in the soil and rocks and may reappear on the surface at lower elevations as a spring or as seepage into streams and rivers which eventually re-enter the ocean. Still some lies in the groundwater reservoir or aquifer and may be tapped by a mechanical tube well or an open well.

The hydrological cycle illustrated in the Figure is the system by which water circulates from the oceans through the atmosphere and back to the ocean overland and underground. Available freshwater is a rare form of water, for 99 percent is either saline (97 percent of all water is in the ocean) or frozen (2 percent in the ice caps and glaciers). Most of the remainder (1 percent) is groundwater with minute proportions in freshwater lakes, soil moisture, rivers and biological systems.

WORLD WATER RESOURCES

Every day the hydrological cycle renews the world's freshwater resources through evaporation and precipitation. The average annual rainfall over land is 110 000 km^3, but some 70 000 km3 evaporate before reaching the sea. The remaining 40 000 km3 are potentially available for human use. Global freshwater consumption is currently around 4 000 km3, only 10 percent of the annual renewable supply.

These numbers suggest that plenty of water is available for human use but a closer look reveals a more complicated situation. The 40 000 km^3 of available water are distributed very unevenly and two-thirds of it runs off in floods. That leaves around 14 000 km^3 as a relatively stable supply. A substantial share of this supply should be left to follow its natural course in order to safeguard wetlands, deltas, lakes and rivers.

For example, 6 000 km^3 of water is needed to dilute and transport the estimated 450 km^3 of waste water now entering the world's rivers each year. Without substantial investment in waste water treatment and more effective regulation, even more water will have to be diverted to dilute and transport wastes.

Precipitation, withdrawals and availability of water vary widely around the world. Per caput availability is highest in Latin America and lowest in North Africa and the Near East, while withdrawals are highest in North America and lowest in Africa. Per caput water availability in Europe and North America is not expected to change greatly by 2000, while Asians, Africans and Latin Americans will face less per caput water availability as their populations continue to grow. At present, Asia accounts for over one-half of the world's water withdrawals. Forecasts to the year 2000 suggest that Asia will consume 60 percent of the world's water, followed by 15 percent in North America, 13 percent in Europe and less than 7 percent in Africa. Latin America's share of world water consumption is forecast to be less than 5 percent in 2000, although the region's consumption has nearly quadrupled since 1950.

WATER SCARCITY

Human actions bring about water scarcity in three ways: through population growth, misuse and inequitable access. Population growth contributes to scarcity simply because the available water supply must be divided among more and more people. Every country has a more or less fixed amount of internal water resources, defined as the average annual flow of rivers and aquifers generated from precipitation. Overtime, this internal renewable supply must be divided among more and more people, eventually resulting in water scarcity.

TABLE : Per caput water availability by region, 1950-2000

Region	1950	1960	1970	1980	2000
	(..........................		'000 m3		..........................)
Africa	20.6	16.5	12.7	9.4	5.1
Asia	9.6	7.9	6.1	5.1	3.3
Latin America	105.0	80.2	61.7	48.8	28.3
Europe	5.9	5.4	4.9	4.4	4.1
North America	37.2	30.2	25.2	21.3	17.5

Source: N.B. Ayibotele. 1992. The world's water: assessing the resource. Keynote paper at the ICWE, Dublin, Ireland.

When annual internal renewable water resources are less than 1 000 m^3 per caput, water availability is considered a severe constraint on socio-economic development and environmental protection.

Table 7 lists the countries where per caput internal renewable water availability will fall below 1 000 m^3 by the end of this decade. Most countries facing chronic water scarcity problems are in North Africa, the Near East and sub-Saharan Africa. Countries with less than 2 000 m^3 per caput face a serious marginal water scarcity situation, with major problems occurring in drought years. By the end of the 1990s, water availability is expected to fall below 2 000m^3 per caput in more than 40 countries.

In many countries, while scarcity is less of a problem at a national level, serious water shortages are causing difficulties in specific regions and watersheds. Notable examples include northern China, western and southern India and parts of Mexico.

People also bring about water scarcity by polluting and overusing existing supplies. This type of scarcity can be regarded as the consumption of the resource's "capital".

For instance, an aquifer represents resource capital, providing what is generally a renewable source of water "income" that can be tapped for human consumption. Sustainable use of the aquifer leaves the capital intact so that future generations can continuously use the renewable portion or income. If pumping is greater than recharge, the aquifer is depleted and the capital is consumed.

Overuse of groundwater has become a major problem in China, India, Indonesia, Mexico, the Near East, North Africa, Thailand, the western United States and many island countries where seawater intrusion results.

The overpumping of aquifers not only results in a water source that is too depleted to serve as a supply, it may also cause the land above the aquifer to settle or subside, resulting in widespread structural damage in extreme cases. Bangkok and Mexico City are well-known examples.

TABLE : Countries predicted to have scarce water resources in 2000

Country[1]	Population in 2000	Water availability	
		Internal renewable water resources	Water resources including river flows from other countries
	(millions)	*(....m³ per caput....)*	
Egypt	62.4	29	934
Saudi Arabia	21.3	103	103
Libyan Arab Jamahiriya	6.5	108	108
United Arab Emirates	2.0	152	152
Jordan	4.6	153	240
Mauritania	2.6	154	2843
Yemen	16.2	155	155
Israel	6.4	260	335
Tunisia	9.8	384	445
Syrian Arab Republic	17.7	430	2008
Kenya	34.0	436	436
Burundi	7.4	487	487
Algeria	33.1	570	576
Hungary	10.1	591	11 326
Rwanda	10.4	604	604
Botswana	1.6	622	11 187
Malawi	11.8	760	760
Oman	2.3	880	880
Sudan	33.1	905	3923
Morocco	31.8	943	943
Somalia	10.6	1 086	1 086

Finally, a shift in access or distribution patterns may concentrate water resources among one group and subject others to extreme scarcity. In many cities of the developing world, large numbers of people depend on water vendors and may pay 100 times as much as the rate of public utilities.

Numerous recent studies document that large numbers of urban poor pay much higher prices and a much larger share of their income for water than families with access to a city water system. Poor families in some large cities spend up to 20 percent of their income on water. When the cost is so high, they use little water for washing and bathing, which results in serious health problems.

A number of other countries with smaller populations, e.g. Barbados, Cape Verde, Djibouti, Malta, Qatar and Singapore, are also included in the water-scarce category. Source: FAO calculations based on World Bank/WRI data.

TABLE : Ratio of prices charged by vendors to prices charged by public utilities in selected cities

Country	City	Ratio
Bangladesh	Dacca	12-25
Colombia	Cali	10
Côte d'Ivoire	Abidjan	5
Ecuador	Guayaquil	20
Haiti	Port-au-Prince	17-100
Honduras	Tegucigalpa	16-34
Indonesia	Jakarta	4-60
	Surabaja	20-60
Kenya	Nairobi	7-11
Mauritania	Nouakchott	100
Nigeria	Lagos	4-10
	Onitsha	6-38
Pakistan	Karachi	28-83
Peru	Lima	17
Togo	Lomé	7-10
Turkey	Istanbul	10
Uganda	Kampala	4-9

Source: R. Bhatia and M. Falkenmark. 1992. Water resource policies and the urban poor: innovative approaches and policy imperatives. Background paper for the ICWE, Dublin, Ireland.

World water use

The early civilizations of Asia, Africa and Latin America organized cooperative efforts to develop river valleys for irrigated agriculture. Through irrigation technology, societies controlled and manipulated natural water supplies to improve crop production. The result was often reliable and ample food supplies which led to the creation of stable agricultural villages, the division of labour and economic surpluses.

Many scholars still argue over whether irrigation technology facilitated political control and development of the state or whether political developments led to advancement of the technology. No matter the direction of cause and effect, no one disputes the association of development with control over water use.

In today's world, agriculture still accounts for the majority of human water use. Globally, around 70 percent of water withdrawals are for agriculture. Domestic and industrial uses consume the remaining 30 percent.

Domestic uses include drinking-water supplies, private homes, commercial establishments, public services and municipal supplies.

Water uses differ greatly depending on access, quantity, quality and socio-economic conditions. For example, agricultural water use is higher as a proportion of total water use in the low-income countries (91 percent) than in the high-income group (39 percent).

TABLE : Sectoral water withdrawals, by income group

Country income group	Annual withdrawals per caput (...m³...)	Withdrawals by sector Agric.	Ind.	Dom.
		(................	%..........	)
Low-income	386	91	5	4
Middle-income	453	69	18	13
High-income	1 167	39	47	14

Source: World Bank. 1992. World Development Report 1992, based on WRI data.

Nevertheless, on a per caput basis, the high-income countries use more water for agricultural purposes than the low-income countries. The trends in world water use during this century are presented in Figure 12. Overall, global water consumption has increased almost tenfold.

Agriculture's share, which was 90 percent in 1900, will have dropped to an estimated 62 percent by 2000. During this same period, industrial consumption will have grown from 6 percent to 25 percent, while consumption by cities will have increased from 2 percent to nearly 9 percent. By 2000, around 35 percent of available water supplies will be in use, compared with less than 5 percent at the beginning of the century.

Water quantity and quality requirements also differ widely depending on the type of use. Net agricultural requirements are especially large in relation to other uses. For instance, around 15 000 m3 of water are normally sufficient to irrigate 1 ha of rice. This same amount of water can supply: 100 nomads and 450 head of stock for three years; or 100 rural families through house connections for four years; or 100 urban families for two years; or 100 luxury hotel guests for 55 days.

BOX : WATER AND POLLUTION

The quality of water from different sources varies widely. Precipitation absorbs gases from the atmosphere and removes particles from the air. When the precipitation strikes the ground it becomes surface water runoff or enters the ground. The surface water flows into larger and larger channels, ponds, lakes and rivers until some of it reaches the sea. Along its course, surface water picks up both organic and mineral particles, bacteria and other organisms as well as salts and other soluble substances. The water in lakes and swamps sometimes acquires odours, tastes and colours from algae and other organisms and from decaying vegetation.

Since ancient times, heavy metals from mining and pathogens from cities have caused serious, although localized, contamination. Since the industrial revolution, water pollution problems have become first regional, then continental and now global in nature. Much water is polluted when it is used in industry and agriculture or for domestic purposes. Mining is the major cause of metal contamination, whereas other industries contribute to acidification. The intensification of agricultural activities has led to the contamination of groundwater by fertilizers and other chemicals. Moreover, irrigation projects often cause a rapid rise in the level of groundwater, which leads to waterlogging and soil salinity.

Since 1977, the UNEP/ WHO Global Environment Monitoring System (GEMS) has been working with Unesco and WMO to develop a global water quality monitoring network. More than ***50*** *water variables are monitored to provide information on the suitability of water for human consumption and for agricultural, commercial and industrial use. Recent assessments have found that the main water pollutants are: sewage, nutrients, toxic metals and industrial as well as agricultural chemicals.*

Conclusions drawn from the GEMS assessment include: the nature and level of freshwater pollution strongly depends on socio-economic development; the most common water pollutant is organic material from domestic sewage, municipal waste and agro-industrial effluent; and the high water nitrate levels found in Western Europe and the United States are a result of the nitrogen fertilizers and manure used for intensive agriculture. The GEMS assessment also noted a dramatic increase in the use of fertilizers in developing countries, particularly where intensive irrigation allows for double or triple cropping.

Other conditions highlighted in the GEMS report include deforestation, eutrophication, suspended particulate matter (SM) and salinity.

Deforestation, i.e. the clearing of land for agriculture and urban development, often leads to water contamination. When the soil is stripped of its protective vegetative covering, it becomes prone to erosion. This in turn leads to higher water turbidity, because of the increased amounts of suspended matter, to nutrient leaching and to a decreased water-retention capacity of the soil. There is also concern about the destruction of wetlands, which destroys the habitat of many species and removes natural filter mechanisms, permitting many common pollutants to reach water supplies.

Eutrophication is the enrichment of waters with nutrients, especially phosphorus and nitrogen. It can lead to enhanced plant growth and depleted oxygen levels as this plant material decays. It is not always a human-induced problem, but is often linked to organic waste and agricultural runoff. Today 30 to 40 percent of the world's lakes and reservoirs are eutrophic. Not all interventions have proved successful, but eutrophication can be reversible if mid-and long-term strategies are enacted. Laws and measures introduced to reduce tripolyphosphates (used mostly in detergents) and to remove phosphorus from waste water have had positive effects.

SM consists of materials that float in suspension in water. There are three main sources of SM: natural soil erosion, matter formed organically within a water body and material produced as a by-product of human activity. SM settles on the sediment bed and forms deposits in rivers, lakes, deltas and estuaries. Evidence of human-induced SM from Roman and Mayan times has been discovered in lake beds, implying that this was one of the first types of water pollution. River damming affects the amount of SM flowing from rivers to the oceans because reservoirs act as effective sinks for SM. An estimated 10 percent of the global SM discharge to the sea is trapped in reservoirs. Approximately 25 percent of the water currently flowing to the oceans has been previously stored in a reservoir. Damming can also greatly modify water quality; waters flowing out of reservoirs not only have reduced SM quantities, they are also depleted of nutrients and are often more saline, which consequently has detrimental effects on downstream agriculture and fisheries.

Salinity is a significant and widespread form of freshwater pollution, particularly in arid, semi-arid and some coastal regions. The primary cause of salinization is a combination of poor drainage and high evaporation rates which concentrate salts on irrigated land. Salinity can adversely affect the productivity of irrigated crops and is also detrimental to industrial and household water users. It is not a new phenomenon; salinization of soil and water in the flood plain of the Tigris and Euphrates Rivers contributed to the decline of the Mesopotamian civilization some 6 000 years ago. The estimated global gross area of irrigated land is 270 million ha. About 20 to 30 million ha are severely affected by salinity while an additional 60 to 80 million ha are affected to some degree. Waterlogged soil, which aggravates the problem of salinity, is usually caused by overwatering and a lack of proper drainage systems. Runoff from agricultural areas fertilized with manure and chemicals pollutes watercourses and groundwater by increasing levels of nutrients.

The present level of water pollution warrants that steps be taken to control further contamination of water resources. More serious action needs to be taken in water resource management, waste water treatment and the provision of safe public water supplies. In developed and developing countries there should be controls and regulations regarding the treatment and recycling of industrial effluents, while efforts must be made to replace harmful products and ban dangerous pesticides.

There is compelling evidence that at least 20 to 30 percent of the water currently used in households and industries can be saved by adopting appropriate regulatory and policy instruments (tariffs, quotas, groundwater extraction charges). The twin benefits of clean water and reduced demand can be obtained if the recycling or reuse of water is encouraged in industries through pollution control legislation and economic incentives (water tariffs based on economic costs, effluent charges and low-interest loans for effluent and sewage treatment plants). Similar savings may be possible in irrigated agriculture by investments in canal lining, by encouraging less water-intensive crops (through relative output prices) and by raising irrigation rates.

Source: UNEP. 1991. Freshwater pollution. UNEP/ GEMS Environmental Library. No. 6. Nairobi.

Industry requires large amounts of water, but most of it is recycled back into the water system. The major problem is that much of this water is returned polluted with wastes, chemicals and heavy metals. Over 85 percent of total withdrawals by industry are recycled as waste water.

Domestic water demand is moderate in comparison with agriculture and industry but its quality requirements are high. Domestic and municipal water uses include drinking, washing, food preparation and sanitation.

WATER AND HEALTH

Two of the most troubling domestic water supply issues for policy-makers are access and health. Nearly one billion people in the world are without clean drinking-water. Providing easier access to safe drinking-water significantly improves health conditions. Personal hygiene increases when water availability rises above 50 litres per day (which generally means that it must be delivered to the house or yard). An estimated 1.7 billion persons contend with inadequate sanitation facilities. The lack of sewage collection and treatment is a major source of surface and groundwater pollution.

Health officials identify five categories of disease related to water: (i) water-borne diseases (typhoid, cholera, dysentery, gastroenteritis and infectious hepatitis); (ii) water-washed infections of the skin and eyes (trachoma, scabies, yaws, leprosy, conjunctivitis and ulcers); (iii) water-based diseases (schistosomiasis and guinea-worm); iv) diseases from water-related insect vectors such as mosquitoes and blackflies; and v) infections caused by defective sanitation (hookworm).

The World Bank's World Development Report 1992 estimates that providing access to safe water and adequate sanitation could result in two million fewer deaths from diarrhoea among young children and 200 million fewer episodes of diarrhoeal illnesses each year.

Water as a Strategic Resource

Water, even when plentiful, is frequently drawn into the realm of politics. Domestic laws and well-established customs can help resolve water-related disputes at national and village levels but international law has not developed fast enough to deal with the growing number of water-related conflicts between many countries and regions. In 1989, Egypt's then Minister of State for Foreign Affairs, Boutros-Ghali, declared: "The national security of Egypt is in the hands of the eight other African countries in the Nile basin."14 As Postel notes, Boutros-Ghali highlights the importance of water to Egypt's economy as well as the advantage upstream countries have over downstream neighbours.

The increasing value of water, concern about water quality and quantity, and problems of access and denial have given rise to the concept of resource geopolitics or "hydropolitics". In this context, water joins petroleum and certain minerals as a strategic resource. Its increasing scarcity and value will only intensify the prevalence of water politics and relevant international conflicts.

Several countries depend heavily on river flows from other countries. Botswana, Bulgaria, Cambodia, the Congo, Egypt, the Gambia, Hungary, Luxembourg, Mauritania, the Netherlands, Romania, the Sudan and the Syrian Arab Republic all receive over 75 percent of their available water supplies from the river flows of upstream neighbours. More than 40 percent of the world's population lives in river basins that are shared by more than one country.

Along with land and energy sources, water has been the focus of disputes and, in extreme cases, even wars. The division of the Indus waters and its tributaries among India and Pakistan provided a salutary warning example. War was only just avoided in the early years of independence by a binding agreement, backed by massive international aid, to build two huge water storage dams and a system of canals. Water could then be channelled to the areas of Pakistan that were deprived of water when some of the Indus tributaries were diverted into Indian territory.

The costs to all parties of this settlement were high but certainly less than the human and financial costs of a conflict. Many other international rivers, including the Nile, Euphrates, Ganges and Mekong, are prospective risk points for disputes. The future of the Jordan waters is already an integral component of regional peace talks and illustrates how complicated hydropolitics can be. The fact that groundwater resources are also involved in the talks adds another dimension of difficulty.

BOX: The international conference on water and the environment: Development issues for the 21st century

The International Conference on Water and the Environment (ICWE) was held in Dublin, Ireland, from 26 to 31 January 1992. The conference provided the major input on freshwater problems for UNCED, convened in Rio de Janeiro, Brazil, June 1992. The ICWE was attended by 500 participants from 114 countries, 38 NGOs, 14 intergovernmental organizations and 28 UN bodies and agencies.

The major work of the ICWE was undertaken by six working groups which addressed:

- *integrated water resources development and management;*
- *water resources assessment and impacts of climate change on water resources;*
- *protection of water resources, water quality and aquatic ecosystems;*
- *water and sustainable urban development and drinking-water supply and sanitation;*
- *water for sustainable food production and rural development and drinking-water supply and sanitation;*
- *mechanisms for implementation and coordination at global, national, regional and local levels.*

The two main outputs of the conference are the Dublin Statement and Report of the Conference, which set out recommendations for action based on four guiding principles. First, the effective management of water resources demands a holistic approach linking social and economic development with the protection of natural ecosystems, including land and water linkages across catchment areas or groundwater aquifers; second, water development and management should be based on a participatory approach that involves users, planners and policy-makers at all levels; third, women play a central part in the provision, management and safeguarding of water; and, finally, water has an economic value in all its competing uses and should be recognized as an economic good.

The Water Sector and Natural Resource Policy

In January 1992, the ICWE concluded that scarcity and misuse of freshwater pose a serious and growing threat to sustainable development and protection of the environment.15 The conference emphasized that human health and welfare, food security, economic development and ecosystems are all at risk, unless water and land resources are managed more effectively in the future.

To address water problems at local, national and international levels, the ICWE recommended a range of development strategies and policies based on four principles. While the conference participants readily agreed on the wording of the first three principles, the fourth provoked a long and contentious debate. Principle 4 declares that water has an economic value in all its competing uses and should be recognized as an economic good.

For many, it is difficult to reconcile the concept of water as an economic good with the traditional idea of water as a basic necessity and human right. Older elementary economic textbooks explain this conceptual puzzle-why diamonds, which have so little utility, are expensive while freshwater, which is so essential to life, is cheap. More recent texts leave water out of these vignettes. Like fresh air, water was once considered a classic free good; now that it is growing scarce, while not yet expensive, it is at least acknowledged to be valuable.

Scarcity is one of the most important issues in considering the various socio-economic tradeoffs in allocating water among different users. Allocation policies and decisions determine who will have access to water and under what conditions, and what impact this will have on society and the economy.

The cheapness of water is often more apparent than real. It is a free good not because water provision is without cost-obviously this is far from true-but because governments have chosen to charge less than full costs for water services for one or more reasons. These subsidies are now coming under scrutiny. The ICWE's final report acknowledges that failure in the past to recognize water's economic value and the real cost of service provision has led to wasteful and environmentally damaging uses. Moreover, the conference report states that managing water as an economic good is an important way of achieving efficient and equitable use, as well as encouraging the conservation and protection of scarce water resources.

Water may be considered a "free" good in the form of rain, but when this free good is captured and delivered to customers by canal, pipe or other means, it becomes a water service. There is generally much less resistance to water service fees than there is to water charges. It is in this context that the ICWE and UNCED called for a new approach to the assessment, development and management of freshwater resources. The proposed approach involves the management of freshwater as a finite and vulnerable resource and the integration of sectoral water plans and programmes within the framework of national economic and social policy.

BOX : FRAGMENTED PLANNING AND WATER RESOURCES IN SOUTHERN INDIA

The World Bank's water resources management policy paper presents several examples from southern India to illustrate the kinds of problem caused by fragmented decision-making. The Chittur River's highly variable flows have traditionally been diverted at many points into small reservoirs to irrigate the main rice crop. The diversion channels are large enough to accommodate flood flows following the monsoon rains. Thus, when a storage dam was constructed, the uppermost channel was able to absorb virtually all the regulated flow. The upper tanks now tend to remain full throughout the year, concentrating benefits and adding to evaporation losses. The more extensive lower areas have reverted to uncertain rain-fed cultivation, and total agricultural value added has decreased. Construction of the storage dam without adequate consideration of downstream users or the existing storage capacity of the basin is one example of how individual project development in isolation can cause significant economic losses.

The construction of the Sathanur Dam on the Ponnani River in Tamil Nadu to serve a left bank command area deprived productive delta areas of irrigation water. While the rights of downstream irrigators are recognized in the dam operating rules, most of the regulated flow is diverted upstream; water losses have greatly increased in the wide sandy bed and no surface water has reached the sea for 20 or more years. Continued spills in about 50 percent of all years were used to justify the subsequent construction of the right bank command, further aggravating shortages in the delta and leading to continual conflicts between the two Sathanur commands. Meanwhile, additional storage dams on upstream tributaries are adding to evaporation losses in what was already a fully developed basin. Irrigation in the productive delta has declined further and the Sathanur commands in turn are suffering. The high-value crops that were once grown on the main river are being replaced by cultivation on less productive lands, served by tributaries that are more variable than the main river.

The Amaravati River, a tributary of the Cauvery, is the most disputed major river in India. In the absence of a Cauvery agreement, Karnataka (the upstream riparian state) has steadily developed large irrigation schemes, depriving the delta (Tamil Nadu's rice bowl) of its accustomed supplies. Meanwhile, Tamil Nadu has been developing the Amaravati. As at Sathanur, water releases are made from the Amaravati Dam for the traditional areas, but these are far downstream and the substitution of regulated flood flows has encouraged the development of private pumps along the river bank. Even though the new electric connections have now been banned, little can be done to control illegal connections or diesel pumps and, consequently, little water now reaches the lowest commands, let alone the Cauvery. Meanwhile, new storage dams are being constructed on tributaries both in Kerala and Tamil Nadu, further depriving not only the old lands but also the new lands and the pump areas.

Source: World Bank. 1993.

Water resources management: a policy paper.

A more integrated and broader approach to water sector polices and issues is important because of water's special nature as a unitary resource. Rainwater, rivers, lakes, groundwater and polluted water are all part of the same resource, which means global, national, regional and local actions are highly interdependent.18 Water use in one part of the system alters the resource base and affects water users in other parts.

Dams built in one country frequently reduce river flows to downstream countries for years afterwards, thereby affecting hydroelectric and irrigation capacity. When a city overpumps a groundwater supply, streamflows may be reduced in surrounding areas; when it contaminates its surface water, it can pollute groundwater supplies as well. Certain human actions at local levels may contribute to climate change, with long-term implications for the hydrological system worldwide.

Water policies, laws, projects, regulations and administrative actions often overlook these linkages. Governments generally tend to organize and administer water sector activities separately: one department is in charge of irrigation; another oversees water supply and sanitation; a third manages hydropower activities; a fourth supervises transportation; a fifth controls water quality; a sixth directs environmental policy; and so forth.

These fragmented bureaucracies make uncoordinated decisions, reflecting individual agency responsibilities that are independent of each other. Too often, government planners develop the same water source within an interdependent system for different and competing uses. This project-by-project, department-by-department and region-by-region approach is no longer adequate for addressing water issues.

To help resolve the growing number of water resource issues, policy-makers are increasingly being called on to review and explain the conditions, problems and progress in the overall water sector. This integrated approach requires water managers to understand not only the water cycle (including rainfall, distribution, ecosystem interactions and natural environment and land-use changes), but also the diverse intersectoral development needs for water resources.

The next section further explores this important concept of linking the water sector with the national economy and provides a conceptual basis for understanding the role of economic policy-making.

WATER RESOURCES: ECONOMICS AND POLICY

In early civilizations, water played a relatively simple role. It was needed for transportation and drinking and it provided a fishing and hunting source. Overtime, sedentary agricultural societies evolved and water use became more important. Families began settling near springs, lakes and rivers to supply livestock and crops with water, gradually developing technologies to divert water for irrigation and domestic purposes. Babylonian, Egyptian, Hittite, Greek, Etruscan, Roman, Chinese, Mayan, Incan and other empires constructed water delivery systems such as long aqueducts to carry water to large cities. In fact, until the middle of the twentieth century, most societies were able to meet their growing water needs by capturing reliable and relatively inexpensive sources.

When water is plentiful relative to demand, water policies, rules and laws tend to be simple and only casually enforced. As populations grow and economies expand, water sectors evolve from an "expansionary" phase to a "mature" phase. At a certain point during the expansionary phase, the financial and environmental costs of developing new water supplies begin to exceed the economic benefits in the least productive (marginal) uses of existing supplies. The real location of existing supplies, rather than the capture of unclaimed supplies, then becomes the least costly method to maximize benefits.

A water sector in the "mature" phase is characterized by rising marginal costs of providing water and increasing interdependencies among users. In this phase, conflicts over scarcities and external costs arise. (External costs result when one user interferes with another's supply, e.g. when an upstream user pollutes a river and raises costs for downstream users.) These conflicts eventually become so complex that elaborate management systems are needed to resolve disputes and allocate water among different users and economic sectors.

Developing effective water sector policies is troublesome for a number of reasons. First, water has unique physical properties, complex economic characteristics and important cultural features that distinguish it from all other resources. Second, water resource management is administratively complicated because it involves legal, environmental, technological, economic and political considerations. In most societies, political considerations dominate decisions on water resource use. Nonetheless, most policy options are framed and discussed in economic terms. For example, water resource management depends on the government's ability to establish an appropriate legal, regulatory and administrative framework. In fact, markets are based on a system of enforceable private property rights. Private water markets require secure and transferable property rights, including the right to exclude other users.

This section attempts to provide a conceptual basis for understanding water policy interventions while examining the circumstances under which water policies work or fail. It comprises three parts: the first examines the relationship between the water sector and the overall economy; the second explains the social, physical and economic nature of water; the third assesses the advantages and disadvantages of broad alternative approaches to public water policy and also reviews policy issues related to the economic organization of water resource management.

Linking the Water Sector with the National Economy

Economic policy-makers tend to confront policy issues one at a time, stating policy objectives in single dimensional terms. This approach presents difficulties because a policy aimed at achieving a single objective usually has unintended and unrecognized consequences. Water managers and policy-makers need to assess the entire range of government interventions to understand fully the economic, social and environmental impacts on a given sector, region or group of people.

Improving water resource management requires recognizing how the overall water sector is linked to the national economy. Equally important is understanding how alternative economic policy instruments influence water use across different economic sectors as well as between local, regional and national levels and among households, farms and firms. For too long, many water managers have failed to recognize the connection between macroeconomic policies and their impact on, for example, technical areas such as irrigation.

Macroeconomic policies and sectoral policies that are not aimed specifically at the water sector can have a strategic impact on resource allocation and aggregate demand in the economy. A country's overall development strategy and use of macroeconomic policies-including fiscal, monetary and trade policies-directly and indirectly affect demand and investment in water-related activities. The most obvious example is government expenditures (fiscal policy) on irrigation, flood control or dams.

A less apparent example is trade and exchange rate policy aimed at promoting exports and earning more foreign exchange. For example, as a result of currency depreciation, exports of high-value, water-consuming crops may increase. If additional policy changes reduce export taxes, farmers are provided with an even greater incentive to invest in export crops as well as in the necessary irrigation.

National development strategies can directly influence water allocation and use in other ways. In the case of a food self-sufficiency strategy, the government may subsidize water-intensive inputs to encourage farmers to produce more rice. By providing financial incentives for rice producers, the government is influencing the demand for water and private irrigation investment through price policies.

Apart from the direct effects on water use resulting from such price policies, the increased demand for irrigation water also has intersectoral, intrasectoral, distributional and environmental implications.

The agricultural sector is provided with an economic advantage in access to water vis-à-vis the industrial sector (intersectoral); water used for rice gains an economic advantage over water used for other crops (intrasectoral); rice producers with more land and access to water gain over those with less land and water (distributional); and increased pesticide and fertilizer use are likely to affect water quality (environmental).

Sectoral policies affect water use and allocation in non-agricultural sectors in a variety of ways. For example, in the western United States, 70 to 80 percent of the region's water yield results from snowmelt from the high-elevation forests, many of which are under public jurisdiction.

Water yields are significantly affected by timber harvest policies on these lands. Rangeland management policies on lower elevations also alter vegetation conditions and thus affect the rate of evapotranspiration, in turn affecting streamflow and groundwater recharge. In such cases, it is important for downstream city water managers to recognize, understand and become involved in the decisions of other sectors such as livestock and forestry.

BOX : Economic policies and water use in the syrian arab republic

After struggling throughout the 1980s, the Syrian economy has performed well over the past few years. The end of a two-year drought allowed agriculture and agro-industries to recover in 1991. During the drought, the government was forced to import large quantities of wheat and barley, thereby draining foreign currency reserves. In addition, the lower water levels meant a reduction in hydropower generation, increasing the need for thermal power and, in turn, lowering crude oil exports.

Two of the Syrian Arab Republic's major national development objectives are: achieving food self-sufficiency to reduce dependency on imports; and expanding agricultural exports to earn more foreign exchange. To support these objectives, the government has invested 60 to 70 percent of the entire agricultural budget in irrigation over the past ten years.

Several factors explain this special attention for irrigation development. The irrigated area comprises only 15 percent of the cultivated land yet produces over 50 percent of the total value of agricultural production. A large part of wheat production as well as all major industrial crops, including cotton, tobacco and sugar beet, are produced on irrigated farms. Production on the remaining rain-fed area, representing 85 percent of the total area, varies greatly from year to year. At present, agriculture accounts for about 85 percent of the country's water consumption, but competition is increasing. During the 1980s, industrial water demand increased by nearly 900 percent. Current projections suggest that water requirements will be two to three times greater by 2010.

The government's effort to promote food self-sufficiency has produced a second generation of water-related problems. To encourage growth in agricultural production and enhance rural incomes, interest rates, seeds, fertilizers, pesticides, transport and energy prices are subsidized. The government also establishes purchase prices and buys industrial crops, major cereals and feedgrains; e.g. the 1992 domestic wheat price was almost twice the international price.

These policies are contributing to the proliferation of wells in the Syrian Arab Republic. Digging wells to pump groundwater accounts for 80 percent of the newly irrigated land since 1987. With irrigation, farmers obtain higher yields, more stable production and greater profit. Since water is free, the only investment expense required is the well and the pumping gear-a one-time fixed cost. Farmers obtain subsidized credit to purchase subsidized fuel for operating imported pumps purchased with overvalued currency (an implicit subsidy). With these economic opportunities, most farmers want to dig wells or pump surface water.

Other current economic pressures are also influencing farmers' decisions to dig wells and expand irrigation. For example, as incomes in urban areas increase, consumers are demanding more fruit and vegetables. At the same time, recent changes in trade and exchange rate policies are making Syrian agricultural products more competitive in regional markets. Farmers who inititally planned only on supplementary irrigation for winter wheat are finding summer vegetables and irrigated fruit production increasingly profitable.

With the continuing importance of structural adjustment and stabilization programmes, many developing countries are implementing fundamental changes in macroeconomic and sectoral polices. Typical adjustment programmes call for a greater reliance on markets, more open trade, fiscal austerity and a phasing out of producer and consumer subsidies (input and product markets). Budget-reducing measures imply increased competition between and within sectors for funding new water projects. In these situations, the overall economic, social and environmental implications of choices must be carefully addressed. For example, when governments must choose between financing either irrigation projects or hydroelectric power projects, there is an additional social opportunity cost of the irrigation water in countries that are dependent on imported energy sources.

At the same time, when water scarcity keeps some farmers on uneconomical lands such as steep watersheds, the country suffers twice: once in terms of reduced production compared with what would be possible with irrigation; and again in terms of erosion and resource depletion, with erosion possibly shortening the life of existing waterworks.

In most countries, pressure has increased not only to modify investment allocations but also to recognize and accommodate new demands for water. The direct implications for water managers include fewer capital investments in new water projects, the elimination of irrigation subsidies, increased efforts to recover its cost and more emphasis on demand management to improve the efficiency of existing supplies.

The Social, Physical and Economic Nature of Water

Policy-makers throughout the world treat water as more than a simple economic commodity. Because water is essential to life, they often reject competitive market allocation mechanisms. Many societies believe that water has special cultural, religious and social values. Boulding observed that "the sacredness of water as a symbol of ritual purity exempts it somewhat from the dirty rationality of the market". In many cultures, goals other than economic efficiency play an unusually large role in selecting water management institutions. Some religions, such as Islam, even prohibit water allocation by market forces.

The international community recognizes that access to water is a basic human right. The ICWE asserted that "...it is vital to recognize first the basic right of all human beings to have access to clean water and sanitation at an affordable price".

The connection between water and human life is most dramatic in arid regions, where crop irrigation is essential to food production. In Egypt, little food can be grown without the help of the Nile for irrigation. However, the focus on water's special status tends to obscure the fact that, in most societies, only a tiny fraction of water consumption is actually for drinking and preserving life. In fact, a large portion of urban water is used for convenience and comfort. In the arid western United States, per caput water withdrawal by households frequently exceeds 400 litres per day, about half of which is used to irrigate lawns and gardens. Most of the remainder is for flushing toilets, bathing and washing cars.

Another important influence on water resource policy is societies' partiality for technical solutions. In most countries, water management is typically relegated to the engineering domain. Indeed, most water managers are engineers, who are trained to solve technical problems. As inadequate public policies are increasingly blamed for water-related problems, a strong case is emerging for emphasizing human behaviour as an additional component of water systems.

Physical Attributes of Water

Water has two additional features that further complicate management efforts: bulkiness and mobility. The value per unit of weight tends to be relatively low (placing water among the commodities that are termed "bulky"). Unlike petroleum, the costs of transporting and storing water are generally high relative to its economic value at the point of use. In crop irrigation, the water applied may yield additional economic values of less than $0.04 per tonne of water. Water is also difficult to identify and measure because it flows, evaporates, seeps and transpires. This evasive nature means that exclusive property rights, which are the basis of a market economy, are hard to establish and enforce.

Many water management problems are site-specific and so elude uniform policy treatment. While water consumption and quality requirements are tied to local populations and development levels, local water availability usually changes with climatic variations throughout the year and over longer cyclical swings. These supplies may be highly variable and unpredictable in time, space and quality. In regions throughout India, for instance, most rainfall is concentrated during a three-month period and there are large year-to-year variations. In addition, forecasts of significant global climate change-attributable to both natural and human causes-raise concerns about longer-term supply trends.

Water projects that attempt to compensate for extreme seasonal variations such as floods and droughts frequently require enormous investments. The economies of size are so large in these cases that unit costs continue to exceed the range of existing demands. This is a classical "natural monopoly" situation in which a single supplying entity is the most economically efficient organizational arrangement.

On the other hand, most economies of size for pumping groundwater are achieved at relatively small outputs and multiple suppliers can therefore operate efficiently. However, aquifers are usually hydraulically linked with rivers or streams-part of a river's volume may come from underground flows and rivers may replenish groundwater stocks. This hydraulic linkage is affected when an aquifer is heavily pumped. A lowered groundwater table may draw water from a connected stream, reducing its flow to surface water users.

Climate change, water resources and agriculture

To date, research has not been able to provide clear conclusions about the prospective impacts of climate change and global warning. Among the potential impacts of climate change is its effect on the hydrological cycle and water management systems. For instance, an increase in floods and droughts will increase the frequency and severity of disasters. Relatively small changes can cause severe water resource problems, especially in semi-arid regions and humid areas where demand or pollution has led to water scarcity.

The statement adopted by the Second World Climate Conference, held in Geneva in 1990, concluded that the design of many costly structures to store and convey water, from large dams to small drainage facilities, is based on analyses of past records of climatic and hydrological parameters. Some of these structures are designed to last from 50 to 100 years or even longer. Records of past climate and hydrological conditions may no longer be a reliable guide for the future. The possible effects of climate change should be considered in the design and management of water resource systems. Data systems and research must be strengthened to predict water resource impacts, detect hydrological changes and improve hydrological parameterization in global climate models.

Agricultural impacts could be significant but researchers are uncertain whether global agricultural potential will increase or decrease. Increases in drought risk are potentially the most serious effect of climate change on agriculture. Disease and pest patterns, raised sea levels and storm surges are additional problems. It also appears that many areas will have increased precipitation, soil moisture and water storage, thus altering patterns of agricultural ecosystems and other water uses.

Aquifer management is often complicated by the aggregate impact of the actions of many individuals. Even though each individual may have a negligible impact when taken alone, the sum total can be of major importance. One example is the rapid spread of tube well irrigation in South Asia. One tube well has little effect on the total water supply, but thousands of tube wells can quickly deplete an aquifer. Establishing effective policies to regulate these many small, scattered decision-makers is exceedingly difficult.

ECONOMIC ATTRIBUTES OF WATER USE

Water provides four types of important economic benefits: commodity benefits; waste assimilation benefits; aesthetic and recreational benefits; and fish and wildlife habitats. Individuals derive commodity benefits from water by using it for drinking, cooking and sanitation. Farms, businesses and industries obtain commodity benefits by using water in productive activities. These commodity benefits represent private good uses of water which are rivals in consumption (e.g. one person's or industry's water use precludes or prevents its use by others). Government policies and regulations that concentrate on improving market access and competition are important means for improving the productive and allocative efficiency of the commodity uses of water.

The second and increasingly important economic benefit of water is waste disposal. Water bodies have a significant, but ultimately limited, assimilative capacity, meaning that they can process, dilute and carry away wastes.

Recreation and aesthetic benefits and fish and wildlife habitats were once regarded as luxury goods outside the concern of governments. Today, these two types of benefit are gaining increased attention. In developed countries, more and more people are focusing their recreational activities around lakes, rivers and seas. In developing nations, as incomes and leisure time grow, water-based recreation is becoming increasingly popular and an adequate supply of good-quality water helps provide a basis for attracting the tourist trade. Examples are cruises on the Nile in Egypt and visits to the Iguazú Falls on the Brazil-Argentina border. Likewise, information and knowledge about how humans have an impact on ecosystems have raised concern about the fish and wildlife benefits provided by water. Fish and wildlife habitats are related to both commodity and recreational uses.

Waste assimilation and recreational and aesthetic values are closer to being public goods than private goods. Public goods are non-rivals in consumption-one person's use does not preclude use by others. For example, the enjoyment of an attractive water body does not deny similar enjoyment to others. Non-rival goods require large amounts of resources to exclude unentitled consumers from using the good. Exclusion costs are frequently very high for water services such as flood control projects and navigation systems. Goods and services that are non-rivals in consumption are normally better suited to public sector interventions, including ownership, provision and regulation.

Aquifer Overdraft

An aquifer is a geological formation, actually or potentially containing water in its pores and voids. Aquifers consist of the porous rock or soil media (sand, gravel or rock materials) within which water is collected and through which it flows. Moisture from rain or snow that escapes evaporation collects in streams as surface water or seeps into the ground. Soil water not taken up by plants seeps downwards until it reaches the water-saturated zone. Water in aquifers is called groundwater. Groundwater deposits are economical to use for human purposes if they are close to the surface (and thereby inexpensive to pump) and are of good quality.

Aquifers vary greatly in their nature and extent. The quantity, quality and ease of extraction can be determined accurately only after extensive exploration. Underground geology varies widely and is expensive to map. Aquifers may be very thin or hundreds of metres thick; some are local in character, while others extend for hundreds of kilometres. The Ogallala-High Plains Aquifer in the central-western United States underlies more than 10 million ha over six states.

Relative to surface water, groundwater moves very slowly-in some cases only a few metres per year. While aquifers may have accumulated over thousands of years, modern pumping devices can easily exhaust them more rapidly than the natural recharge rate. It is also possible to divert surface water to recharge an existing aquifer artificially and make it available for future use.

Aquifer status reports from many parts of the world suggest that all is not well with our groundwater resources. Symptoms of management problems begin with pumping rates that exceed the natural recharge. Primary symptoms are: an exceedingly rapid exhaustion of groundwater stocks and the consequent increase in pumping costs; the intrusion of poorer-quality water into the deposit being exploited; salt water intrusion from rapid pumping near seacoasts; and mineralized deposits interspersed with better-quality water.

Subsidence of overlying lands is another adverse impact of aquifer overexploitation. As water is withdrawn, the soil and rock particles comprising the aquifer are compressed into a smaller volume and, consequently, crack the earth's surface. This results in damage to buildings, roads, railroads, etc. Another consequence of overpumping may be the interruption of flows in neighbouring wetlands and streams; deprived of their water source, they are reduced in size or may dry up altogether. Other adverse effects from overpumping result when residential or farmers' wells dry up because of the presence of larger and deeper wells.

From a broad perspective, aquifer exploitation can bring about either or both of two types of social dilemma. First, overdraft is an example of a class of resource problems, usually called "common pool" problems. A common pool resource can be defined by two characteristics. The first is subtractibility (meaning that a unit of resource withdrawn by one individual is not available to another individual user). The second is the high cost of excluding potential beneficiaries from exploiting the resource. Fugitive or mobile resources, such as water, petroleum or migratory fish and wildlife, are typical examples of resources with high exclusion costs.

Common pool problems or dilemmas arise when individually rational resource use leads to a non-optimal result from the perspective of the users as a group. Three conditions are necessary to produce a common pool resource dilemma: first, large numbers of users withdraw the resource; second, the actions and characteristics of the individual users and the extraction technology bring about suboptimal outcomes from the group's viewpoint; third, there must be an institutionally feasible strategy for collective resource management that is more efficient than the current situation.

The roots of the problems associated with common pools are found in the inadequate economic and institutional framework within which the resource is exploited. Common pool resources have been typically utilized in an "open access" framework, within which resources are used according to a rule of capture. When no one owns the resource, users have no incentive to conserve for the future and the self-interest of individual users leads them to overexploitation. The characteristics of the economic institutions governing their use is the fundamental issue in managing common pool resources.

The second type of social dilemma associated with groundwater exploitation is the imposition of external costs or externalities. In the presence of significant externalities, the calculation of costs and benefits by exploiters does not yield a collectively optimal rate of exploitation.

Economic Organization of the Water Sector: Markets or Governments?

Most countries rely on a mix of market policies and direct government interventions to manage water resources. Each system has its own advantages and disadvantages.

A competitive market has the potential to allocate resources (water supplies) efficiently among competing demands. Producers and consumers acting in their own self-interest reach the price at which available supplies are allocated. Private producers, guided by prospective profit, seek to buy inputs as cheaply as possible, combine them in the most efficient form and create products that have the highest value relative to cost.

Consumers' incomes, tastes and preferences influence expenditure patterns, which encourage firms to produce the commodities people are willing and able to buy. Prices are forced upwards for the commodities most desired, and producers allocate resources in the direction of the greatest potential profits. The firms producing desired goods most efficiently are rewarded by profit while the unsuccessful are eliminated, so production occurs at the least cost. However, the needs of potential consumers with limited incomes may either not be met at all or be met only partially.

While the private market has the potential to produce the maximum private-valued bundle of goods and services, the public sector also plays an important role. Public actions incorporate a broader range of social goals than the private sector. The public sector can ameliorate income inequalities, promote development in disadvantaged regions, regulate private activities that harm the environment and control other undesirable effects of a private, profit-oriented monopoly.

Market Failures

If water as a commodity, or the economic system in which water is used, meets the preconditions for a market system, government interventions can be minimized. In competitive markets, government's primary role is to emphasize "incentive structures" and to establish "rules". Some of the most important rules are the laws governing the establishment of property rights and the enforcement of contracts.

Market economies experience shortcomings called market failures.26 Market failures occur when incentives offered to individuals or firms encourage behaviour that does not meet efficiency criteria or, more generally, because efficiency or economic criteria fail to satisfy national social welfare objectives. In these cases, the public sector may intervene to influence water provision and allocation. Market failures affecting water resources include externalities, public goods and natural monopolies. In other cases, even efficient markets may not meet societies' equity criteria so public intervention is necessary to compensate for distributional inequity.

Externalities are inherent in water sector activities. An example is the detrimental effect of saline return water flows (caused by irrigation) on downstream water users. Another example is the waterlogging of downslope lands through inefficient irrigation practices. Most irrigators do not normally consider the external costs they impose on others, so governments attempt to protect affected individuals through regulations, taxes, subsidies, fees or technical standards. For instance, irrigation practices can be regulated by setting and enforcing standards to control salinity and waterlogging.

In recent years, the "polluter pays" principle has attracted increased attention in industrialized countries (and to a lesser extent in developing countries). This principle requires producers to pay the "full" cost of their production process, including externalities such as polluting water.

Water storage projects and flood control programmes represent examples of public goods. The market does not adequately supply public goods because private entrepreneurs cannot easily exclude non-paying beneficiaries and capture a return on investment. For example, it is not possible to exclude people living along a river from the benefits of a flood protection plan on that river.

A firm that experiences decreasing costs throughout its range of production is easily able to dominate the entire market and become a natural monopoly (a common situation in the water sector). Decreasing costs imply increasing returns; thus, the first firm to begin production can always underprice new entrants. Urban water supply systems, hydropower plants and canal irrigation projects are subject to this type of market failure. Unregulated monopolies can restrain production and charge excessive prices; they also have little incentive to innovate. A water supplier acting as a natural monopoly has the power to impose exorbitant costs-even economic ruin-on its customers.

Public regulation or public ownership can mitigate the undesirable effects of a private, profit-oriented monopoly. When increasing returns exist, the lowest-cost production is that of a single producer. Society is likely to benefit by regulating or owning the monopoly rather than by encouraging competitive suppliers. More than one competitive supplier would present much higher distribution costs.

While free competition is viewed as the most efficient system for allocating resources, potential market imperfections can accentuate income disparities. Societies' public welfare goals often incorporate a broad range of social objectives. Primary among these is ameliorating income inequalities between members of the society and sometimes among political subdivisions or regions. In these situations, the government may direct investment and subsidies towards specific regions or groups. Water projects provide important investment strategies both for human welfare (drinking-water and food supplies) and for infrastructure to support economic development.

Government Failures

Even in the event of market failures, public sector interventions or non-market approaches may not lead to the socially optimum solution. In many cases, non-market responses to market failures lead to less than optimal outcomes. In particular, some government agency performance incentives result in a divergence from socially preferable outcomes (both in terms of allocative efficiency and distributional equity criteria). The problem areas relevant to water sector services are:

- *"Products" are hard to define.* The outputs of non-market activities are difficult to define in practice and difficult to measure independently of the inputs that produced them. Flood control or amenity benefits of water storage reservoirs are examples of water system outputs that are hard to measure.
- *Private goals of public agents.* The internal goals, or "internalities", of a public water agency as well as the agency's public aims provide the motivations, rewards and penalties for individual performance. Examples of counterproductive internal goals include budget maximization, expensive and inappropriate "technical-fix" solutions and the outright non-performance of duties. In addition, agencies may adopt high-tech solutions, or "technical quality", as goals in themselves. For example,

they may recommend sprinkler or drip irrigation systems when other less expensive but reliable methods are more economical. Finally, irrigation agency personnel may be persuaded, by gifts or other inducements, to violate operating rules for a favoured few.27

- *Spillovers from public action.* Public sector projects can also be a major source of externalities. Salinity and waterlogging of downslope lands can occur just as easily from inappropriately managed public irrigation projects as from private irrigators.
- *Inequitable distribution of power.* Public sector responsibilities, however noble their intent, may not be scrupulously or competently exercised. Yet the monopoly control of water supplies by public agencies provides certain groups or individuals with so much power over the economic welfare of water users that procedures to protect those of limited influence should be of prime importance.

Economic Structure and Irrigation

For many years, the economic systems in a number of developing countries discriminated against agriculture through policies such as high levels of protection for domestic manufacturing sectors, overvalued exchange rates and taxes on agricultural exports. Most developing countries today are at some stage of structural reform, attempting to adjust and transform their economies towards a more liberal economic trade regime-modifying government involvement and increasing market influence.

The developing world's recent record in consolidating macroeconomic stability with solid economic growth is very mixed. Where success is evident, most of the economic transformation has taken place at the macro level and much remains to be done to effect the consequent adjustments at the micro level, at the level of water users in other words.

Even with widespread acceptance of the need for macroeconomic price policy reforms for all other sectors since the early 1980s, the dominant supporting actions for agriculture have been non-price policies. For non-agricultural sectors, the new policy mix includes minimizing state involvement in the pricing and marketing of inputs and outputs, privatization and limiting government borrowing.

Despite the irrigation sector's often being sheltered or even benefiting from the effects of these economic policy reforms, government subsidy cuts are inevitably affecting the scope and efficiency of agricultural support services. In most countries, there is a pressing need to discuss how various policy options, including both public interventions and market-oriented, private sector activities, may assist the irrigation sector in the process of economic reform.

4

Priorities for Agriculture and Rural Development

BACKGROUND

Although agriculture contributes only 21% of India's GDP, its importance in the country's economic, social, and political fabric goes well beyond this indicator. The rural areas are still home to some 72 percent of the India's 1.1 billion people, a large number of whom are poor. Most of the rural poor depend on rain-fed agriculture and fragile forests for their livelihoods. The sharp rise in foodgrain production during India's Green Revolution of the 1970s enabled the country to achieve self-sufficiency in foodgrains and stave off the threat of famine. Agricultural intensification in the 1970s to 1980s saw an increased demand for rural labor that raised rural wages and, together with declining food prices, reduced rural poverty.

Sustained, although much slower, agricultural growth in the 1990s reduced rural poverty to 26.3 percent by 1999/00. Since then, however, the slowdown in agricultural growth has become a major cause for concern. India's rice yields are one-third of China's and about half of those in Vietnam and Indonesia. With the exception of sugarcane, potato and tea, the same is true for most other agricultural commodities. The Government of India places high priority on reducing poverty by raising agricultural productivity. However, bold action from policymakers will be required to shift away from the existing subsidy-based regime that is no longer sustainable, to build a solid foundation for a highly productive, internationally competitive, and diversified agricultural sector.

ISSUES AND CHALLENGES

Slow Down in Agricultural and Rural Non-Farm Growth: Both the poorest as well as the more prosperous 'Green Revolution' states of Punjab, Haryana and Uttar Pradesh have recently witnessed a slow-down in agricultural growth. Some of the factors hampering the revival of growth are:

- Poor composition of public expenditures: Public spending on agricultural subsidies is crowding out productivity-enhancing investments such as agricultural research and extension, as well as investments in rural infrastructure, and the health and education of the rural people. In 1999/2000, agricultural subsidies amounted to 3 percent of GDP and were over 7 times the public investments in the sector.
- Over-regulation of domestic agricultural trade: While economic and trade reforms in the 1990s helped to improve the incentive framework, over-regulation of domestic trade has increased costs, price risks and uncertainty, undermining the sector's competitiveness.
- Government interventions in labor, land, and credit markets: More rapid growth of the rural non-farm sector is constrained by government interventions in factor markets — labor, land, and credit — and in output markets, such as the small-scale reservation of enterprises.
- Inadequate infrastructure and services in rural areas.

Weak Framework for Sustainable Water Management and Irrigation:

- Inequitable allocation of water: Many states lack the incentives, policy, regulatory, and institutional framework for the efficient, sustainable, and equitable allocation of water.
- Deteriorating irrigation infrastructure: Public spending in irrigation is spread over many uncompleted projects. In addition, existing infrastructure has rapidly deteriorated as operations and maintenance is given lower priority.

Inadequate Access to Land and Finance:

- Stringent land regulations discourage rural investments: While land distribution has become less skewed, land policy and regulations to increase security of tenure (including restrictions or bans on renting land or converting it to other uses) have had the unintended effect of reducing access by the landless and discouraging rural investments.
- Computerization of land records has brought to light institutional weaknesses: State government initiatives to computerize land records have reduced transaction costs and increased transparency, but also brought to light institutional weaknesses.
- Rural poor have little access to credit: While India has a wide network of rural finance institutions, many of the rural poor remain excluded, due to inefficiencies in the formal finance institutions, the weak regulatory framework, high transaction costs, and risks associated with lending to agriculture.

Weak Natural Resources Management: One quarter of India's population depends on forests for at least part of their livelihoods.

- A purely conservation approach to forests is ineffective: Experience in India shows that a purely conservation approach to natural resources management does not work effectively and does little to reduce poverty.
- Weak resource rights for forest communities: The forest sector is also faced with weak resource rights and economic incentives for communities, an inefficient legal framework and participatory management, and poor access to markets.

Weak delivery of basic services in rural areas:

- Low bureaucratic accountability and inefficient use of public funds: Despite large expenditures in rural development, a highly centralized bureaucracy with low accountability and inefficient use of public funds limit their impact on poverty. In 1992, India amended its Constitution to create three tiers of democratically elected rural local governments bringing governance down to the villages. However, the transfer of authority, funds, and functionaries to these local bodies is progressing slowly, in part due to political vested interests. The poor are not empowered to contribute to shaping public programs or to hold local governments accountable.

PRIORITY AREAS FOR THE WORLD BANK SUPPORT

1. Enhancing Agricultural Productivity, Competitiveness, and Rural Growth

Enhancing productivity: Creating a more productive, internationally competitive and diversified agricultural sector would require a shift in public expenditures away from subsidies towards productivity enhancing investments. Second it will require removing the restrictions on domestic private trade to improve the investment climate and meet expanding market opportunities. Third, the agricultural research and extension systems need to be strengthened to improve access to productivity enhancing technologies. The diverse conditions across India suggests the importance of regionally differentiated strategies, with a strong focus on the lagging states.

Improving Water Resource and Irrigation/Drainage Management: Increase in multi-sectoral competition for water highlights the need to formulate water policies and unbundle water resources management from irrigation service delivery. Other key priorities include: (i) modernizing Irrigation and Drainage Departments to integrate the participation of farmers and other agencies in irrigation management; (ii) improving cost recovery; (iii) rationalizing public expenditures, with priority to completing schemes with the highest returns; and (iv) allocating sufficient resources for operations and maintenance for the sustainability of investments.

Strengthening rural non-farm sector growth: Rising incomes are fueling demand for higher-value fresh and processed agricultural products in domestic markets and globally, which open new opportunities for agricultural diversification to higher value products (e.g. horticulture, livestock), agro-processing and related services. The government needs to shift its role from direct intervention and overregulation to creating the enabling environment for private sector participation and competition for agribusiness and more broadly, the rural non-farm sector growth. Improving the rural investment climate includes removing trade controls, rationalizing labor regulations and the tax regime (i.e. adoption of the value added tax system), and improving access to credit and key infrastructure (e.g. roads, electricity, ports, markets).

2. Improving Access to Assets and Sustainable Natural Resource Use

Balancing poverty reduction and conservation priorities: Finding win-win combinations for conservation and poverty reduction will be critical to sustainable natural resource management. This will involve addressing legal, policy and institutional constraints to devolving resource rights, and transferring responsibilities to local communities.

Improving access to land: States can build on the growing consensus to reform land policy, particularly land tenancy policy and land administration system. States that do not have tenancy restrictions can provide useful lessons in this regard. Over the longer term, a more holistic approach to land administration policies, regulations and institutions is necessary to ensure tenure security, reduce costs, and ensure fairness and sustainability of the system.

Improving access to rural finance: It would require improving the performance of regional rural banks and rural credit cooperatives by enhancing regulatory oversight, removing government control and ownership, and strengthening the legal framework for loan recovery and the use of land as collateral. It would also involve creating an enabling environment for the development of micro-finance institutions in rural areas.

3. Strengthening Institutions for the Poor and Promoting Rural Livelihood

Promoting Community-Based Rural Development: State Government efforts in scaling up livelihood and community-driven development approaches will be critical to build social capital in the poorest areas as well as to expand savings mobilization, promote productive investments, income generating opportunities and sustainable natural resource management. Direct support to self-help groups, village committees, user's associations, savings and loans groups and others can provide the initial 'push' to move organizations to higher level and access to new economic opportunities.

Moreover, social mobilization and particularly the empowerment of women's groups, through increased capacity for collective action will provide communities with greater "voice" and bargaining power in dealing with the private sector, markets and financial services.

Strengthening Accountability for Service Delivery: As decentralization efforts are pursued and local governments are given more prominence in the basic service delivery, the establishment of accountability mechanisms becomes critical. Local governments' capacity to identify local priorities through participatory budgeting and planning needs to be strengthened. This, in turn, would improve the rural investment climate, facilitating the involvement of the private sector, creating employment opportunities and linkages between farm and non-farm sectors.

IRRIGATION, FOOD PROCESSING, FERTILIZERS & FISHERIES

From a nation dependent on food imports to feed its population, India today is not only self—sufficient in grain production, but also has a substantial reserve. The progress made by agriculture in the last four decades has been one of the biggest success stories of free India. Agriculture and allied activities constitute the single largest contributor to the Gross Domestic Product, almost 33% of it. Agriculture is the means of livelihood of about two—thirds of the work force in the country.

This increase in agricultural production has been brought about by bringing additional area under cultivation, extension of irrigation facilities, the use of improved high yielding variety of seeds, better techniques evolved through agricultural research, water management, and plant protection through judicious use of fertilizers, pesticides and cropping practices.

Crops

The 1970s saw a multi-fold increase in wheat production that heralded the Green Revolution. In the next decade rice production rose significantly; in 1995-96, rice production was 79.6 million tons. Total grain production crossed 191 million tons in 1994-95, a big leap from 51 million tons in 1950-5 1. During the Seventh Plan, the average grain production was 155 million tons, 17 million tons more than the Sixth Plan average. To carry improved technologies to farmers, a National Pulse Development Program, covering 13 states, was launched in 1986. The Special Food Production Program augmented efforts to boost pulse production further. In 1995-96, pulse production was 13.2 million tons. With some States offering more than the statutory minimum price, sugarcane production also received a boost, in 1995-96 a record 283.0 million tons was registered.

Irrigation

As efforts continued to increase the irrigation potential in the country, the last 40 years saw the gross irrigated area reach 8~ million hectares. Flood forecasting has become an important activity over the years. Over 500 hydrological stations collect and transmit data through 400 wireless stations for issuing forecasts for 157 sites. About 5000 forecasts are issued in a year with 94% accuracy. The country also receives international support, with the World Bank as a primary source, for developing the water resources. International cooperation is also envisaged in setting up a National Center for Information on Water and Power. As there is a broad seismic belt in the country, particularly along the Himalayan, the Kutch region and ports of Maharashtra, a scheme is being evolved to collect all data on seismic activity at various dam sites.

Fertilizers

The fertilizer industry in India has grown tremendously in the last 30 years. The Government is keen to see that fertilizer reaches the farmers in the remote and hilly areas. It has been decided to decontrol the prices, distribution and movement of phosphatic and potassic fertilizers. Steps have been taken to ensure an increase in the supply of non-chemical fertilizers at reasonable prices. There are 53 fertilizer quality control laboratories in the country. Since bio—fertilisers are regarded as an effective, cheap and renewable supplement to chemical fertilizers, the Government is implementing a National Project on Development and Use of Bio-fertilisers. Under this scheme, one national and six regional centers for organizing training, demonstrating programs and quality testing of bio-fertilisers has been taken up. It was a challenging decision of the Government to take Bombay High gas through a 1,700-km pipeline to feed fertilizer plants located in the consumption centers of North India. However, the major policy which has ensured the growth of the fertilizer industry is the thrust on accelerating fertilizer consumption by fixing, on the one hand, low and uniform price for fertilizers, and on the other hand providing the manufacturers adequate compensation through the retention price and subsidy scheme. As expected, fertilizer nutrient demand has gone up from 0.29 million tons in 1960-61 to 13.9 million tons at the end of 1995-96, compared to 12.15MT during 1992-93.

Fisheries

Fish production achieved an all-time high of 4.9 million tons at the end of 1995-96. Programs that have helped boost production include the National Program of Developing Fish Seeds, Fish Farmers' Development Agencies and Brackish Water Fish Farmers' Development Agencies. The Central Institute of Fisheries Nautical and Engineering Training trains the necessary manpower. To diversify fishing methods and introduce processed fish products on a semi-commercial scale, an Integrated Fisheries Project has been launched. A National Fisheries Advisory Board has also been established.

Food Processing

A Ministry of Food Processing Industries was established in July 1988 to ensure better utilization of farmers' output by inducting modem technology into the processing of food products, thus augmenting the income of farmers and generating employment opportunities in rural areas. A new seeds policy has been adopted to provide access to high quality seeds and plant material for vegetables, fruit, flowers, oil-seeds and pulses, without in any way compromising quarantine conditions. Initiatives have been taken to encourage private sector investment in the food processing industry.

Agricultural Research

The apex body for education, research and extension education in the field of agriculture is the Indian Council of Agricultural Research (ICAR), established in 1929. India's transformation from a food deficit to a food surplus country is largely due to ICAR's smooth and rapid transfer of farm technology from the laboratory to the land.

ICAR discharges its responsibilities through 43 research institutes, four national research bureaus, 20 national research centers, nine project directorates, 70 all-India coordinated research projects, and 109 Krishi Vigyan Kendras (farm science centers). Besides, the program of Agricultural Education is coordinated by ICAR with the curricula and other normative guidance given to the 26 Agricultural Universities and four National Research Institutes.

Oilseeds Production

A Technology Mission on Oilseeds was launched in 1986 to increase production of oilseeds in the country and attain self-sufficiency. Pulses were brought under the Technology Mission in 1990. Before the Mission was launched in 1985-86, oilseed production was 10.83 million tons; during 1995-96, it was estimated at 22.42 million tons, which is a record.

Soybean, rapeseed and mustard largely contributed the increase in production. Production of pulses has seen many ups and downs, which is expected to be checked under the Mission. The country grows mainly nine oilseeds, with groundnut, rapeseed and mustard accounting for 62% of total production. Lately, soybean and sunflower have shown major growth potential.

Drinking Water

A Technology Mission on Drinking Water and Related Water Management has been constituted to cover the residual problem villages and provide potable water at 40 liter per capita per day, and 70 liters per capita per day in desert areas inclusive of 30 liters for cattle. The Mission is tackling the problem through 55 mini-missions in project districts and countrywide problem oriented sub-missions. A Village Level Operation and Maintenance (VLOM) pump called India Mark-11 has been developed and is being exported to 40 countries. By March 31, 1993, over 79% of the rural and about 85% of the urban population was provided drinking water facilities.

PRECISION FARMING: DREAMS AND REALITIES FOR INDIAN AGRICULTURE

Ever since the man appeared on the earth, he has been harnessing the natural resources to meet his basic requirements. Reference to soil, water and air as basic resources, their management and means to keep them pure are mentioned in the Vedas, Upanishads and in ancient Hindu literature. The phenomenal increase in population of both man and animal in the last century and fast growing industrialization and urbanization in last few decades have overstrained the natural resource base, which are getting degraded much faster than ever before. Thus, the attention of whole world is focused on how to increase production to feed the burgeoning population and the question uppermost in every ones mind is "Can we produce enough food in a sustainable manner without damage to the natural resource base?"

Belying all predictions made to the contrary, India could achieve unprecedented increase in the food grain production as a result of expansion of irrigation and technological advancement in agriculture. While it has been a satisfying experience, Indian agriculture would need a new vision to make rapid progress in the ensuing millennium. To achieve the required growth will not be easy as some of the existing production systems are based on unsustainable use of the resources. The signs of fatigue in the natural resources have already appeared which is a cause for serious concern to the planners, decision-makers and researchers alike.

Precision Agriculture is the application of technologies and principles to manage spatial and temporal variability associated with all aspects of agricultural production for improving production and environmental quality. The success in precision agriculture depends on the accurate assessment of the variability, its management and evaluation in space-time continuum in crop production. The agronomic feasibility of precision agriculture has been intuitive, depending largely on the application of traditional arrangement recommendations at finer scales. The agronomic success of precision agriculture has been quite convincing in crops like sugar beet, sugarcane, tea and coffee. The potential for economic, environmental and social benefits of precision agriculture is largely unrealized because the space-time continuum of crop production has not been adequately addressed.

Successful implementation of precision agriculture depends on numerous factors, including the extent to which conditions within a field are known and manage, the adequacy of input recommendation and the degree of application control. The enabling technologies of precision agriculture can be grouped in to fine major categories: Computers, Global Positioning System (GPS), Geographic Information System (GIS), Remote Sensing (RS) and Application control.

Aspects of precision agriculture encompass a broad array of topics including variability of the soil resource base, weather, plant genetics, crop diversity, machinery performance and most physical, chemical and biological inputs used in crop production. Precision agriculture must fit the needs and capabilities of the farmer and must be profitable.

Content Issues and the Gateway Debate

Despite all the natural advantages, India's productivity of food grains per hectare is no more than three-fourths of the world average and less than half of that in agriculturally advanced countries, per capita food grain availability even after the Green Revolution, has been less than two thirds of the world average. Only five states in India, namely Himachal Pradesh, Punjab, Haryana, Uttar Pradesh and Madhya Pradesh – produce more grain than their populations can consume. The combined population of the five states is less than one-third of the total of the country. More than two thirds of the population lives in states that are still food-deficit. This requires transport of lakhs of tonnes of food grain, involving high costs and pilferage. Our effort should have been to make all the states self-sufficient with respect to food grains and if some disturbances occurred due to unnoticed natural calamities the nation must be in an ever ready position to mitigate such challenging tasks.

The Indian green revolution is also associated with negative ecological / environmental consequences. The status of Indian environment shows that, in India, about 182 million ha of the country's total geographical area of 328.7 million ha is affected by land degradation of this 141.33 million ha are due to water erosion, 11.50 million ha due to wind erosion and 12.63 and 13.24 million ha due to water logging and chemical deterioration (salinization and loss of nutrients) respectively. On the other end, India shares 17 per cent of world's population with 2.5 per cent of geographical area, 1 per cent of gross world product, 4 per cent of world carbon emission and hardly 2 per cent of world forest area. The Indian status on environment is though not alarming when compared to developed countries, it gives an early warning to take appropriate precautionary measures.

The growth rate of grain production during the Ninth plan has been less than the population growth rate. The poor agricultural performance has not been because of the vagaries of monsoon. From 1997-98 to 2002-03, rainfall was between 92 and 106 per cent of the normal. Per capita availability of grain and per capita calorie intake, which were less than the minimum required for adequate nutrition, have further declined. According to Human Development Report 2003, the percentage of the undernourished in India, which was 21 a few years ago, has now reached 24.

The Government claims that India has emerged as the seventh largest exporter of food grains in the world. This is nothing to be proud of, if we take into account that the total Indian grain export in 2002-03 did not add up to even 4 per cent of the total world exports; and the value of our grain exports did not add up to even the value of our imports of vegetable oils and pulses. The more crucial question, however, is whether it is morally justifiable to export grain when 24 per cent of the population remains under-nourished.

The decline in agricultural growth and increase in rural poverty have been due to the long persisting government indifference towards the farm sector, which is evident from plan outlays on Agricultural and Allied activities, Rural Development and Irrigation, which added up to 37.1 per cent of the total during the first plan were brought down to only 19.4 per cent during the Ninth plan. However, the main reason, for poor performance of the farm sector has been the long persisting adverse terms of trade policies for agriculturists in addition to the mismanagement of natural resources leads to ever ending crisis.

THE NEED FOR PRECISION FARMING

The 'Green revolution' of 1960's has made our country self sufficient in food production. In 1947, the country produced a little over six million tonnes of wheat, in 1999; our farmers harvested over 72 million tonnes, taking the country to the second position in wheat production in the world. The production of food grains in five decades, has increased more than three fold, the yield during this period has increased more than two folds. All this has been possible due to high input application, like increase in fertilization, irrigation, pesticides, higher use of HYV's, increase in cropping intensity and increase in mechanization of agriculture.

i) Fatigue of Green Revolution

Green revolution of course contributed a lot. However, even with the spectacular growth in the agriculture, the productivity levels of many major crops are for below than expectation. We have not achieved even the lowest level of potential productivity of Indian high yielding varieties, whereas the worlds highest productive country have crop yield levels significantly higher than the upper limit of the potential of Indian HYV's. Even the crop yields of India's agriculturally rich state like Punjab is far below than the average yield of many high productive countries (Ray et al., 2001).

ii) Natural Resource Degradation

The green revolution is also associated with negative ecological/ environmental consequences. The status of Indian environment shows that, in India, about 182 million ha of the country's total geographical area of 328.7 million ha is affected by land degradation of this 141.33 million ha are due to water erosion, 11.50 million ha due to wind erosion and 12.63 and 13.24 million ha are due to water logging and chemical deterioration (salinisation and loss of nutrients) respectively. On the other end, India shares 17 per cent of world's population, 1 per cent of gross world product, 4 per cent of world carbon emission, 3.6 per cent of CO2 emission intensity and 2 per cent of world forest area. One of the major reasons for this status of environment is the population growth of 2.2 per cent in 1970– 2000. The Indian status on environment is, though not alarming when compared to developed countries, gives an early warning. In this context, there is a need to convert this green revolution into an evergreen revolution, which will be triggered by farming systems approach that can help to produce more from the available land, water and labour resources, without either ecological or social harm (Swaminathan, 2002). Since precision farming, proposes to prescribe tailor made management practices, it can help to serve this purpose.

The Basic Components of Precision Farming

Precision farming basically depends on measurement and understanding of variability, the main components of precision farming system must address the variability. Precision farming technology enabled, information based and decision focused, the components include, (the enabling technologies) Remote Sensing (RS), Geographical Information System (GIS), Global Positioning System (GPS), Soil Testing, Yield Monitors and Variable Rate Technology.

Precision farming requires the requisition, management, analysis and output of large amount of spatial and temporal data. Mobile computing systems were needed to function on the go in farming operations because desktop systems in the farm office were not sufficient. Because precision farming is concerned with spatial and temporal variability and it is information based and decision focused. It is the spatial analysis capabilities of GIS that enable precision agriculture. GPS, DGPS has greatly enabled precision farming and of great importance to precision farming, particularly for guidance and digital evaluation modeling position accuracies at the centimeter level are possible in DGPS receivers. Accurate guidance and navigation systems will allow for farming operations at height and under unfavorable weather conditions even. In India, we have all these technologies available and they can be implemented through agricultural training centers by giving training to agriculture officers in these technologies.

Basic Steps in Precision Farming

The basic steps in precision farming are,

i. Assessing variation

ii. Managing variation and

iii. Evaluation

The available technologies enable us in understanding the variability and by giving site specific agronomic recommendations we can manage the variability that make precision agriculture viable. And finally evaluation must be an integral part of any precision farming system. The detailed steps involved in each process are clearly depicted in a diagramme.

Assessing Variability

Assessing variability is the critical first step in precision farming. Since it is clear that one cannot manage what one does not know. Factors and the processes that regulate or control the crop performance in terms of yield vary in space and time. Quantifying the variability of these factors and processes and determining when and where different combinations are responsible for the spatial and temporal variation in crop yield is the challenge for precision agriculture.

Techniques for assessing spatial variability are readily available and have been applied extensively in precision agriculture. The major part of precision agriculture lies in assessing to spatial variability. Techniques for assessing temporal variability also exist but the simultaneous reporting a spatial and temporal variation is rare. We need both the spatial and temporal statistics. We can observe the variability in yield of a crop in space but we cannot predict the reasons for the variability. It needs the observations at crop growth and development over the growing season, which is nothing but the temporal variation. Hence, we need both the space and time statistics to apply the precision farming techniques. But this is not common to all the variability/ factor that dictate crop yield. Some variables are more produced in space rather with time, making them more conducive to current forms of precision management.

Managing Variability

Once variation is adequately assessed, farmers must match agronomic inputs to known conditions employing management recommendations. Those are site specific and use accurate applications control equipment.

We can use the technology most effectively. In site-specific variability management. We can use GPS instrument, so that the site specificity is pronounced and management will be easy and economical. While taking the soil/plant samples, we have to note the sample site coordinates and further we can use the same for management. This results in effective use of inputs and avoids any wastage and this is what we are looking for.

The potential for improved precision in soil fertility management combined with increased precision in application control make precise soil fertility management as attractive, but largely unproven alternative to uniform field management. For successful implementation, the concept of precision soil fertility management requires that within-field variability exists and is accurately identified and reliably interpreted, that variability influences crop yield, crop quality and for the environment. There fore inputs can be applied accurately.

The higher the spatial dependence of a manageable soil property, the higher the potential for precision management and the greater its potential value. The degree of difficulty, however, increases as the temporal component of spatial variability increases. Applying this hypothesis to soil fertility would support that Phosphorus and Potassium fertility are very conducive to precision management because temporal variability is low. For N, the temporal component of variability can be larger than its spatial component, making precision N management much more difficult in some cases.

Evaluation

There are three important issues regarding precision agriculture evaluation.

- Economics
- Environment and
- Technology transfer

The most important fact regarding the analysis of profitability of precision agriculture is that the value comes from the application of the data and not from the use of the technology. Potential improvements in environmental quality are often cited as a reason for using precision agriculture. Reduced agrochemical use, higher nutrient use efficiencies, increased efficiency of managed inputs and increased production of soils from degradation are frequently cited as potential benefits to the environment. Enabling technologies can make precision agriculture feasible, agronomic principles and decision rules can make it applicable and enhanced production efficiency or other forms of value can make it profitable.

The term technology transfer could imply that precision agriculture occurs when individuals or firms simply acquire and use the enabling technologies. While precision agriculture does involve the application of enabling technologies and agronomic principles to manage spatial and temporal variability, the key term is manage. Much of the attention in what is called technology transfer has focused on how to communicate with the farmer. These issues associated with the managerial capability of the operator, the spatial distribution of infrastructure and the compatibility of technology to individual farms will change radically as precision agriculture continues to develop (Pierce and Peter, 1999).

Technology Transition

Precision agriculture is dependent on the existence of variability in either or both product quantity and quality. If this variability does not exist then a uniform management system is both the cheapest and most effective management strategy and precision farming is redundant. Thus, in precision farming,

"Variability of production and quality equals opportunity". Having said this, the nature of the variation is also important in determining the potential for PA in a system. For example the magnitude of the variability may be too small to be economically feasible to manage.

Alternatively the variability may be highly randomized across the production system making it impossible to manage with current technology. Finally the variability may due to a constraint that is not manageable. Thus the implementation of precision farming is limited by the ability of current variable rate technology (VRT-machinery/technology that allows for differential management of a production system) to cope with the highly variable sites and the economic inability to produce returns from sites with low variability using precision farming (VRT).

Due to these constraints PA is at present operating on a zonal rather than a completely site-specific basis. As VRT improves and the capital cost of entering PA decreases, the minimum size of management zone needed to effectively implement PA will decrease till eventually a truly site-specific management regime is possible.

Until this occurs there is need to be able to quantify both the variability of a production system and the size of the minimum manageable zone (MMZ). If the variability in the production system dictates management zones smaller than the MMZ than PA is not relevant to the system. At the present time (but may be in future). It will be interesting to see how the concept of the management zone develops and to see how it compares with the concept of terroir.

Present Scenario

Though precision farming is very much talked about in developed countries, it is still at a very nascent stage in developing countries, including India. Space Application center, ISRO, in collaboration with Central Potato Research Institute, Shimla, has initiated a study on exploring the role remote sensing for precision farming.

The study on precision agriculture has already been initiated in India, in many research institutes. Space Application Center

(ISRO), Ahmedabad has started experiment in the Central Potato Research Station farm at Jalahandhar, Punjab to study the role of remote sensing in mapping the variability with respect to space and time. M S Swaminathan Research Foundation, Chennai, in collaboration with NABARD, has adopted a village in Dindigul district of Tamil Nadu for variable rate input application. Indian Agricultural Research Institute has drawn up a plan to do precision farming experiments in the institutes' farm. Project Directorate for Cropping Systems Research (PDCSR), Modipuram and Meerut (UP) in collaboration with Central Institute of Agricultural Engineering (CIAE), Bhopal also initiated variable rate input application in different cropping systems. In coming few years precision farming may help the Indian farmers to harvest the fruits of frontier technologies without compromising the quality of land.

Prospects

Precision farming, though in many cases a proven technology is still mostly restricted to developed (American and European) countries. Except for a few (Wang, 2001), there is not much literature to show the scope of its implementation in India.

We feel that, one of the major problems is the small field size. In India more than 57.8 per cent of operational holdings have size less than 1 ha. However, in the major agricultural states of Punjab, Rajastan, Haryana and Gujarat there are more than 20 per cent of agricultural lands have operational holding size of more than 4 ha. These are individual field sizes. However, when we consider contiguous field with same crop (mostly under similar management practices) the field (rather simulated field) sizes are large. Using aerial data, has found that in Patiala district of Punjab, more than 50 per cent of contiguous field sizes are larger than 15 ha. These contiguous fields can be considered a single field for the purpose of implementation of precision farming.

Misconceptions about Precision Agriculture

There are several mistaken preconceptions about precision agriculture.

a). Precision agriculture is a cropping rather than an agricultural concept

This is due to cropping systems, in particular broad-acre cropping, being the face and driving force of PA technology. However precision farming concepts are applicable to all agricultural sectors from animals to fisheries to forestry. In fact it might be argued that precision farming concepts are more advanced in the dairy industry where the "site" becomes an individual animal, which is recorded, traced and fed individually to optimize production. These industries are just as concerned with improved productivity and quality decreased environmental impact and better risk management as the cropping industry however precision farming concepts have yet to be applied on the same scale in these areas. For example a grazer's use of advance warning meteorological data and market predictions to estimate fodder reserves and plan livestock numbers is a form of precision farming.

b). Precision agriculture in cropping equals yield mapping

Yield mapping is a crucial step and the wealth of information farmers are able to obtain from a yield map makes them very valuable. However they are only a stepping-stone in a precision farming management system. The bigger agronomic hurdle lies in retrieving the information in the yield map and using it to improve the production system. The advance of PA adoption (usefulness) in this country is may soon be bottlenecked at this point due to the lack of decision support systems (DSS) to help agronomists and farmers understand their yield maps. Yield maps may not tell the whole story either with other data sources, e.g. crop quality and soil maps, economic indicators or weather predictions, proving further information necessary for correct agronomic interpretations.

c). Precision agriculture equals sustainable agriculture

Precision agriculture is a tool to make agriculture more sustainable however it is not the total answer. Precision farming aims at maximum production efficiency with minimum environmental impact. Currently it is the potential for improved productivity (and profitability) that is driving precision farming rather than the more serious issue of long-term sustainability. Precision farming will not fix problems such as erosion and salinity by itself although it will help to reduce the risk of these problems occurring. Sensible sustainable practices still need to be used in conjunction with precision farming.

Obstacles

There are many obstacles to adoption of precision farming in developing countries in general and India in particular. Some are common to those in other regions but the others are specific to Indian conditions are as follows.

- Culture and perceptions of the users
- Small farm size
- Lack of success stories
- Heterogeneity of cropping systems and market imperfections
- Land ownership, infrastructure and institutional constraints
- Lack of local technical expertise
- Knowledge and technical gaps
- Data availability, quality and costs

Opportunities

Despite the many obstacles listed earlier, business opportunities for precision farming technologies including GIS, GPS, RS and yield monitor systems are immense in many developing countries. The scope for funding new hardware, software and consulting industries related to precision agriculture is gradually widening. In Japan, the market in the next 5 years is estimated at about US $ 100 billion for GIS and about US $ 50 billion for GPS and RS (Srinivasan, 2001). Punjab and Haryana states in India, where farm mechanization is more common than in others, may be the first to adopt precision farming on a large scale.

Recently, the governments of certain Asian countries initiated special efforts to promote precision farming. In Japan, the Ministry of Agriculture has allocated special funds for research on remote sensing applications of precision farming.

A quasi-governmental institute "Bio-oriented Technology Research Advancement Institute (BRAIN)" is also funding research on precision farming. In Malaysia, the Malaysian Agricultural Research and Development Institute (MARDI) is promoting research on precision farming of upland rice. In other countries, the private sector, which holds or leases a large acreage, is likely to adopt precision farming sooner than the small holders.

Precision farming is useful in many situations in developing countries. Rice, wheat, sugar beet, onion, potato and cotton among the field crops and apple, grape, tea, coffee and oil palm among horticultural crops are perhaps the most relevant.

Some have a very high value per acre, making excellent cases for site-specific management. For all these crops, yield mapping is the first step to determine the precise locations of the highest and lowest yield areas of the field. Researchers at Kyoto University recently developed a two-row rice harvester for determining yields on a micro plot basis (Iida et al., 1998).

Precision farming can bring several benefits to the sugar beet industry in Hokkaido, where the marketing system was changed in 1986 from a quantity (fresh weight) to quality (sugar yield) basis.

Heavy N fertilization, a common practice here, results in excessive N levels and a decreased sugar concentration. It is now possible to estimate sugar and amide N concentration in leaves using reflectance in visible bands and root yield using reflectance in visible and infrared bands (Okano et al., 1997).

Incorporation of such data into a GIS along with precise positioning of non-uniform areas using GPS can be used to vary fertilizer dose within a field, thereby improving productivity. Although weighing conveyor technology has been known for some time, effective yield measurement still remains the main problem in crops such as sugar beet, onion and potato. Further, the preparation of product quality maps for these crops is as important as yield maps. In India, a few researchers in the private sector initiated studies on precision agriculture in high value crops like cotton, coffee and tea. In cotton, remote sensing coupled with GIS can assist in improved precision of insect pest management and harvesting.

In Sri Lanka, researchers at the Tea Research Institute are examining precision management of soil organic carbon. In so far as dairy farming in Asia is concerned, precision farming techniques can help in improving efficiency of methods, timing and rate of application of animal wastes leading to high application efficiency and low environmental pollution. While considering soil and climatic conditions.

For instance, factors determining the risk of NO3 leaching, release of N2O through denitrification and contamination of surface and ground water by runoff can be mapped and analysed. Likewise, poorly managed areas in grass lands can be identified and the optimum period for cutting on a plot basis determined.

Nutrient stress management is another area where precision farming can help Indian farmers. Most cultivated soils in India are acidic and spatial variation in pH is high. Detecting nutrient stresses using remote sensing and combining data in a GIS can help in site-specific applications of fertilizers and soil amendments such as lime, manure, compost, gypsum and sulphur. This in turn would increase fertilizer use efficiency and reduce nutrient losses.

In semi arid and arid tropics, precision technologies can help growers in scheduling irrigation more profitably by varying the timing, amounts and placement of water. For example, drip irrigation, coupled with information from remotely sensed stress conditions (e.g., canopy temperature) can increase the effective use of applied water from 60 to 95 per cent there by, reducing runoff from 23 to 1 per cent and deep percolation from 18 to 4 per cent.

Pests and diseases cause huge losses to Indian crops. If remote sensing can help in detecting small problem areas caused by pathogens, timing of applications of fungicides can be optimized. Recent studies in Japan show that pre-visual crop stress or incipient crop damage can be detected using radio-controlled aircraft and near-infrared narrow-band sensors. Like wise, airborne video data and GIS have been shown to effectively detect and map black fly infestations in citrus orchards, making it possible to achieve precision in pest control.

Perennial weeds, which are usually position-specific (Wilson and Scott, 1982) and grow in concentrated areas, are also a major problem in developing countries. Remote sensing combined with GIS and GPS can help in site-specific weed management.

Although through cost-benefit analysis has not been done yet, the possible use of precision technologies in managing the environmental side effects of farming and reducing pollution is appealing.

Strategies

Precision farming is still only a concept in many developing countries and strategic support from the public and private sectors is essential to promote its rapid adoption.

Successful adoption, however, comprises at least three phases including exploration, analysis and execution. Data on crop yield, soil variables, weather and other characteristics are collected and mapped in the exploratory stage, which is important for increasing the awareness among farmers of long term benefits. The approaches to data collection and mapping must, therefore, reflect local needs and resources.

In the analysis stage, factors limiting the potential yield in various areas within a field and their interrelationships are examined using GIS-based statistical modeling. Sadler et al. (1998) showed that quantitatively important yield variation may occur over distances as short as 10m, however, only some factors such as soil structure, water status, pH, nutrient levels, weeds, pests and diseases can be controlled but not the others (soil texture, weather, topography).

After determining the significance of each source of variability to profitability of a particular crop and relative importance of each controllable factor, management actions can be prioritized. It must be remembered that in some low yielding areas, the reason for poor yields may be the lack of sufficient soil nutrients in the first place. In such cases, application beyond just replenishment is necessary.

Lastly, execution phase includes variable application of inputs or cultural operations. In most developing countries of Asia. However, it is not always necessary and/or possible to use variable rate applicators. Efforts must, therefore, initially focus on limiting indiscriminate use of inputs in conventional methods. Once the economic and environmental benefits are known widely, variable rate technology would be rapidly implemented at least in high value crops.

To spur adoption of precision farming methods in developing countries, pilot demonstration projects must be conducted at various growers locations by involving farmers in all stages of the project.

The pilot projects must attempt to answer the grower's needs and emphasize the operational implementation of technology and complete analysis of the costs and savings involved. Documentation of pilot projects would help in examining the operational weaknesses and identification of remedial measures. The projects can be used to train innovative farmers and early adopters, expose the neighboring nonparticipating farmers to the new technologies, and show the usefulness of the technology for short and long-term management.

The role of agricultural input suppliers, extension advisors and consultants in the spread of these technologies is vital. For instance, public agencies should consider supplying free data such as remotely sensed imagery to the universities and research institutes involved in precision farming research.

Also, professional societies of agronomy, agricultural informatics, and engineering must provide training guidance in the use of technologies. The involvement of inter/disciplinary teams is essential in this. Small farm size will not be a major constraint, if the technologies are available through consulting, custom and rental services. The role of agricultural cooperatives is important in dissemination of precision farming technologies to small farmers. If precision farming is considered a series of discrete services: map generation, targeted scouting, it is possible to fit these services within the structure of a progressive agricultural cooperative in each developing country.

Changes in agricultural policies are also necessary to promote the adoption of precision farming. There are basically two policy approaches: regulatory policies and market based policies. The former refer to environmental regulations on the use of farm inputs and later refer to taxes and financial incentives aimed at encouraging growers to efficiently use farm inputs. In most developing countries the lack of penalties for pollutant generation has partly contributed to an excessive use of inputs.

Subsidies on inputs and outputs and mechanisms that prevent the price system from rationing limited resources are also common. The latter include state-guaranteed crop prices, tariffs, import quotas, export subsidies.

Inputs such as water and fossil fuels are usually sold at prices that are well below the real resource cost of their use, which consists not only production costs but also includes scarcity value and costs of pollution. In such cases, the formulation of policies that reflect the real scarcity value of natural resources and penalize pollution and policies such as green payments for farmers adopting techniques that would lower environmental costs can promote the adoption of precision farming technologies (Branden et al., 1994).

In most developing countries, the pollution effects of agriculture have been largely ignored so far because of inability to effectively monitor such effects. The advent of precision farming, and the computerization of input and output flows, will now enable such monitoring. Higher taxes on pollution farms are often recommended, but there is strong opposition to the implementation of the polluter-pays-principle concept in most countries including India.

At the same time, some consumers in India would like to see a drastic reduction in the use of pesticides and fertilizers, and are willing to pay as much as 4 to 6 times the normal price for produce such as organic vegetables, soybean and wheat. When the price elasticity of input use is low and the input costs are only a small part of the total production expenditure, as in the case of fertilizers and pesticides. Very high taxes are required to reduce their use adequately. Given the unfeasibility of such high taxes, a hybrid policy may be implemented for controlling pollution. A tax-free quota of N can be combined with taxes on additional N use.

At the research level, many issues remain to be resolved. Although some progress has been made at Space Application Center, Ahmedabad, yield monitors for small farm conditions are yet to be developed.

The development of standards for the hardware and software (image transfer formats and GPS transfer formats, map projection formats) is another issue. Crop models and decision support systems must be improved by considering local resources. Data for calibration of models must be made available to increase their accuracy and/or predictability.

The ability to finance a creative information venture in agriculture will affect the speed of diffusion of precision farming technologies. Commercial banks, as well as other sources of funding, have to be educated regarding the potential of precision farming. In many developing countries, it may be worthwhile to develop programmes of subsidized credit to enable R&D activities on precision farming.

CONCLUSION

Precision farming in many developing countries including India is in its infancy but there are numerous opportunities for adoption. I believe that progressive Indian farmers, with guidance from the public and private sectors, and agricultural associations, will adopt it in a limited scale as the technology shows potential for raising yields and economic returns on fields with significant variability, and for minimizing environmental degradation. Although it is recognized that agriculture is a major polluter of the environment in many developing countries, farmers will not adopt precision farming unless it brings in more or at least similar profit as compared to traditional practice. The support from governments and the private sector during the initial stages of adoption is, therefore vital. It must be remembered that not all elements of precision farming are relevant for each and every farm.

For instance, introduction of variable rate applicators is not always necessary or the most appropriate level of spatial management in Indian farms. Likewise, not all farms are suitable to implement precision farming. Some growers are likely to adopt it partially, adopting certain elements but not others. Precision farming cannot be convincing if only environmental benefits are emphasized. On the other hand, its adoption would be improved if it can be shown to reduce the risk. We must be cautious, however, is not overselling the technologies without providing adequate product support. The adoption of precision farming also depends on product reliability, the support provided by manufacturers and the ability to show the benefits. Effective coordination among the public and private sectors and growers is, therefore, essential for implementing new strategies to achieve fruitful success.

5

Groundwater Development and Socio-economic Aspects in India

At the end of the 20th century, the population of India crossed one billion mark. India has mainly an agricultural economy where land holdings are generally small. Due to steep rise in population, the demand of water has increased considerably over the last 50 years resulting in overdraft and water quality deterioration.

The paper discusses major aspects of groundwater development and connected socio-economic issues.

INTRODUCTION

In India about 70% people live in rural areas. However, in recent years there is a greater trend of migration of the rural population to urban areas. Due to steep increase in population along with associated activities, water is becoming a scarce resource coupled with quality deterioration.. It is estimated that the entire utilizeable water resources of the country would be required for various uses by the year 2025 A.D.

The maximum use of water is for irrigation. Surface water is Government owned but groundwater is private i.e. it belongs to the land owner.

There has been an indiscriminate use of water as there is no control on its use either by the Government or public organizations. Recently attempts are being made for an equitable distribution of this scarce resource for the economic development and well being of the society.

GROUNDWATER OCCURRENCE

The vast expanse of alluvial formations in north India deposited by the Ganga-Brahamputra river system, is most productive. It consists of thick pile of sand, silt and clay with occasional beds of gravel, extending to a depth of about one km. Tubewell irrigation is being practiced in this area from the last more than one hundred years. The area is bestowed with good rainfall and hence good recharge.

The sedimentary formulations comprising of sandstone, shale and limestone, varying in age from Pre-Cambrian to Tertiary, occur as isolated pockets in different parts of the country. Permeability of older formations is quite low and therefore well yields are poor. However, rocks of younger ages (Mesozic and Tertiary) are more productive forming artesian aquifers at places.

The main volcanic suite of rocks is represented by Deccan Traps occupying an area of about 500, 000 km^2 in the western and central parts of the country. A number of basaltic flow units are identified of Upper Cretaceous to Lower Eocene age. Part of the Deccan Trap area has semi-arid climate. Low rainfall and rugged topography results in poor recharge to groundwater.

Crystalline (igneous and metamorphic) rocks of Pre-Cambrian age occupy nearly two-third part of the country. The permeability is poor except in weathered and fractured parts. Groundwater from weathered horizons is tapped by large diameter shallow (30-25m) wells. Small diameter (4 to 6 cm) bore wells of depth 30 to 70 m tap deeper fractured zones. Geophysical and remote sensing techniques have greatly increased the success rate of well drilling. Natural recharge from rainfall is being supplemented by artificial recharge.

WATER RESOURCES AVAILABILITY AND DEMAND

The average annual rainfall in India is about 1170 mm depth with a total volume of 4000 km^3..However, its distribution is greatly uneven in space varying from about 100 mm in the western parts to more than 1100 mm in the north-eastern parts of the country.

The total utilizeable water potential is 1140 km3, out of which 690 km3 is from surface water and 450 km3 from groundwater. Water utilization for the year 2000 and the projected demands for the year 2025 are given in Table below.

Table: Estimates of Annual Water Demand in India (in Km³)

1. Purpose/Year	2000	2025
2. Domestic use	33	52
3. Industrial	30	120
4.Energy	27	71
5. Irrigation	630	770
6. Other uses	30	37
7. Total	750	1050
Distribution		
Surface water	500	700
Groundwater	250	350

Table above indicates that out of total water utilized in the country, 84% is used for irrigation, about 4.4% for drinking and municipal use, 4% for industry, 3.6% for energy development and the remaining 4% for other purposes. Table above also shows that nearly the entire utilizeable water resource of the country would be required to be put to use by the year 2025. This is mainly on account of increased demand of water for irrigation required to grow more food grains for the increasing population which is estimated to reach about 1.25 billion by the year 2025.

Groundwater Development

Out of the total replenishable groundwater which is estimated to be about 450 km^3,the present development is nearly 40%.However, its development has not been uniform. Groundwater contributes to about 50% of the total irrigated area of the country and 85% of the rural water supply is met from groundwater.

There has been a significant increase in the demand of groundwater for agriculture, domestic and industrial uses, which has caused over-exploitation of groundwater in some areas causing excessive lowering of water levels, seawater intrusion in coastal aquifers, and upconing of saline water in inland areas. In contrast to this, in canal irrigated areas, due to poor drainage and excessive irrigation, a rising trend of water level has taken place resulting in water logging and soil salinization. About 25,000 km^2 area under canal irrigation is affected by water logging.

The use of groundwater for irrigation has considerably increased from a meager 6.5 km^3 in 1951 to over 50 km^3 in 1997.The number of wells has also considerably increased from merely 4 million in 1951 to nearly 17 million in 1997. The investment from all sources in the development of groundwater has also grown from less than Rs.600 million (US $ 12 million) during the First Plan (1951-1956) to over Rs. 12 billion (US $ 2.4 billion) during the Eighth Plan period (1992-1997). The institutional finance for groundwater development is about 60% of the total outlay for groundwater development while public outlay is 20% and the balance is met from the private sources (Kapoor, 2000).

About 75% landholders are small and marginal farmers having less than 2 hectares of land per family. The area owned by them is about 30% of the total cultivated area in the country. At per the present norms, Government provides subsidies @ 33% to marginal and 25% to small farmers for the construction of wells and purchase of pump sets.

The Central Ground Water Board (CGWB) has established a country wide observation well network for monitoring water levels. A total decline of 4 m i.e. 20 cm/year has been noted during 1981-2000 in several states of the country. In the NCT (National Capital Territory) of Delhi, in some areas, a decline of as much as 5 to 10 m is noted. In several cases the water levels have fallen below the suction lift of existing pumping equipment.

The CGWB has categorized areas based on the present stage of groundwater development and past water level trends. Based on these criteria, about 300 blocks, all over the country, have been classified as 'over-exploited' where groundwater development is more than 100 percent and 160 blocks are 'dark' where the stage of groundwater development is between 85 and 100 percent. Such a categorization provides guidelines to financial institutions for providing loans to farmers for the construction of additional wells. 'Grey' and 'white' areas are those where groundwater development has been 65-85% and < 65 % respectively. Overexploited areas are not worthy of additional groundwater development while in dark areas development should be undertaken with care. In grey and white areas there is a scope of further groundwater development.

According to a study carried out by the International Water Management Institute(IWMI), India is among the 50 most water poor countries. This study is based on the Water Poverty Index (WPI). India is ranked 47th in WPI while Canada, Norway, Finland, Iceland, Guyana and Surinam are among the water rich countries. At the lower end of the scale lie Ethiopia, Rwanda and Malawi. Almost all the water rich nations are in the northern hemisphere and all those with less water are in Africa. The WPI is based on resource, access, use, capacity and environment. The WPI is not an indication of only water availability but it takes into account the effectiveness of its use also.

GROUND WATER RIGHTS

Under the Indian Constitution, the land owner has an absolute right on the groundwater under his land. Therefore, a land owner can abstract any amount of water irrespective of its effects in the adjoining areas. It also means that 30% of the landless rural population do not have the water rights. Such an approach violates the fundamental rights to life of a person in a socialistic society. Therefore, the above water rights have to be modified to ensure equitable availability of water to all the citizens irrespective of land holdings.

There are also inter-state problems in the sharing of not only surface water but also of groundwater as major aquifers run across the state administrative units. Therefore, water should be recognized as a national-rather than a regional-resource which needs cooperation amongst states on these issues.

GROUNDWATER LEGISLATION

Recognizing the importance of proper groundwater development, a model bill was framed by the Government of India in 1970 and was circulated to the states. On the basis of experiences in the last two decades, the Bill was revised first in 1972 and again in the year 1996.

As a subsequence of this, the Govt. of India constituted the Central Ground Water Authority (CGWA) for the purpose of regulation and control of groundwater management and development including water quality. The CGWA has identified certain areas where for further groundwater development prior permission of the Authority is necessary. However, it is being realized that implementation of such restrictions is difficult. The bureaucratic setup of the Government is often unable to solve the local problems without involving local people. This also requires mass awareness about the adverse effects of overexploitation and degradation pf groundwater quality. Local elected bodies, viz. village councils (panchayats) should be involved in decision making. Non-Government Organizations (NGOs) can also play an important role as people will listen to them with greater care due to their involvement in other local developmental activities, such as health and education.

GROUNDWATER QUALITY

In addition to salinity (both inland and coastal), high concentration of fluoride, arsenic, iron & nitrate are the main contaminants in groundwater. Unscientific disposal of industrial waste and sewage also causes widespread pollution of groundwater mainly in the urban and industrialized areas.

High concentration of fluoride (more than the permissible limit of 1.5 mg/l) is reported both from the hard rock (granites & gneisses) as well as alluvial aquifers. People living in such areas were drinking high fluoride waters without realizing its presence which caused various bone diseases. The cause of high fluoride in groundwater is geological, being a result of the dissolution of fluoride bearing minerals. Defluoridation plants have been installed in areas where such problems exist.

A very serious problem detected recently is the presence of As in groundwater of several districts in the Ganga river delta, covering parts of Bangladesh and eastern part of India (West Bengal). About half a million people in eight districts of West

Bengal suffer from various arsenic related skin and other diseases. Shallow aquifers in the depth range of 15 to 75 m have higher concentration of As (0.3 to 1.1 mg /l) while the deeper aquifers (>150 m_) contain negligible amount of As. The origin of As in groundwater of West Bengal (India) and Bangladesh is controversial.However, it is regarded to be geological derived from the As rich pyrite present in peat and clay formations in the deltaic alluvium (Mukherje et al., 2002). Mitigation is difficult given the scale of the problem as well as social and economic factors. Options include use of deep groundwater (>150 m), rain water harvesting and treatment of contaminated groundwater (BGS, 2000).

Inland salinity is predominant in canal irrigated areas due to water logging. People living in these areas are also exposed to malaria and other diseases.

Over-exploitation of groundwater in the coastal aquifers of Saurashtra in Gujarat state, Tamilnadu in south India and coastal parts of Orissa in the east has led to seawater intrusion and thereby water quality deterioration.

FUTURE STRATEGIES OF GROUNDWATER DEVELOPMENT

In order to meet the future demands of groundwater, some aspects of groundwater exploration, development and management, which are necessary, are listed below:

(1) Groundwater development in water logged areas

It is estimated that about 25000 km^2 area under canal irrigation suffers from water logging and soil salinity due to high water table and lack of proper drainage. Such areas can be reclaimed by the conjunctive use of groundwater and surface water.

(2) Evaluation of Deep Aquifer Systems

Studies by the Oil and Natural Gas Corporation (formerly Oil and Natural Gas Commission) and Central Ground Water Board indicate the presence of deep aquifers (500 to 1000m) in the Ganga Brahamputra alluvium (Jones, 1987). In hard rocks areas also, there is possibility of finding groundwater at depths more than 100 m in fractured rocks (Singhal,1999). These areas are to be further explored mainly from the point of view of recharge mechanism and water quality.

(3) Groundwater Development in the Eastern parts of the Country

In the eastern parts of the country the present stage of groundwater development is estimated to be about 25% mainly due to the fragmented nature of land holding, non-availability of public funding and power supply (Kapoor, 2000). These areas are worthy of groundwater development.

(4) Inter-Basin water Transfer

The Government of India has taken up an ambitious programme of long distance transfer of surplus surface water to water-deficient areas. Necessary investigations are required to study the possible impact of inter-basin water transfer on groundwater régime and its environmental impact. This also requires consensus amongst various states and necessary political leadership.

(5) Groundwater Development in Drought Prone Areas

Drought is a recurring feature causing great miseries including stress on water availability for various uses. In view of this, high priority is required to provide safe drinking water to rural population and schools. With this in view, the Government of India, under the Accelerated Rural Water Supply Programme (ARWSP), has allocated Rs 2070 million (US $ 420 million) for the year 2003 to drill wells which will be used only during drought period as a crisis-management measure.

(6) Groundwater-Seawater Interaction

India has a long coast line stretching to about 3000 km. In certain areas, over-exploitation of groundwater has resulted in seawater intrusion in coastal aquifers. Study of groundwater-seawater interaction including quantitative assessment of fresh groundwater discharge into the sea is necessary for the optimum development of groundwater resources of coastal aquifers. The International Association of Scientific Hydrology (IASH) has also proposed recently various types of research in this field (IASH,2002).

(7) Artificial Recharge

The importance of artificial recharge including rain water harvesting is being increasingly realized to conserve the water resources. In some mega-cities, roof-top rain water harvesting has been made mandatory under the new building codes. Underground storage by artificial recharge will also prevent floods.

(8) Availability of funds

One of the problems in groundwater development has been the availability of funds especially to small and marginal farmers for the well construction.

(9) Water Quality Monitoring

The effect of natural processes and man's activities on groundwater quality needs regular monitoring for taking up timely corrective measures. Necessary mass awareness and education is also an important component

(11) Active Participation of Women

Women's participation in water resources projects especially in those involving water supply and sanitation at village level will greatly improve the implementation and sustainability of the projects.

CONCLUSIONS

The growing population of the country needs more water for various uses. However water can be constraint, if not prudently developed and managed. The real life problems facing India in the water resources sector are about the water rights including sharing of surface and groundwater resources between the various states and individuals, general shortage of water in rural and urban areas, deterioration in water quality and degradation of the environment. These aspects need due attention by administrators, scientists, engineers and social workers to ensure equitable distribution of water for the sustenance of mankind without endangering the needs of future generation.

AN OVERVIEW OF INSTREAM FLOWS

States that straddle the 100th meridian have long wrestled with the complex issues surrounding Great Plains and Mountain states water rights. The home state of Prairie Fire, Nebraska, has often postponed the resolution of many aspects of various struggles over water rights.

Even in the recently adjourned session of the Unicameral, days were spent attempting to balance the interests of surface water and groundwater users, given that many of Nebraska's rival basins are now fully appropriated or even overappropriated. The Nebraska Legislature did not take the first step to recognize the obligation to protect streams as a fish and wildlife resource until 1984. Even so, in the intervening years, only slightly over 2% of Nebraska's streams and rivers have received instream flow protection.

Instream flows-defined simply as the water flowing in a stream channel and its variations in flow levels across different seasons and wet, dry and normal years-have received renewed attention as the water struggles continue between surface water users and groundwater users. The subject has an enormously complex history. Accordingly, we decided to publish a comprehensive, albeit lengthy, essay on instream flows in Nebraska. We hope that our efforts, combined with Gene Zuerlein's, will succeed in equipping our readers with the knowledge needed to effectively engage in the many water discussions that lie ahead in this, the Century of Water.-Publisher

Nebraska's obligation to protect streams and fish and wildlife resources (recognized as the Public Trust Doctrine) originated in the 6th century A.D. in Roman history. Justinian, emperor of Rome at the time, codified a law stating "By the law of nature, these things are common to mankind-the air, running water, the sea, and consequently, the shore of the sea." England adopted this Public Trust Doctrine as common law, which was subsequently exported to the original 13 colonies here in the United States.

Following the fight for independence, the Public Trust Doctrine was adopted as part of the basic laws in each state. Under U.S. Constitutional provisions, rights and obligations not specifically reserved for federal jurisdictions were transferred equally to all new states joining the union. When Nebraska accepted statehood in 1867, it accepted certain rights, common laws and obligations provided to the 13 original states and each additional state. Among others, each state accepted the common law known as "The Public Trust Doctrine (PTD).

The Constitution of the State of Nebraska states "The use of the water of every natural stream within the State of Nebraska is hereby dedicated to the people of the state for beneficial purposes" (Article XV, Sec. 5). "The right to divert unappropriated water of every natural stream for beneficial use shall never be denied except when such denial is demanded by the public interest" (Article XV, Sec. 6).

Pre-1984

The public trust doctrine revolves around the concept that government owes its citizens special duties of stewardship regarding common property resources which the state holds in trust for the public. The public trust doctrine holds that government must act as a fiduciary (one to whom property or power is entrusted for the benefit of another) in its management of the trust resources. The beneficiaries of this trust are the citizens of the state, including future generations. Common property resources, including water, fish, wildlife, air and land, are held by the states in their sovereign capacity and are subject to the public trust.

When covered wagons rolled across Nebraska in the mid-to late 1800s, there were no laws governing use of surface waters. Naturally, controversy occurred over who could use it, and 22 years after Nebraska became a state, the legislature enacted a law on March 27, 1889, which recognized and protected rights to appropriate surface waters of the state. This act established the fundamental principals to the appropriative system: first in time, first in right. Six years later, the Comprehensive State Code Act of April 4, 1895, created the State Board of Irrigation and firmly established the current appropriation system for surface water rights. Eventually, this state agency became known as the Department of Water Resources, and in more recent times, the Nebraska Department of Natural Resources (NDNR).

While the appropriation system worked well during the development years of the state, it may not be the best for future generations because much more than three or four instream flow purposes need to be protected.

It is pretty much recognized today that human welfare is dependent upon ecological health and that when rivers no longer support living things, they will no longer support human affairs as well. How much can we depart from the natural flow patterns of any particular river and still retain enough semblance of the natural character to meet ecosystem needs? Protecting rivers should really be about preserving the processes and functions needed to sustain ecosystems and the many amenities they provide to society as a whole.

Although pumping groundwater was in its infant stages in the 1920s, the "correlative use doctrine" was legally recognized in Nebraska in 1933. Basically, correlative use means that in times of water shortages adjacent users must share and share alike. Management of groundwater resources up to this point has, for the most part, been relegated to 23 political subdivisions of the state called Natural Resources Districts (NRDs) with some oversight by the Nebraska Department of Natural Resources. These NRDs, organized on a watershed basis in 1974, are charged with regulating groundwater pumping. Up until passage of LB 962 in 2004, two sets of laws, one governing surface water appropriations and one governing groundwater pumping, existed, with neither recognizing the conjunctive aspect of both sources of water.

Both surface and groundwater resources have been extensively developed since 1889. In water year 1975, 93.2% of all water used in the state was for irrigating 5,400,000 acres. Groundwater irrigation accounted for 66.7% and surface water irrigation accounted for 26.5%. By 1986 approximately 7,200,000 acres were under irrigation. Nine years later (1995), more than 7,448,700 acres were irrigated. Groundwater provided 82.6% and surface water provided 17.4% of the water consumptively used. During 2001, there were 8,175,000 acres irrigated in Nebraska.

While irrigation was expanding in Nebraska, other authorities recognized the potential risk and were advocating change. The

1976 "Missouri River Basin Commission's Platte Level B Study" boldly stated:

> *"Progressively greater use of groundwater for irrigation and other uses as well as direct uses of the surface waters, particularly for irrigation, are having adverse effects on wetlands, natural lake levels and on stream flow regimes. These adverse effects will continue, unless there is recognition in state law and policy of the need to maintain certain minimum stream flows to ensure the maintenance of the fishery resources, wildlife, and other environmental resources."*
>
> *In 1976, portions of 21 streams in northeastern Nebraska became totally dry and fish kills during the summer were the most numerous in recorded history. Drought, excessive stream withdrawals and groundwater mining contributed to the lowering of stream levels. For example, on the dry Platte, some surface water appropriators reverted to digging holes in the bed of the river so they could get their stingers to suck up the last drops of subsurface water for irrigation. In advocating for an instream flow law, one concerned citizen stated, "The Nebraska environment must not be blindly sacrificed in the name of economic development." Another citizen stated, "The past few years have demonstrated that water, like any other natural resource, is exhaustible. It is evident from dewatering of Nebraska streams that the water laws of Nebraska have not kept up with the needs of the environment."*

In 1978, the Legislature passed LB 957 and LR 300, directing the Natural Resources Commission (now Nebraska Department Natural Resources or NDNR) to accelerate state water planning. This led to nine Policy Issue and one Summary and Review Policy Issue Studies. One of these studies, "Instream Flows," specifically identified streams and rivers which contained unappropriated water. It also recommended flows required for: fishery needs in 13 streams/rivers, canoeing in six rivers, compact flows for the Little Blue and Big Blue, on-stream hydroelectric generation flows for four rivers and Minnechaduza Creek, recharge of Lincoln's well field along the lower Platte, and flows for whooping crane habitat on the Niobrara River. In the summary section of this report, it distinctly states that "Nebraska's present system for acquiring and administering appropriative rights was adopted in 1895 and has undergone little change ... under Nebraska law an appropriator may impound or divert the entire flow of a stream if necessary to satisfy his water right regardless of the impact on stream flow values" (emphasis added).

Post-1984

In 1984, after almost a decade of debate and study on the need for instream flows and 95 years after Nebraska water laws were first adopted, the Legislature passed LB 1106. For the first time in state history, a statutory mechanism to protect instream flows in streams and rivers with unappropriated flows materialized. This legislation was significant because it finally recognized that surface water appropriations for instream flow values of fish, wildlife and recreation could be obtained. The Legislature gave responsibility (but no money) for obtaining instream flows to the Nebraska Game and Parks Commission and the 23 Natural Resource Districts in the state. During the 23 years since 1984, only 255 miles (2.1%) of Nebraska's 12,371 miles of streams and rivers have been protected with instream flow appropriations.

Protected reaches include eight miles on Long Pine Creek (a tributary to the Niobrara River), 147 miles on the middle Platte and 100 miles on the lower Platte River. One has to wonder where the state of Nebraska would be now in protecting its public trust waters if each NRD had just filed for one instream flow appropriation to protect the main river in their district during the past 23 years. While all initial applications for instream flow protection have been contentious, many river basins are now fully or overappropriated. Most basins have no instream flow appropriations for fish, wildlife or recreational resources and consequently many of the amenities flowing water could provide to our society are in jeopardy unless actions are taken to change state policy to better protect stream resources for future generations.

In 2004, the Legislature passed LB 962 to make the NDNR and 23 NRDs more proactive in anticipating and preventing conflicts between groundwater and surface water users. In fully or overappropriated basins, the NDNR must work with the NRDs to develop and implement integrated management plans. The NDNR must also annually evaluate each remaining river basin to determine if it is fully appropriated. However, unless there is an instream appropriation in the basin, there is no mandatory requirement under LB 962 for NDNR's evaluations to protect public trust instream resource values. All they can do is listen to concerns about the many other amenities a river provides. If streams continue to be depleted, biological opinions regarding instream flows needs for threatened or endangered species may very well be another factor to consider in fully appropriated river basins. The fact remains that until adequate flows through an instream appropriation are actually granted, new surface water appropriations and groundwater pumping permits are likely to continue to be issued until a stream is declared "fully appropriated." Since the majority of streams and rivers do not have instream flow protection, once a fully appropriated status is declared for a basin, water will have to be leased (or someday purchased) similar to what is being contemplated for the fully appropriated Republican River Basin and major portions of the Platte River Basin.

A new provision of LB 962 allows leasing of the consumptive portion of a surface water appropriation (e.g., an irrigation diversion appropriation) for instream flows or other uses within a basin for a period of time up to 30 years. This is a start, but it may also be more appropriate for those who are going to have to provide tax dollars to allow for perpetual purchasing of such water in the long term.

During 2006, when assessing hydrological connections along streams and rivers, the NDNR adopted a hydrologically connected area regulating rule called "10-50." Under this rule, groundwater supplies are considered to be hydrologically connected to a stream or stream reach if the groundwater is draining to the stream.

In accordance with NDNR Rule 457 NAC 24.001.02, the area within which groundwater is hydrologically connected to a stream is the area within which "pumping of a well for 50 years will deplete the river, or a base flow tributary thereof, by at least 10% of the amount pumped in that time." Wells within the geographic boundary defined by the 10-50 rule can legally be regulated to prevent a basin from becoming overappropriated, but wells outside the 10-50 line may not be regulated even though they may also contribute to depletions of stream flows.

The provision to allow leasing of the consumptive part of a surface water appropriation will have merit in the recently approved 2006 Platte River Recovery Implementation Program, where the state of Nebraska will have to pick up the costs of replacing any depletions from designated target flows which occurred after July 1, 1997, because of the Cooperative Agreement signed by the governors of Nebraska, Wyoming, Colorado, and the U.S. Department of the Interior Director on this date. While the purpose of the Cooperative Agreement is to improve and maintain habitat for the endangered whooping crane, interior least tern and piping plover (threatened) in the critical reach of the central Platte River, and endangered pallid sturgeon in the lower Platte River reach, better flows in the central and lower Platte will help many other species and their habitats as well, not to mention other amenities to communities and citizens living along these reaches. Tough decisions remain to be made to fulfill this obligation.

It seems prudent that the state of Nebraska could save taxpayers a lot of money if rivers and streams were protected before they become fully or overappropriated. Since the waters of the state are public trust resources belonging to all citizens, it begs the question: How well have the state of Nebraska and its officials protected the public trust?

The United States has passed through four eras of public land and resources management, each with its own legislative policies and environmental ethic.

There was settlement and development of the original public domain (1789-1834); next, a public land resource stewardship with a conservation ethic began with President Theodore Roosevelt in the early 1900s; after World War II there was ensuing national growth, including many water development projects such as dams (1941-1962); last, there was the environmental law era of 1962-1990. These four eras paved the way for the present era of watershed restoration and collaborative stewardship.

State-of-the-art understanding of the dynamic nature and ecology of streams and rivers and their importance to providing ecosystem goods and services to mankind has increased tremendously in the last two decades. While the task of protecting instream flows to sustain these uses is a daunting one, those responsible for protecting the public trust must join hands with fellow citizens if future generations are to have any hope of enjoying what present generations enjoy as part of their quality of life here in Nebraska.

The need for ecosystem management of large rivers and their floodplains has never been greater. Significant economic advantages, as well as increased biodiversity, can result from restoration of impaired systems.

Because ecosystem goods and services rendered by rivers and streams were not well understood historically, they were underappreciated. As a society, we are just beginning to awaken to the true cost of ignoring them. In many cases, it will be cheaper to restore them than to exploit them beyond sustainability.

Nebraska's surface and ground waters have been extensively developed for many purposes, but irrigated agriculture is the largest consumptive user of water in the state. Some would construe the development and over-exploitation of our surface and groundwater to be a "Tragedy of the Commons."

In this context, state property right laws (e.g., when a surface water appropriation to divert is issued and perfected, it becomes a property right, or the unlimited issuance of irrigation well permits to pump groundwater by NRDs) have failed to safeguard important public trust natural resources which belong to all citizens.

Together, they are impacting many stream and riverine natural resources which contribute to the physical, social, biological and economic aspects of Nebraska's economy. Collectively, some people refer to these resources as ecosystem goods and services. Essentially, they are environmental flow regimes of a particular magnitude, frequency and timing necessary to ensure that a river system remains environmentally, economically and socially healthy for its citizens. Environmental flow regimes are heartbeats for rivers and should not be flatlined.

Although this sounds bleak for managing public trust natural resources on a sustainable basis, much work remains to be done. There are some rivers with unappropriated water left which can be protected with instream flows.

On May 24, 2006, the Nebraska Game and Parks Commission (NGPC) Board of Commissioners passed a resolution directing staff to protect existing instream flows already granted and to secure instream flows on streams with high-value natural resources, particularly the heartbeat of the Niobrara River with its high-quality tributaries.

(Note: The Central Platte NRD instream flow appropriations on the central Platte, reaching from Lexington to Columbus, are up for a 15-year review in 2009, and the NGPC complimentary instream flow appropriations on the central and lower reaches of the Platte are up for a 15-year review in 2013.)

Should more and more basins become fully or overappropriated and streams and rivers dry up more frequently, the state of Nebraska could very well have to lease or purchase water back to restore and protect public trust/public interest values. Depending upon assumptions made and analyses conducted, it could cost millions of tax dollars to accomplish this. Since surface water is a public resource regulated by the NDNR and groundwater is a public resource regulated locally by NRDs, it remains to be seen whether or not the fortitude to prevent or solve overexploitation of both exists.

Funding for NRDs primarily comes from local property tax levees, but state officials may not be open to raising state taxes on all citizens in the future to bail out local NRDs whose decisions result in overexploitation of groundwater in their basins, thus resulting in depletion of hydrologically connected stream/river flows and, subsequently, the loss of current and future ecosystem goods and services.

More than three out of four Americans participate in active outdoor recreation each year. Yet many people fail to realize that having fun and staying healthy in the outdoors is essential to the growth of our economy. According to the Outdoor Industry Foundation, the active outdoor recreation economy contributes $730 billion annually to the US economy.

During 2006, an independent economist from ECONorthwest by the name of Ernie Niemi out of Eugene, Ore., evaluated the potential to grow Nebraska's economy by capitalizing on natural-resource-related, amenity-driven growth in Nebraska. His report, entitled "Natural-Resource Amenities and Nebraska's Economy: Current Connections, Challenges, and Possibilities," is available from the Nebraska Game and Parks Commission. His conclusion: Natural-resource-related amenities may be able to stimulate economic growth through four mechanisms.

* Improving the quality of life by making the state attractive to entice entrepreneurs.
* Improving feedback to the farm sector by increasing off-farm job opportunities.
* Expanding recreational and other commercial uses of natural resources.
* Protecting environmental values by sustaining species and keeping the web of life together.

A significant proportion of Nebraska's future economic vitality could potentially revolve around its streams and rivers if natural attributes are protected enough so they can generate amenities citizens are seeking. Examples where this is happening include ecotourism on the central Platte for bird-watching; ecotourism on the Niobrara for canoeing and tubing; and ecotourism on the Missouri River from boating and many other recreational uses.

The Missouri River has an active recovery program for the endangered pallid sturgeon, least tern and piping plover, as well as for the diversity of habitats needed to support a healthy riverine ecosystem. A healthy Missouri River means that historically forgotten amenities will be more prominent in the future to help grow Nebraska's (and other basin states') economy by paying dividends to many Nebraska citizens seeking fun places to connect with nature, the outdoors and rivers. While Nebraska's instream flow provisions are the most restrictive among western statutory laws, they could be improved upon considerably. Adequate instream flows benefit both ecological and economic interests.

They are the essence of what makes a river and contribute to many ecosystem goods and services, including filtration and dilution of sewage and associated effluents for water quality; livestock watering; increased land values; cooling water for electrical generating plants; hydro-generating plants; drinking water sources and groundwater recharge; recharging riparian wetlands; subirrigating wet meadow grasslands; fish, wildlife and recreational uses; and many, many other things important to the quality of life here in Nebraska.

However, the question remains: when stream and river flows can legally be diverted or diminished by some combination of surface water diversions and/or groundwater depletions to the point where the lifeblood is drained out of them and they no longer flow, has the state of Nebraska fulfilled its obligation of protecting the public property rights embodied by the public trust? Has the public interest of present and future generations been served?

6

Greening Agriculture in India

There has been a spurt in domestic and international demand for greening agriculture across the countries as a result of initiatives of multiple actors such as institutions/organizations, industrial and trading firms, farming communities, civil society and their representatives. The dynamic of the role played these actors has determined the extent of greening of the agricultural production activities in both developing and developed countries. This growing demand for green agriculture products is both a constraint as well as window of opportunity not only for the Indian agriculturists but also for producers, suppliers and traders of agriculture inputs (fertilizer, pesticide etc.) and outputs. Given this outlook, this paper in the first section attempts to understand the current status of the market for agricultural inputs especially for chemical fertilizers & pesticides within the India as a background for understanding the greening initiatives in the country contextually. The second section dwells into the agricultural greening initiatives in India by focusing on both the market for green inputs and outputs. It also attempts to analyse the market potential both by looking at domestic and international agriculture market. Finally it evaluates the role played by different agencies in promoting green agriculture market in the country and concludes by incorporating some suggestions so as to improve market potentials for green input and output market.

INTRODUCTION

Agriculture and allied sector contributes 24% of the total GDP and provide employment to around 67% Indian population (Planning Commission, 2002). Use of chemical fertilizers and pesticides have played a positive role in increasing agricultural productivity and in making India self-sufficient in food grain production. Yield of food-grain in India increased from 644 k.g. per hectare in 1966-67 to 1636 k.g. per hectare in 2000-2001(www.indiastat.com) i.e. this registered an impressive increase by around two and half times.

This was mainly brought about by a more than 12 fold increase in the consumption of chemical fertilizers (from 1.1 million ton to 13.56 million tons) during the same period (Pawan Wadhwa, 2001). This apart, inorganic chemical use in agriculture has also contributed towards increasing productivity of cash crops.

After this prolonged dependence on inorganic and mineral components for agriculture growth there has been an increasing demand for rethinking agricultural growth strategy. Agriculture sustainability (Pretty J., 1998), soil degradation (soil productivity and soil structure), bio-diversity (CSE, 1998), impact on human health and on environment as a whole are the some of the concerns that are being raised for reviewing part of the agricultural growth potentials based on the current strategy.

Search for alternates with a focus on long-term sustainability of agriculture has been enhanced in the last decade. In developed countries the initiatives towards greening agriculture have been prompted both by market attractiveness as well as state support activities. Usage of bio-fertilizer & bio-pesticides, organic farming (Bernhard Berger, 2001), Biodynamic farming (Planning Commission, 2001) low input agriculture (http://www.ileia.org/), permaculture (Allan Atkisson, 1991), sustainable agriculture (Pretty J. 1998), integrated farming practices (integrated pest management and integrated nutrient management), are some of the practices that are being espoused by proponents both in developed and developing countries.

All these practices have evolved as alternatives to chemical use in agriculture keeping in view the increasing demand for green agriculture products across the world(Gilk Paul, 2003). This growing demand for green agriculture products is both a constraint as well as window of opportunity not only for the agriculturists but also for producers, suppliers and traders of agriculture inputs (fertilizer, pesticide etc.) and outputs. As a result of increasing domestic and international demand for greening agriculture across the countries both economic and non-economic actors such as institutions/organizations, industrial and trading firms, farming communities, civil society and their representatives played significant role in determining the extent of greening the agricultural production activities. In order to understand the greening initiative in agriculture contextually, it is pertinent to have an overview of trends in chemical inputs into the agriculture in India.

Hence in the following we present a brief overview of the same in Indian agriculture.

AGRICULTURAL INPUTS MARKET TRENDS & POTENTIALS IN INDIA

Chemical Fertilizers

After independence the use of fertilizers in India in the last 50 years has grown nearly 170 times. In 1950 use of fertilizer per hectare in India was 0.55 Kg but by 2001-02 this figure has increased to around 90.12 Kg per hectare. Green revolution during 1960s and subsequent increased intensification of agriculture were major causes behind this growth as seen in Fig. No. 1. Fertilizers and pesticides have become major cost of production in India along with the cost of other input like seeds, and labor cost.

Fig: 1 Consumption of Total Plant Nutrient per hectare of Gross Cropped Area

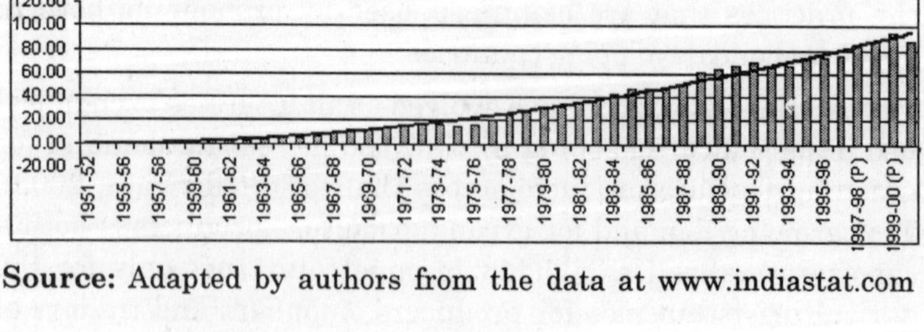

Source: Adapted by authors from the data at www.indiastat.com

Given the differences in the intensity of agriculture and cropping patterns across the country there are wide variations in the extent of fertilizer consumption patterns across India. For instance states like Punjab, Andhra Pradesh, Haryana, Karnataka, Tamilnadu, West Bengal and Uttar Pradesh have very high average fertilizer consumption per hectare in comparison to the states like Rajasthan, Madhya Pradesh, Himachal Pradesh, Orissa, Goa and northeastern states.

Per hectare fertilizer use in Andhra Pradesh as high as 179.2 Kg in 2000-01 and on the other hand in most of Eastern states it was less than 10Kg per hectare and in Rajasthan it was only 29.78 kg/hectare.

Fig: 2 Trends in Economics of Fertilizer Input on Wheat Production in India (1971-2002)

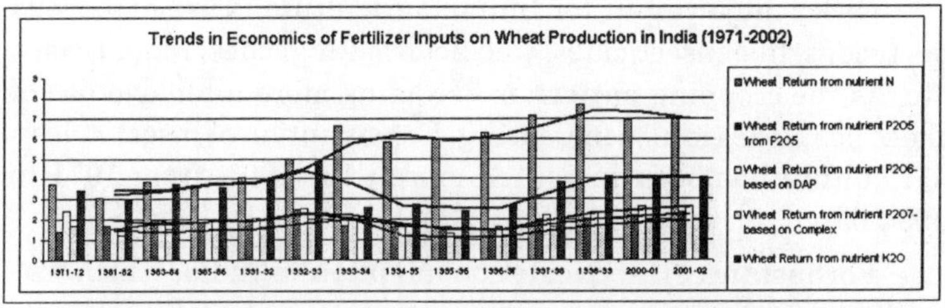

Unfortunately increase in chemical usage has not inevitably led to increasing incomes of the farmers at the same rate at which it enhanced the agricultural production costs. The marginal income from land because of additional unit of chemical fertilizer and pesticide is decreasing. Another reason for increasing cost is decreasing govt. subsidies on farm inputs. The fertilizer subsidy bill for 2002-03(BE) is Rs. 11,228 crore that is Rs.716 crore less than the revised estimate of Rs. 1,944 crore and budgeted expenditure of Rs12,808 crore for 2001-02 (Economic Survey, 2002-03).

Use of fertilizer in improper ratio of N: P: K is also a major problem for Indian agriculture. While the recommended ratio is 4:2:1 this ratio of N: P: K has been around 8.5:2.6:1. This "induces initial vegetative growth, susceptible to pests, diseases, lodging and causes poor floral induction and delayed maturity thereby reducing the yield" (Hegde N. G. 2000).

Fig: 3 Trends in Economics of Fertilizer Input on Rice Production in India (1971-2002)

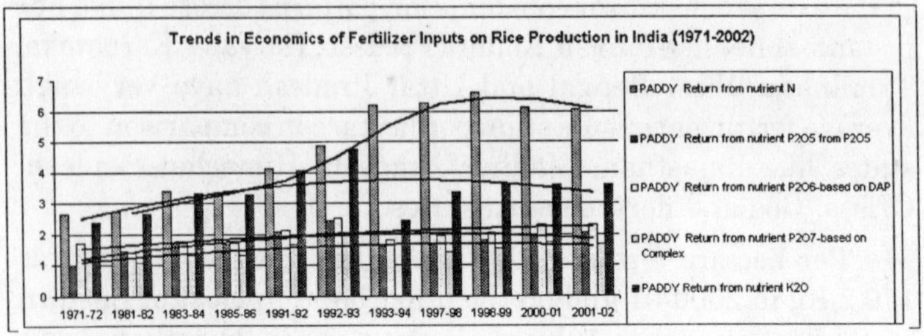

Source: Adapted by authors from the data collected at www.indiastats.com

Pesticides

Other major input for Indian agriculture is use of various pesticides, like insecticides, weedicides, fungicides, rodenticides etc. As the cropping pattern is becoming more intensive use of these pesticides is also increasing. Consumption of insecticide in agriculture has been increased more than 100% from 1971 to 1994-95.

For instance, insecticide consumption in India, which was to the tune of 22013 tonnes has increased to 51755 tonnes by 1994-95 (www.indiastat.com). Consumption of all of these pesticides in same duration has increased more than two times, that is from 24305 tonnes to 61357 tonnes.

Fig: 4 Consumption of Pesticides in India

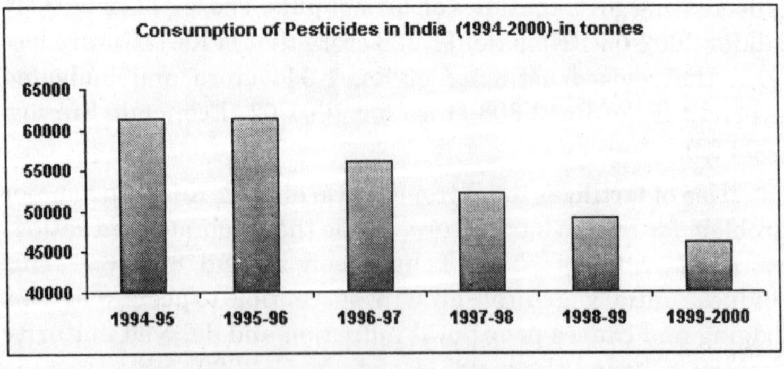

Source: Indian Chemical Statistics 2000-01

But in recent past, change has been observed in trends of pesticides consumption. As a consequence of adoption of bio intensive Integrated Pest Management Programme in various crops the consumption of chemical pesticide (Tech. Grade) has come down from 66.36 thousand MT during 1994-95 to 43.59 thousand MT during 2001-02 with a reduction of 27.69%(Thirty Seventh Report of Standing Committee on Petroleum and Chemicals, 2002). Consumption pattern of pesticides in India is also very different from world. In India insecticide account for 76% of the total domestic market while herbicides & fungicides have a significantly higher share in the global market.

There are wide ranges of regional variations in pesticide consumption in the country. In the year 2000-01, States of Haryana, Punjab and Uttar Pradesh by consuming more than 5,000 MT (technical grade) pesticides annually come under category I state in consumption of pesticides. States viz., Andhra Pradesh, Gujarat, Karnataka, Kerala, Madhya Pradesh, Maharashtra, Rajasthan, Orissa and Tamil Nadu, which consumed between 1000 MT and 5000 MT fall in the category II states. States viz., Assam Bihar and Himachal Pradesh that consumed pesticide between 100 and 1000 MT come under category III. States viz., Arunachal Pradesh, Jammu & Kashmir, Manipur, Mizoram, Nagaland, Tripura, Delhi and Union Territory (UT) of Pondicharry consumed pesticides between 10 and 100 MT annually fall under category IV. States viz., Goa, Meghalya, Sikkim and UTs viz., Andman & Nicobar Islands, Candigarh, Dadara & Nagar Haveli, Daman & Diu and Lakshadweep consumed less than 10 MT pesticide annually as fall in the last category in pesticide consumption (Thirty Seventh Report of Standing Committee on Petroleum and Chemicals, 2002).

One of the consequences of indiscriminate use of pesticide is the adverse health impact on society in general and vulnerable population like children in particular. Some of the well-known health effects of pesticide exposure include acute poisoning, cancer, neurological effects and reproductive and developmental harm (CSE, 1997). The major causes of concern in this respect are bio-accumulation of pesticides and the prolonged time period that it takes to express the negative health consequences.

GREEN INPUT MARKET-SPATIAL & TEMPORAL TRENDS

It is very difficult to estimate the total size of green inputs market in India because of its diversity in terms of products and also due to the nature of it being unorganized market. Green inputs into agriculture include bio-fertilizers, bio-pesticides, compost, Farm Yard Manure (FYM), green manure etc. As most of this inputs are either not traded and even if they are traded, it is only at informal levels available information regarding production capacity, demand and sales is at best sketchy estimation and hence inadequate. The limited number well-established firms that have their presence in this market today as a result it this is predominately controlled by the small and local producers of bio-fertilizer, vermi compost and other input producers who are in large numbers. Relatively speaking there is more rigour in estimation of bio-fertilizer market in India, because of the presence of some large producers in production of bio-fertilizers and comparatively this is more organized than other green inputs market. Based on the gross cropped area in India (190 million hectare) and recommended doses of bio-fertilizers, potential demand is estimated to be about 6,27,000 MT. This demand can further be segregated into different categories of bio-fertilizer, such as Rhizobium, Azotobactors, Azospirillium, BGA, and Phosphate Solubilizer etc. whose demand differ widely as shown in Table:1 But by looking at the product segregation as seen in Table:1 potentials for different strains of bio – fertilizers in India:

Table 1: Estimated Total Potential Demand for Bio-fertilizers in India

Category of Bio-Fertilizer	Amount in Million Tonnes
Rhizobium	35,730Mt
Azotobacter	162,610Mt
Azospirillum	77,160Mt.
BGA	267,510Mt
Phosphate solubilizer	275,510Mt
TOTAL	818,730Mt

Source: Abhay Phadke, 2001

For year 2000 proposed production target for bio-fertilizer was 39,165Mt, which was only 4.8% of the total estimated demand (Abhay Phadke, 2001). But the actual production and the distribution of bio fertilizers are below the targeted (as seen in Table.2). This shows the huge gape between potential market demand and production and also provides an opportunity for bio-fertilizer producers. There has been a positive trend in India, with respect to production of bio-fertilizers. As it can be seen from Table 2 that while the total production of bio-fertilizer in India in 1992-93 was 2005.0 tons and it has increased to 8010.1 tons by 1998-99. Similarly the consumption/distribution of bio-fertilizer has also increased 1600.01 tons to 6700.27 tons during the same time period.

Table: 2 Installed production capacity, total production and distribution of bio-fertilizer in India (1992-99)

Year	Installed Production Capacity (Tons)	% Growth Rate in Installed Capacity	Total Production (Tons)	% Growth Rate in Production	Total Consumption/ Distribution (Tons)	% Growth Rate in Consumption/ Distribution
1992-93	5400.5		2005.0		1600.01	
1993-94	6125.5	13.42	3084.0	53.82	2914.37	82.15
1994-95	8114.5	32.47	5800.5	88.08	4988.90	71.18
1995-96	10680.4	31.62	6692.3	15.37	6288.32	26.05
1996-97	12647.0	18.41	7406.6	10.67	6681.44	6.25
1997-98	N.A.	0.00	7104.6	-4.08	6295.63	-5.77
1998-99	16446.0	30.04	8010.1	12.75	6700.27	6.43

Source: The Fertilizer Association of India Bio-fertilizer Statistics 1999-2000

But the growth rate in installed bio-fertilizer capacity is comparatively more stable than the growth rate in total production, consumption & distribution of bio-fertilizers (Table: 2). For total production of bio-fertilizers growth rate had reduced to 12.75%

during 1998-99 from 53.82% in 1993-94 and during same period the growth rate of consumption & distribution had reduced to 6.43% from 82.15%. This is an indication that there is not only a need but also a role for market development for green agriculture inputs in India.

Fig: 5 Installed production capacity and total production of bio-fertilizer in India (1992-99)

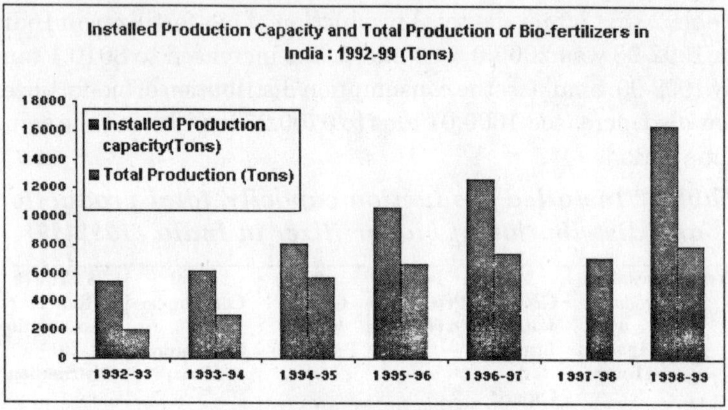

Source: Adapted by authors from FAI, 2001.

Fig: 6 Total Consumption / Distribution of Bio-fertilizer in India (1992-99).

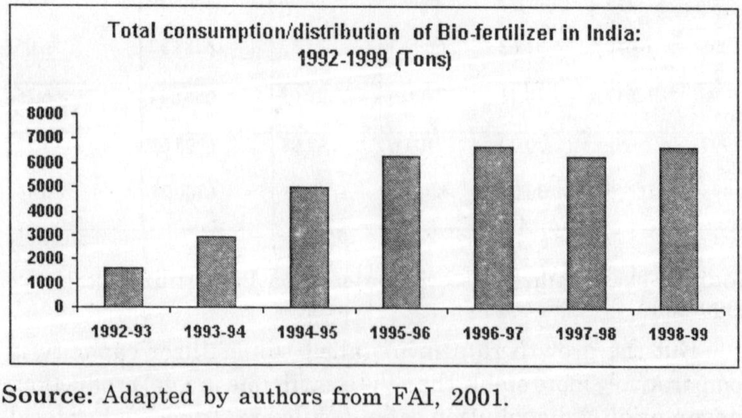

Source: Adapted by authors from FAI, 2001.

Inspite of the impressive growth rate of more than 200% in production capacity and around 300% growth rate experienced in production and consumption of bio-fertilizers in India within 6 years (i.e., from 1992-93 to 1998-99) yet it is only around 1.5% of the estimated demand potential for bio-fertilizers in the country.

Fig:7 Trends in Bio-fertilizer Production in Uttar Pradesh (1997-2003*)

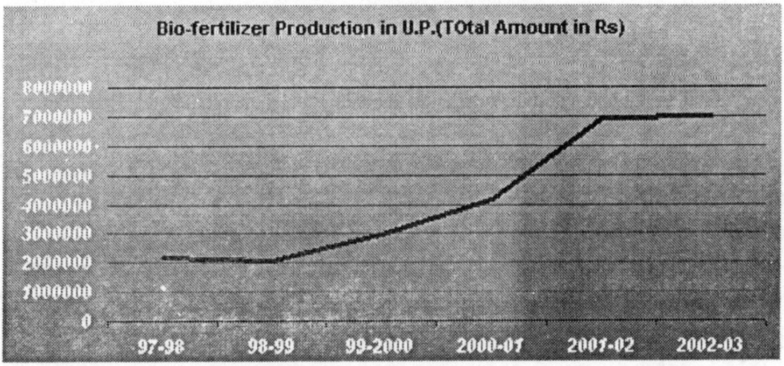

*Production for 2002-03 is estimated

Source: Adapter by Authors from the data given by Department of Agriculture, Govt. of U.P, 2002

Fig: 8 Consumption of bio-fertilizer in Punjab (1999-2002)

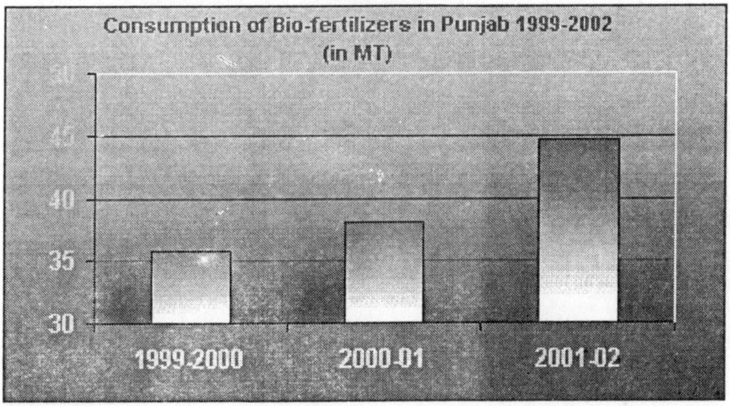

Source: Compiled by authors from different bio-fertilizer producers in Punjab

Region wise production trend analysis in India shows wide variations across the country. Western India has the highest bio-fertilizer production capacity as it can be seen that for the 1999-2000 the estimated production in this region was 5098.2 tons and it was expected grow upto 6429.9 tons by 2000-01 (FAI, 1999-2000). Southern India has the second largest bio-fertilizer producing region with 4491.6 tons for 1999-2000 and 6117.5 tons for 2000-01. Inspite of the huge agricultural production base in Northern India the production of bio-fertilizer stood at 207.2 tons for 1999-2000. At state level Maharashtra is highest bio-fertilizer producer state with 3173.0 tons of likely production for 2000-01 followed by Karnataka with likely production of 3152.5 tons for same year (FAI, 2001). Other states are also showing the trends of increasing orientation towards bio-fertilizers. For example in last four years value of bio-fertilizer distributed in Uttar Pradesh has increased from around Rs 2 Lakh in 1997-98 to Rs. 7 Lakh in 2001-02 (Fig: 7). Punjab is also showing increasing trends for bio-fertilizer market inspite of the fact that the sale of bio-fertilizer in Punjab was started in only 1997-98 by 2001-02 market has grown to 45 mt/year (Fig: 8).

Increase in use of vermi-compost has been observed for kitchen gardens and for cultivation of high value cash crops but the information about actual quantity used is not available. Area under green manure is one indicator that is showing negative trends because the area under intensive cropping is increasing. Increase in irrigation facilities are indirectly contributing towards reduction of area under green manure is as seen in Table 3.

Table: 3 Area under Green Manure in India (1995-97)

Area Under Green Manure in India

Year	**Area in Lakh Hectares**
1994-95	35.872
1995-96	34.411
1996-97	22.512

Source: FAI, 1999-2000.

Other green inputs for agriculture in India are used in very minimal quantity. Some of the popular bio-pesticides include neem based formulation and *Bacillus thuringingiensis* (Bt). Consumption of bio-pesticides in India has increased from 83 MT

(Tech. Grade) during 1994-95 to 686 MT during 1999-2000 and in case of neem based pesticide formulation it has increased 40 MT to 71 MT during the same period in case of *Bacillus thuringiensis* (Bt) (THIRTY-SEVENTH REPORT STANDING COMMITTEE ON PETROLEUM & CHEMICALS, 2002).

GREEN OUTPUTS MARKET TRENDS & POTENTIALS IN INDIA

Demand for green agricultural products is a stimulant for growth for input market. In other words if there is demand in market for organically produced farm products will encourage farmers to implement the organic farming practices and also to use organic input like bio-fertilizers, bio-pesticides, varmi-compost, green manure and FYM.

Table: 4 Major products produced in India by organic farming

Major products produced in India by organic farming

Type of Product	Products
Commodity	Tea, Coffee, Rice, Wheat
Spices	Cardamom, Black pepper, white pepper, Ginger, Turmeric, Vanilla, Tamarind, Clove, Cinnamon, Nutmeg, Mace, Chili
Pulses	Red gram, Black gram
Fruits	Mango, Banana, Pineapple, Passion fruit, Sugarcane, Orange, Cashew nut, Walnut
Vegetables	Okra, Brinjal, Garlic, Onion, Tomato, Potato
Oil seeds	Mustard, Sesame, Castor, Sunflower
Others	Cotton, Herbal extracts

Source: Garibay S V and Jyoti K, 2003

Estimating area under organic agriculture in India is a difficult task as there is no central agency that collects and compiles this information.

Different agencies have estimated the area under organic agriculture differently for instance the study undertaken by FIBL and ORG-MARG (Garibay S V and Jyoti K, 2003) the area under organic agriculture to be 2,775 hectares (0.0015% of gross cultivated area in India). But other estimation undertaken by SOEL-Survey shows that the land area under organic cropping is 41000 hectare.

The total numbers of organic farms in the country as per SOEL-Survey are 5661 but FIBL and ORG-MARG survey puts it as 1426. Some of the major organically produced agricultural crops in India include crops like plantation, spices, pulses, fruits, vegetables and oil seeds etc (Table: 4).

India is best known as an exporter of organic tea and also has great export potential for many other products. Other organic products for which India has a niche market are spices and fruits.

Org-Marg's survey also proves this fact as around 30% of respondents that includes producer, exporters and traders has responded that organic tea is produced in India and this is highest response for any single crop, next are spices, fruits, vegetables, rice and coffee (Garibay S V and Jyoti K, 2003). There is small response for cashew, oil seed, wheat and pulses. Among the fruit crops Bananas, Mangos and oranges are the most preferred organic products.

Export Market: Organic agricultural export market is one of the major drivers of greening of agriculture in India. The current production of organic crops is around 14,000 tons (Garibay S V and Jyoti K, 2003). Out of this production, tea and rice contributes around 24% each, fruits and vegetables combine makes 17% of this total production. From India around 11,925 tons of organic product is exported, that makes around 85% of total organic crop production.

Major export market for Indian producers are Australia, Belgium, Canada, France, Germany, Italy, Japan, Netherlands, Sweden, Singapore, South Africa, Saudi Arabia, UAE, UK, and USA. Estimated quantity of various products that are exported from India in 2002 is shown in Table 5.This shows that around 3000 tons of tea was exported and in quantity term it was the highest, next major exports are rice (2500 tons), fruits & vegetables (1800 tons), cotton (1200 tons) and wheat (1150 tons) (Garibay S V and Jyoti K, 2003).

Table: 5 Major organic products exported from India

Product	Sales (Tons)
Tea	3000
Coffee	550
Spices	700
Rice	2500
Wheat	1150
Pulses	300
Oil Seeds	100
Fruits & Vegetables	1800
Cashew Nut	375
Cotton	1200
Herbal Products	250
Total	11,925

Source: Org-Marg, 2002

The burgeoning US and European green markets provides enormous scope for Indian exporters. International Trade Centre's (ITC) overview of estimation of organic food world-wide shows that there is strong growth in retail sales from US $ 10 billion in 1997 to US$ 17.5 billion in 2000 and about US$ 21 billion in 2001 (in 16 European countries, USA and Japan). If the demand of so called 'green product' in Japan that is not certified as organic product is excluded from total estimation, than also it is US$ 16 billion for 2999 and reached around US$ 19 billion in 2001. Though the current market share for organic produced is estimated between one to two percent of total food products market, but the forecasting by experts show that this market is likely to grow at a higher pace. According to experts in medium term around five percent of the market is expected to be organic market share (Minou Yussefi and Heldge Willer, 2003).

Europe is largest market of organic produces in world and consumes around half of the world produce of organic production (Minou Yussefi and Helga Willer, 2003). EU is a net importer of cereals, oilseeds, potatoes and vegetables. For 2001, European market for organic food was estimated to be around US$ 9 billion but with expected annual growth rate of around 20% (Table: 6) depending upon the market, and for 2003 the retail sales for organic food in this market is expected to US$ 10-11billion (Rudy Korbech-Olesen, ITC, UNCTAD/WTO). Within Europe, Germany is largest market for organic products with sales value of around 2.5 billion Euros ($2.3 billion (US)). On an average the per capita spending on organic produces in Europe was euro 23 for 2000. In terms of per capita consumption of organic products countries like Denmark (72 Euros per head), Switzerland (Euros 68), Austria (Euros 40) and Germany (Euros 31) fared much better than others (Fig: 9). While some of the European countries like Italy not only meet their internal demand for organic products but they also cater to the demands of other neighbouring countries. There are other countries like United Kingdom, which are highly dependent on imports to meet their domestic organic product demand.

Fig: 9 Per capita sales of organic produces in selected European Countries in Euro (2000)

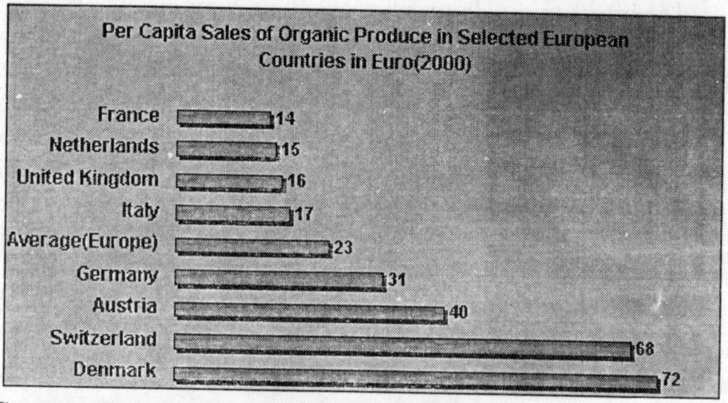

Source: Garibay S V and Jyoti K, 2003

In North America, retail sales of organic products for 2002 was estimated nearly $12 billion (US) out of this US alone is contributing for $11 billion (US). US retail sale for organic product has grown 20-24% per year for the past 12 years and the same growth trends expected to continue for future. Current retail sales for organic food is around 2% of total retail food sale in US (Minou Yussefi and Heldge Willer, 2003).

In Asia largest market for organic food product is Japan and it is estimated to have the retail sales of organic food and beverage of around $(US) 2.5-3.0 billion (Minou Yussefi and Heldge Willer, 2003). Of this total value of organic market, imports are estimated to be to the tune of around $(US) 360 million. Though the organic food market is not more than 0.5% of total food market of Japan but according to the Japanese Integrated Market Institute, import of organic products is likely to grow by 40% (Hiraga, 2002). Other global markets for organic products in Middle East are Saudi Arabia and UAE. Within Africa, South Africa is the only country that has organic market potential. As seen from the global market growth trends for organic foods there are enormous potentials for India to exploit.

Table: 6 Percentage of organic food and medium term growth expected in selected markets

Overview for World Market for organic food & beverages in 2000 (estimates)		
Markets	**% of total food sales**	**% Expected growth - Medium term**
Germany	1.6-1.8	10-15
U.K.	1.0-2.5	15-20
Italy	0.9-1.1	10-20
France	0.8-1.0	10-15
Switzerland	2.0-2.5	10-15
Denmark	2.5-3.0	10-15
Austria	1.8-2.0	10-15
Netherlands	0.9-1.2	10-20
Sweden	1.0-1.2	15-20
Belgium	0.9-1.1	10-15
U.S.A.	1.5-2.0	20

Source: ITC, January2002

Total commodity wise demand (in volume terms) has been estimated in some selected export markets (Germany, Holland,

UK, Switzerland, USA, and Japan) by the FIBL & ORG-MARG survey which shows that for Banana it is 6,410 tons, for wheat and soy bean 1,000 tons, for pineapple around 900 tons and for mango this is around 650 tons (Garibay S V and Jyoti K, 2003).

The attractiveness of organic market gets enhanced also because of the price premium that these products have over the conventionally produced products. Price premium for various organic produces vary in different countries depending upon the distribution channels and market conditions. This premium varies from 30-50% (trader level) for different products.

As seen from above there are immense opportunities for organic agricultural exports for Indian to exploit. Some of the prerequisites for exploiting this potential include:

- Farmers capacity to produce the organically the agricultural products which have global market and
- Prior experience of exporters and traders in exporting agricultural commodities to these markets

In the Fig 10 an attempt has been made to develop a matrix by depicting the conventional agricultural commodities, which India has been exporting to various countries across the world as well as the existence of organic market for these commodities in these countries.

Depicting the current conventional agricultural market indicates the capabilities of India in exporting the specific agricultural commodities to different countries and similarly depicting the existence of organic agriculture market for specific commodities in these countries reveal the existence of opportunities for exporting organic agricultural commodities.

In developing this matrix we have used annual exports of agricultural commodities as published in CMIE agricultural sector reports and for exploring organic market in different countries for different commodities we have used the internet resources mentioned at the end of this article.

The matrix reveals that India has demonstrated capabilities of exporting agricultural commodities like rice, wheat, tea, coffee, spices, oil meals, sugar, fruits & vegetables etc to countries like USA, U. K, Germany, Japan, France, Saudi Arabia, South

Africa, CIS Countries, Poland, Netherlands, Italy etc. It also shows that in most of these countries there is a demand for organically produced commodities, which attract price premiums ranging from 10% to 100%. This showcases a window of opportunity that is yet to be exploited to its maximum potentials by Indian exporters and producers of agricultural commodities.

Fig: 10 Conventional agricultural products & their export market and prospective market for Indian organic products.

Agricultural Commodities	Rice	Wheat	Tea	Coffee	Tobacco	Spices	Cashew	Oil meals	Cotton	Castor oil	Sugar	Fruits / vegetables
USA	❀		❀	❀	❀						❀	
UK	❀		❀		❀	❀	❀					❀
Japan			❀	❀		❀	❀	❀				
France						❀	❀				❀	
Germany			❀	❀	❀	❀	❀					❀
Italy				❀								
CIS	❀		❀	❀		❀	❀					
Netherlands			❀	❀			❀					
Switzerland				❀								
Egypt			❀		❀						❀	
UAE	❀		❀		❀	❀	❀					❀
Saudi Arab			❀		❀							❀
Poland			❀	❀								
Belgium				❀	❀							
South Africa	❀											

Existing conventional export market for Indian producers for particular product

Prospective market for Indian organic products.

Source: Adapted by authors by collating information from different Internet sites mentioned in the references

Domestic Market

Given the unorganized nature of the domestic organic agriculture market in India it is difficult to estimate the magnitude and trends in this growing market.

In general, the sale of organic produces is limited to metros like Mumbai, Delhi, Kolkata, Chennai, Bangalore and Hyderabad. To a large extent this sale is also based on individual initiative of the farmers, Non Governmental Organizations and some entrepreneurial traders etc.

The current domestic green products market demand is mainly for fruits, vegetables, rice and wheat. Other products include tea, coffee and pulses (ORG-MARG Survey, 2002). The market prospects other commodities like organic spices, fruits, herbal plants and cotton are relatively high. For next five years it is projected that organic spices would grow by 14%, fruits 8% and herbal plants and cotton it is estimated to be around 7% (ORG-MARG Survey, 2002). Market for different range of organic agricultural products as shown in Table: 7is estimated to reach up to 1568 tons in 2006-07.

Table: 7 Growth forecast for specific organic products in the domestic market

Product	% Projected Growth in the 5 next Years
Spices (all)	14
Pepper	5
Turmeric	4.5
Tea	13
Rice	10
Fruits (all)	8
Banana	15
Mango	5
Orange	5
Pineapple	5
Herbal extracts	7
Cotton	7
Coffee	5
Oil seeds	5
Honey	5
Groundnut	5
Baby food	5
Coconut	5

Source: Org-Marg, 2002

GOVERNMENT ROLE IN PROMOTION OF GREEN AGRICULTURE IN INDIA

Increasing Investments

There has been limited allocation under 9th Plan for bio-fertilizer, bio-pesticide popularization in the Agriculture sector and the provision for this programme was enhanced by expanding the scope of activities whereby promotion organic agriculture has been included as part of the activities targeted in the 10th Plan.

As part of 10th Five year Plan, Government of India has earmarked about Rs. 100 crores for the promotion of organic agriculture in the country. The main components of this initiative include farming of standards, negotiating with different countries and putting in place a system of certification for organic products.

Promoting Input Market

Central Government is also promoting the production and use of bio-fertilizer to make it popular. Government has initiated a project "National Project on Development and Use of Bio fertilizers" for this purpose. Main objectives of this project are as following:

i. Production and distribution of Bio fertilizers (BFs)
ii. Developing Standards for different BFs and Quality control
iii. Releasing of grants for setting up BF units
iv. Training and Publicity

Promoting Green Agriculture Market

To promote the organic agriculture in India government has also taken some initiative in recent past. APEDA (Planning Commission, 2001) is the nodal agency to promote the Indian organic agriculture and its exports opportunities. National Steering Committee under the Chairmanship of Secretary Commerce has already outlined and approved the National Program for Organic Production (NPOP) by May 2001 (www.apeda.com).

Under this program, National Organic Standards have been evolved. This apart, it has also developed Criteria for Accreditation of certification agencies, Accreditation Procedure and Inspection and Certification Procedures. In developing these standards and procedures due attention is paid to the guidelines as enumerated by international organizations such as International Federation for Organic Agricultural Movement (IFOAM), EU Regulations and FAO Codex Standards. As part of this program, a National Logo for organic products on behalf of Govt. of India has also been developed. Some of the other efforts towards promotion of organic exports include attempts to collaborate with all the major organic importing countries. Towards this APEDA is deliberating with European Union for inclusion of India in the list of third countries under Article 11 of the EU regulations No 2092/91 so that India's National Programme for Organic Production gets the required recognition under the EU regulations.

Facilitating Factors for Greening of Indian Agriculture: Organic agriculture provides economic opportunities for different stakeholders. Some of the drivers that facilitate growth of organic agriculture in India are

- Growing export market for organically produced crops (Kortbech-Olesen, 2003).
- Price premium for organically produced agriculture products from10% to 100% (V. Garibay, K. Jyoti, 2003).
- Diverse agro-climate regions across the country that provides environment for wide range of crops that can cater to different market demands.
- Increasing awareness & health consciousness especially among certain sectors of domestic consumers.
- Availability of comparatively cheap labor for labor-intensive organic agriculture
- Huge numbers of small farmers those who do the traditional farming with very limited capacity to pay for most of the chemical inputs into agriculture ((Planning Commission, 2001)
- Presence of Non-Government Organizations (NGOs) as active promoters of Organic farming in different agro-climatic regions (Donthi N. Reddy, 2001)
- Increasing involvement of private companies in field of agricultural extension, trade, consultatio . and other services
- Enhanced Government attention and support for organic agriculture through various policy initiations and action programs.

Factors Constraining Greening of Indian Agriculture

Though there are positive signs for green agriculture in India it is not growing at a pace to enhance its market attractiveness so as to motivate larger section of farming community to opt for organic agriculture. Fig 11 is an exercise to find why the penetration of greening the agriculture in India is limited. Major problems that hinders the growth organic agriculture in India can be listed as follows:

Factors limiting Bio-inputs Market

In exploring the factors limiting bio-input market we attempted to analyse them from multiple stakeholders perspectives presented briefly in the following:

Producers'/Distributors'/Traders' point of view:

- Lack of proper infrastructure for distribution and conservation of bio-inputs is a major constraint hinders the access of these inputs to farmers.
- Existence of poor quality bio-inputs in market reduces the credibility of input providers. Lack of quality control mechanisms for bio-inputs furthers the mistrust among farmers.
- Given the low penetration of bio-inputs market and the limited shelf-life it is disincentivizing the traders to store and sell bio-inputs

From Users' (farmers') point of view:

- Bio-fertilizers and bio-pesticides are perceived as less yielding.
- Some climatic regions and soil conditions are not suitable for specific strains of organic production.
- For some strains limited shelf life is also constrain as most of the bio-input last only for about 4-6 months.
- Given the mandated gestation period of around three years for a conventional farm to become an organic farm the benefits perceived by farmers in general and small and marginal farmers in particular tend to be limited as they have short term orientation. As a result even if they

are aware they are hesitant to switch over to organic (green) agricultural practices.

From Promoters' (Government's) point of view:

- Agricultural departments, research institutions and extension services have for long been oriented towards chemical input agriculture as a result there is a requirement for reorienting these officials towards organic (green) agriculture
- Changing the cropping and cultivation patterns is slow and time-consuming process given the high levels of illiteracy and large number of small and marginal farmers it makes the change process difficult.
- Subsidies on chemical fertilizers and pesticide impede the growth of organic agriculture.

Limiting Factors Organic Produce Market

- Lack of market information in general and organic market information in particular is biggest drawback for Indian agriculture. The current information base is low and even the limited information available does not get disseminated due to lack of adequate channels for dissemination. As a result farmers are in a predicament as they are unable to attune their production practices as per the market changes. Marketing network specifically for organic products has not yet developed both in the domestic as well as export market.
- Quality of Indian food industry is always a constraint for growth, low consistency of quality and contamination in food products is a hindrance in capturing the available market especially the international market.
- Given the high levels of transaction costs for getting farms certified as organic it is a major deterrent for enhancing organic production in the country. As the certification process for organic farming is very lengthy and complex, the cost of certification is also unaffordable for small farmers {Rs.22000 to Rs.29200 per certification} (Garibay S V and Jyoti K, 2003).

- Government has shown limited interest for organic agriculture, though the activities from government side are increasing but till date there is no direct support from government side in terms of subsidy or market support towards organic agriculture.
- Lack of proper infrastructure in terms of roads from remote villages, cold storage facilities and slow transportation infrastructure affects the cost, quality and reach of producers and
- Indian organic agriculture is very fragmented and there are no organizations for managing the entire value chain of organic products.

Large number of these problems listed above are due to the relatively newness of this sector from the point of view of different players.

RECOMMENDATIONS

Focus group discussions with different stakeholders like farmers, traders of green agricultural inputs, government officials involved in promotion of organic agriculture, agricultural scientists, extension officers and NGO's have revealed that multi-pronged initiatives at different levels would contribute towards enhancing greening of Indian agriculture.

From Policy Perspective

Experience elsewhere shows that government has to play a key role in developing organic agricultural production and enhancing marketing opportunities (Scialabba Nadia, 2000). Towards this there is a need to have policy framework to address greening agriculture in India. Policy change in favour of organic agriculture can make positive difference for changing the market condition in terms of encouraging production of bio-inputs, which in turn can propel changes in cropping pattern in favour of organic practices.

Currently the attention given both in terms of policy framework and institutional dynamics towards organic agriculture is only marginal. Though Ministry of Commerce registers farmers wishing to convert to organic operations but farmers are asked to seek technical assistance from the Ministry of Agriculture that is unavailable (Scialabba Nadia, 2000).

Involvement of government not just in standardization and accreditation procedures but also through proactive "support to inspection and certification and market-oriented services are necessary to provide equal opportunities. Otherwise, the export of certified organic products risks becoming that only large farmers, or highly organized groups of small holders, can afford" (Scialabba Nadia, 2000).

From Farmers Perspective

- Existing subsidy structure enhances the use of chemical fertilizers and pesticides as agricultural inputs. Gradual phasing out subsidy on synthetic fertilizers / pesticides and initiating promotion of bio-inputs would contribute towards enhancing organic agriculture production in the country.
- Providing grant assistance in the form of financial assistance for converting the traditional farm in to organic farm and intending support to meet certification fees especially for the small and marginal farmers etc.
- Enlarging the scope of work of the agricultural extension services by focusing on organic agriculture through collaborative engagement with NGOs, who are actively working in the rural areas (Scialabba, Nadia, 2000).
- Special insurance scheme for organic farm that reduces the risk of farmer in case of failure of crop.
- Promote contract farming based on organic agriculture as it has been done in Madhya Pradesh.

From NGO's Perspective

Non-Government Organizations have being playing crucial role in promoting organic agricultural practices in the country. Change of agricultural practices is equivalent to changing the culture and mindset of farmers, which can only be achieved by a long drawn interface. NGOs have demonstrated capabilities to this effect. An illustrative example of public private partnership is the successful story of Spice Board's involvement of NGOs to enhance organic production of spices in Kerala, Tamilnadu, Andhra Pradesh and North Eastern states (Shenoy, 2003)

From Traders Perspective

- Ministry of Commerce & Trade should have a dedicated cell for providing organic agricultural export market potentials in different parts of the world and the price premium that different products attract.
- Establishment of Special Organic Agriculture Trade Zone (OATZ) for domestic as well export market can help the traders in easily accessing the farm products as well as customers for organic products like agro-based food processors and retailers.
- In order to develop organic export networking potentials there is need for inventorizing the early exporters by providing special tax relaxation for traders/exporters those who have organic trading/export.
- In order to enhance the domestic organic agricultural market government need to make efforts towards promotion of organic food processing industries by providing subsidies and financial assistance as well as facilitates to market development. As the shelf life of some of the organic produce is shorter establishment of dedicated cold storage facilities could help in enhancing the prospects of exports.

From Green Input Producers Perspective

- Popularization of existing scheme for promotion of bio-fertilizers and extension of these schemes for other bio-inputs.
- Assistance in marketing of bio-inputs thorough govt. network and also involving the network of co-operative societies at village level for distribution of these bio-inputs.

- Improving infrastructure facilities like roads, transportations, storage facilities etc would enhance forward and backward linkages in the organic products supply chain.
- Promotion of corporate research for organic agronomic practices, bio-control of diseases and pest, bio-fertilizers etc.

From Institutional Perspective

There is urgent need for giving strategic attention to organic farming efforts. This requires inter ministerial coordination among various ministries at the Centre.

Towards this forming a Steering Committee consisting of various Ministries at Central Government level would be a move in the right direction. Such as.

- Ministry of Agriculture,
- Ministry of Commerce & Trade,
- Ministry of Environment,
- Ministry of Science & Technology,
- Ministry of Finance etc.

Such committee would helps on increasing effectiveness of policies & programmes evolved towards promotion of organic agriculture.

At the state level some of the important institutions that require coordinated action plan include: Agriculture universities, State agriculture department, Private business organizations and NGOs

Each of these institutions can enhance their contribution towards greening agriculture by developing a detailed program of action. In the following an attempt has been made to briefly dwell action programs for some of these institutions. For instance:

Agriculture Universities can have action programs by reorienting their current 1) Educational activities 2) Research Agenda and 3) Extension services Programmes as given in the matrix below:

Education	**Research**	**Agriculture Extension**
From:	***From:***	***From:***
• Traditional subjects and practices which are mainly focused on high productivity	• Research that is focused on increasing productivity through high use of chemical fertilizer & pesticides. • Research focused on development of chemical based methods for controlling plant diseases and pests.	• Information dissemination that is focused on conventional land use and cropping practices.
To:	***To:***	***To:***
• Incorporation of new subjects and syllabus with focus on sustainable and organic agriculture. • Introduction to environmental impact of agriculture practices.	Research that give adequate attention to alternative patterns of agriculture with emphasis on environmental benign and sustainable agriculture.	• Global and local market opportunities for organic agriculture produces and price premium they carry. • Organic agronomic practices, organic control of diseases and pests. • Encourage use of Bio-fertilizers and Bio-pesticides.

To build green agricultural input market in India it is not sufficient to incentivize production but there is a need to focus efforts in generating market demand.

7

Demand Management of Water Policies

To help select the most appropriate policy option or programme alternative, policy analysts divide the water sector into supply-side and demand-side components. The supply-side approach is structure-oriented; investments in water projects are combined with engineering and technical expertise to capture, store and deliver water and to make systems operate effectively. The supply side focuses on providing water and related services.

For most of the twentieth century, policy-makers have focused their attention on the supply side. Economists have evaluated public water supply and policy options through benefit-cost analysis (BCA). The main purpose of BCA is to assure that scarce resources (such as labour, capital, natural resources and management) are all employed to their best advantage. BCA attempts to quantify the advantages and disadvantages to society of alternative policies or actions in terms of a common monetary unit.

With new water-related problems arising in many parts of the world, policy-makers are increasingly emphasizing non-structural approaches to water management. A non-structural approach encompasses demand management, scientific research, education and persuasion to coordinate how humans use water. These demand-side policies attempt to address the human causes of water problems such as water quality degradation, overexploitation of aquifers and the decreasing availability of water flows to meet non-consumptive water uses (hydroelectric power, pollution assimilation and fish and wildlife habitats). In part, this user-focused approach entails coordinating and influencing people through organizations and institutions. This focus on water users aims to promote least-cost, environmentally sound water planning and takes both demand and supply options into account. Voluntary associations, government bureaucracies and private businesses are examples of organizations that operate on both the demand (user) side and the supply (delivery) side of water supply systems. On the supply side, large hierarchical organizations usually control the capture, storage, conveyance and distribution of surface water. Demand-side organizations, for example water user associations, are established to represent the interests of irrigators and to introduce and enforce water allocation rules.

This section examines how water institutions and water allocation systems incorporate a user-focused approach to address surface water, groundwater and water quality issues related to agriculture.

INSTITUTIONS AND WATER POLICY

Institutions are defined more broadly than simply government agencies and private organizations. Institutions are "...sets of ordered relationships among people which define their rights, exposure to rights of others, privileges and responsibilities". In this context, institutions set the "rules of the game" within which the economic system operates. For example, the property rights system is considered a water institution because it includes provisions which determine access to water and land. The property rights structure helps define the incentives, disincentives, rules, rights and duties (including informal customs and formal legal systems) that guide human activities and encourage conformist behaviour.30 Thus, property rights are part of an institutional arrangement governing economic activities including water use.

Many demand-side policies attempt to coordinate water use through institutions such as property rights and incentive structures such as prices. Altering the institutional system of permissions, restrictions, incentives and penalties can compel consumers to do what they might not otherwise do. For instance, financial inducements (monetary rewards and penalties) can encourage p^ople to use water in a more socially desirable way.

Two factors significantly influence the form of water institutions in a society: the relative scarcity of water and the transactions costs required to establish and enforce water rights. While scarcity is both supply-and demand-dependent, the human pressures on the demand side are probably the most important. Transactions costs include the resources required to obtain information, negotiate agreements on property rights and police these agreements. Water supply and demand characteristics make transactions costs for water relatively high and the value of water relatively low compared with other resources or commodities.

Many economists are trying to find ways to improve water-use efficiency through improved institutional performance. Research to date suggests that institutions and technological change are altered in response to the same types of incentives. When water is plentiful relative to demand, laws governing water use tend to be simple and enforced only casually. Where water is scarce, more elaborate institutional systems evolve. Higher population and income levels as well as technological advances are prompting many governments to establish formal water-use and water quality management systems.

Establishing an institutional structure for allocating water is a fundamental role of social policy for any nation. The choice of structure is ultimately a compromise between the physical nature of the resource, human reactions to policies and competing social objectives. Not surprisingly, different cultures make tradeoffs based on the relative importance of their particular objectives.

Countries try various means to balance economic efficiency (obtaining the highest value of output from a given resource base) and fairness (assuring equal treatment). Individual freedom, equity, popular participation, local control and orderly conflict resolution are other important objectives which societies must juggle when choosing a structure for water allocation.

Water Allocation Systems

In an "ideal" market-based water allocation system, entitlements (water rights) are well defined, enforced and transferable and they confront users with the full social cost of their actions. This type of market-dependent institutional arrangement requires security, flexibility and certainty.34 Security refers to protection against legal, physical and tenure uncertainties.

The assumption is that users will undertake profitable long-term investments to obtain and use water supplies only if water entitlements are reasonably secure.

A system is flexible if allocations between users, uses, regions and sectors can be changed at a low cost in relation to benefits. Flexibility implies that changes in demand are accommodated easily by reallocating water to higher-valued uses as they emerge. Certainty is also necessary: water-use rules must be easy to discover and to understand.

The three basic types of "water rights" systems are: (i) riparian-only those owning the land in physical contact with a natural watercourse have a right to use it; (ii) prior appropriation-based on beneficial and actual use; and (iii) public administration-a public authority authorizes water distribution and use. Prior appropriation and public administration are the most common systems in use throughout the world.

Property Rights Systems and Surface Water Allocation

Some water allocation systems are relatively decentralized and based on entitlements or rights to specific quantities of water. Examples of these types of system are found in the western United States and southern Australia. In contrast, France uses a more centralized public utility model of water allocation. Chile is the only country with a comprehensive water allocation system that establishes tradeable property rights.

Chile's water law: allows trade between and among economic sectors; protects third party rights; establishes compulsory water user associations and a national water authority to resolve conflicts; and allows for judiciary solutions to those conflicts not resolved by water user organizations or the water authority. Water transfers require authorization at two levels-those of the local water user associations and the national water authority.

While formal tradeable water rights systems have not been established in other developing countries, Rosegrant and

Binswanger document the expansion in surface water and groundwater markets. One recent study on surface water trade in Pakistan reported active markets in 70 percent of watercourses.

A "public utility" model for water allocation and pollution control

France's model for allocating water could be termed a "public utility" model. Administration is centred in six river basin committees (RBCs) and six river basin financial agencies (AFBs) which control water abstraction, treatment and delivery. The RBCs are the centre for negotiations and policy-making regarding water management at the basin level. The AFBs base action plans on extensive water data (quality and quantity needs) and are the centre of knowledge and technical expertise for the government and other interested water users. The RBCs collect fees, award grants and loans, develop long-term plans, collect and analyse water data, conduct studies and finance research.

The RBCs approve 20-or 25-year water development plans and, every five years, establish action plans to improve water quality. They also set two fees to be paid by water users: one for water consumption and the other for point source pollution. The fees provide incentives for users and also form a fund to encourage better water use through grants or soft loans. The RBCs include representatives from national, regional and local government administrations as well as individuals from industrial, agricultural and urban interests.

Those withdrawing water outside the authority (excluding small units) must measure and pay for it. Costs depend on the source (surface or ground) and how valuable it is in the specific basin. This approach also employs the "polluter pays" principle. While pollution assimilation is recognized as a legitimate water use, the entity causing pollution must pay for the costs of remediating the pollution and must compensate for any damages. Reports indicate that the system is self-financing and that it has performed well over 25 years.

The French approach provides feasible and apparently effective solutions to the major concerns about public water management: water scarcity, pollution and conjunctive use of ground and surface water.

It does, however, appear to rely more on centralized administrative discretion and less on the preferences and initiatives of private individuals. For example, water charges are set without regard for scarcity values based on bids and offers by users.

Source: World Bank. 1993. Water resources management: a policy paper.

The water allocation system in the western United States originated last century and evolved out of the customs of miners and farmers. This system is called the "prior appropriation" doctrine because water entitlements are granted according to the date on which a person applies the water to a beneficial use. The phrase "first in time, first in right" describes the basic principle, as the date of appropriation establishes the order in which users may draw from the water source.

In the western United States system, the individual's property interest in water is limited to the right to divert and use a specified quantity. Private individuals cannot "own" water but have "usufructuary" rights. The state retains ownership and determines which uses are beneficial. Beneficial uses were originally limited to private sector, off-stream purposes in agriculture, households and industry. More recently, in-stream uses for recreation and for fish and wildlife habitats are being recognized.

Water rights are generally tied to a specific parcel of land. However, in most states these water rights can be sold, without loss of priority, to another individual for use on another parcel. Rights are protected by the state from other appropriators and cannot be taken from an individual by the government without just compensation for the foregone economic value.

In the prior appropriation system, irrigation water rights are administered by private non-profit cooperative organizations or by public districts, under the supervision of the state government. Financing requirements and cost recovery are normally based on area served rather than on a strict volumetric pricing system. Early in the history of western irrigation, private capital was the main source of funds. In the twentieth century, private financing has mostly been replaced by federal subsidies. In contrast, municipal and industrial water supplies are typically financed by the users, with a full-cost pricing rule.

In recent years, southern Australian states have begun to allocate water through a system of transferable water entitlements. The Australian water law is based on a non-priority permit system under state control and ownership. Individuals obtain a right to use water through a licence issued by a state agency; this right is usually for a specified type of use on a designated tract of land. In contrast to the United States doctrine of prior appropriation, all users share equally in supply shortfalls and permits expire after a specified time period. Recent studies indicate the need to base permits on the water system's capacity in proportion to the quantities assigned in the original permit.

In southern Australia, the transfer of rights is generally limited to water users in the same watershed, with special conditions imposed to protect supply reliability and to prevent third-party damages. Reports evaluating water market performance highlight two points: first, the system is facilitating reallocation from low-value to higher-value uses; and, second, transferable entitlements should be considered as part of a broad package of decentralized decision-making for the entire water sector.

Prices and Surface Water Allocation

In practice, market forces rarely establish prices for water. Instead, prices are set by publicly owned supply agencies or regulated private utilities. Water prices ("rates" in public utility jargon) have an impact on both efficiency and equity as well as influencing agency revenues. The charging scheme for recovering costs and allocating water is a decision variable for the supplying or regulating agency.

Rate-setting can be evaluated within a multiple objective framework in which allocative efficiency, equity of income distribution and fairness in apportioning costs all play a role in evaluating pricing policies. The secondary criteria of simplicity, administrative feasibility and stability are also taken into account.

The most commonly employed pricing policy for water is a flat rate charge, designed primarily to recover costs. Flat rates are not set according to the volume received, although a proxy for volume usually provides the basis for the charge. In agriculture, the most frequent basis for a water charge or service fee is the area irrigated. For residential use in the industrialized world, flat rate charges have been based on the number of residents, the number of rooms, the number and type of water-using fixtures or measures of property value.

Flat rates are criticized because they do not include incentives for rationing water in line with willingness to pay. Such schemes are, however, simple to administer and assure the supplier adequate revenue. The high cost of installing and monitoring meters is suggested as being the main reason for continuing the flat rate approach. This argument is convincing in cases where water is plentiful, supply costs are low and managers doubt the rationing effects of volumetric pricing. In other cases, water managers are turning to volumetric pricing to address water scarcity problems and the high costs of developing new supplies.

Policy-makers who are primarily interested in allocative efficiency (maximizing net social product) as the goal for a pricing scheme advocate marginal cost pricing. The marginal cost represents the incremental cost of supplying a good or service. The marginal cost is a schedule of costs related to quantity and typically rises as further increments are supplied. When water prices are set at the marginal cost, rational consumers demand additional water only as long as willingness to pay (demand) exceeds the incremental costs. In theory, marginal cost pricing yields the most economically efficient allocation.

Price impacts on water use

In Australia, Canada, Israel, the United Kingdom and the United States, studies have demonstrated that water demand drops by 3 to 7 percent when prices charged to households rise by 10 percent. While it is difficult to measure elasticity of demand without metering consumption, some research in developing countries indicates how prices, combined with other policy efforts, affect water use.

China

In Beijing a water quota and high rates for exceeding it led to a 37 percent reduction in industrial water use in the 1980s. During the same period, the industrial sector was able to expand rapidly.

India

A fertilizer plant at Goa reduced water consumption by 50 percent in response to higher water prices. The Goa plant now uses 10.3 m3 to produce 1 tonne of nutrient, paying $0.12 per m3. In contrast, a similar plant at Kanpur pays $0.01 per m3 but uses 24.35 m3 per tonne of nutrient.

Indonesia

In Bogor a water tariff increase ranging from 200 to 300 percent (from $0.15 to $0.42 for the first 30 m3 per month) decreased monthly consumption by around 30 percent for domestic and commercial connections.

Source: R. Bhatia and M. Falkenmark. 1992. Water resource policies and the urban poor: innovative approaches and policy imperatives. Background paper for the ICWE, Dublin, Ireland.

A number of obstacles are encountered in the application of marginal cost pricing. One problem is the variety of definitions of the appropriate marginal cost concept, particularly whether to use a short-run (variable cost) concept or a long-run, full-cost approach. A long debate ensued from the "short-run marginal cost" pricing proposal which emerged from welfare economists' work in the 1930s. For example, Coase strongly objected to setting utility prices at short-run marginal costs, especially where marginal costs are below average costs (thereby incurring a deficit and requiring a public subsidy). Coase also criticized the absence of a market test to determine whether users are willing to pay the full cost of supplying the commodity; the redistribution of income to favour users of decreasing-cost industrial products; and the impetus towards centralization of the economy.

Most of these criticisms can be dealt with by a multipart pricing system: the first part sets marginal price equal to marginal cost while the second part levies an assessment to recover those costs that exceed marginal costs. Even so, multipart schedules often fail to reflect the economic concept of opportunity costs correctly, focusing instead on recovering historical or embedded costs. The relevant opportunity costs include both the cost of securing incremental supplies of water and the value of water in alternative uses. Opportunity costs should be determined after adjusting prices to allow for distortions brought about by government interventions in pursuit of other objectives. In economic jargon, "shadow prices" must be used.

The average cost pricing principle calls for recovering all costs by charging for each unit according to the average cost of providing all units. It is simple and easy to understand, as well as fair and equitable. Beneficiaries pay only the resource costs incurred on their behalf. The desired signals to users are provided, although not in as precise a way as with multipart pricing. Here, too, often only historical costs, not opportunity costs, serve as the basis for calculating average costs.

The ability-to-pay principle rests heavily on the equity criterion. Water charges are dependent on income or wealth rather than on costs. This principle is the most common basis for setting irrigation rates throughout the world and is also regularly applied to village water supplies in developing countries. Economists who view water as a commodity tend to be critical of the ability-to-pay approach. Since charges bear little relation to costs, no allocative test of willingness to pay is provided. This ability-to-pay concept is inherently subjective and political pressures frequently influence the formula in ways that distribute wealth from taxpayers to water users.

In many places throughout the world, water is scarce enough to justify the tangible and intangible costs of establishing formal pricing systems. Flat rates could satisfy cost repayment requirements in the absence of serious shortages. However, when the signals of water scarcity are absent, pressures arise for structural solutions (more construction to capture, store and deliver water) to satisfy incorrectly perceived water "needs".

The inevitability of scarce water supplies suggests the eventual adoption of multipart rate schemes that reflect the real or opportunity costs of water and other resources required for service provision. The literature describing the most desirable form for water markets and the literature dealing with water pricing have converged on the notion of a pricing system that reflects the opportunity cost of water via the mechanism of transferable water entitlements.

Coordinating Groundwater Extraction

Groundwater is an extremely important resource for many developing countries, including Bangladesh, India, Pakistan and the entire Near East region. In India, tube wells accounted for nearly one-half of the net irrigated area by the late 1980s.48 Because it deals with the complex interaction between society and the physical environment, aquifer management presents a formidable problem of policy design. Two types of collective policy decisions must be addressed in the management or regulation of overexploited aquifers. For one type, termed "managing the water", decisions are based on: (i) the appropriate annual rate of pumping; (ii) the geographic distribution of pumping; and iii) whether water supplies are augmented and/or the aquifer artificially recharged. The other type of policy decision, "coordinating the pumpers", determines: (i) the institutions and policies that divide the extraction rate among potential individual users and user classes and that influence pumper behaviour; and (ii) how rules for limiting pumping are monitored and enforced.

The three broad types of institutional arrangement for managing aquifers are prices and charges, quantity-based controls and exchangeable permits.

Prices and charges to control pumping. Charging pumpers is one potential method of achieving economically efficient extraction rates. An appropriately scaled charge or tax confronts pumpers with both the foregone user cost and the external cost (from increased pumping costs) imposed on neighbouring pumpers.

This type of water charge internalizes user costs and external costs and achieves an optimal extraction rate.

In aquifer management, this approach takes care of one important difficulty-pumpers impose costs on themselves (that is, the external costs are reciprocal). The reduction in water use resulting from a tax would be at the expense of redistributing rents to the taxing authority, thus lowering the net income of the aquifer exploiters.

Quantity-based controls. Quantity-based control mechanisms range from simple well permits to exchangeable pumping entitlements. Well and pump permits grant the right to install and operate a well of a particular capacity. Irrigation permits frequently specify the lands on which well water can be used, thereby restricting the transport of water to other sites. To protect existing pumpers, permits for new wells may restrict locations. For example, the state of Colorado in the United States identifies "designated groundwater basins" (for aquifers with limited natural recharge) in which new well permits must meet specific criteria-no more than 40 percent of stocks may be exhausted within a three-mile radius over a 25-year period. In most cases, well permits do not set limits on the quantity of water pumped. The economic limitations imposed by pumping costs and crop prices are assumed to be sufficient to inhibit excessive withdrawals.

Permits with appropriate size and spacing specifications can slow extraction rates. They are relatively easy to monitor and are reasonably palatable to pumpers who strongly reject more stringent regulatory devices. On the other hand, permits are most effective before problems have become severe and complex-in cases when preventing new wells and pumps solves the problem or when pumped water is not exported away from the area overlying the aquifer. In more serious cases, where all existing users must reduce annual extractions, regulating rates of withdrawals must be considered.

A pumping "quota" is a more precise quantity control mechanism. The quota specifies a fixed annual rate of extraction for each water user. The initial quantity might be assigned in proportion to use in a base period (although such an approach might set off a pumping race to establish initial rights) or be based on the proportion of land that is owned overlying the aquifer. The technology for metering withdrawals is neither complex nor expensive so, if the pumpers are willing to be metered, regulatory monitoring and enforcement need not be difficult. In principle, pumping quotas are no different from conventional surface water rights, which entitle owners to fixed shares of each year's available flow.

Anecdotal evidence suggests that farmers who have previously enjoyed an unregulated aquifer believe they are entitled to unlimited withdrawals for use on lands overlying the aquifer. They are frequently reluctant to submit to metering and the meters, once installed, are reportedly subject to high rates of unexplained "breakdowns".

Very small wells for livestock or individual households could be exempted from the permit and quota system. At moderate levels of overdraft, the cost of monitoring every small pump set might outweigh gains from reduced pumping. Also, for income distribution reasons, policy-makers may not want to restrain smallholders.

Transferable pumping entitlements. When a fixed quota is too inflexible in the face of changing water stocks and demand conditions, transferable pumping entitlements are an alternative. The pumping entitlement can be divided into two parts: one component may provide a claim to the stock of water and the other to the annual recharge. Both claims may vary from year to year, with allotments set by the groundwater authority. Annual rights to the basic stock would vary according to current and anticipated economic and hydrological conditions (including energy and commodity prices, interest rates and the remaining stock of groundwater). Rights to the natural recharge and return flows from human uses could be set to reflect a moving average of estimated recharge in recent years.

The transferability of entitlements promotes economic efficiency over the long term, permitting a reallocation to higher-valued uses as economic conditions change. Transferable rights are also consistent with local control criteria and require minimal interference with individual freedom to operate a farm or business enterprise. One recent study suggests that tradeable rights and water markets for groundwater appear to be increasing in India, where as much as one-half of the gross area irrigated by tube wells involves purchased water.

In groundwater management, the quantity-based approaches appear to be preferable to pumping charges. They can yield economically efficient solutions with simpler monitoring and enforcement burdens, while avoiding the redistributive implications of taxes or subsidies. While some new outside controls on pumping are required, they need not be any more repressive than property rights for other resources or commodities.

Conjunctive Groundwater and Surface Water Management

Joint management of interrelated stream-aquifer systems is called conjunctive ground-surface water management. Aquifers interrelated with flowing streams frequently present both distinct management opportunities and problems. Unrestricted access to groundwater may reduce the water available to those holding rights to streamflows. In the state of Colorado in the United States, a problem arose two decades ago for irrigators in the South Platte basin. Groundwater exploitation reduced streamflow, but by only a small fraction of the amount pumped. The most obvious option-placing the pumpers into the existing surface water rights system while protecting those holding existing rights to surface water-would have sacrificed most of the substantial economic benefits of exploiting the aquifer.

After several methods had been experimented, a solution was found based on markets for existing rights to surface water. In the event of a shortage, groundwater users could replace the portion of streamflows taken by pumping the aquifer. They could also replace water by purchasing and delivering rights to reservoir water. Young, Daubert and Morel-Seytoux demonstrated that this decentralized approach is economically superior to the alternative of forcing pumpers into the surface water rights system. The ready availability of substitute water supplies and the existence of flexible water transfer institutions are necessary to implement a solution of this type. Numerous opportunities for this market-based approach do exist, however, in the large alluvial basins of the Indus and Ganges-Brahmaputra.

Preserving Water Quality

Human production and consumption activities generate pollution by extracting and processing raw materials into consumer goods. Some wastes (residuals) from the production process are returned to the environment (e.g. waste chemicals from petroleum refineries discharged to rivers). Similarly, households return unwanted by-products of consumption activities to the environment-to sewers, to the air or to sites receiving solid waste. The materials balance principle, derived from basic laws of physics regarding the conservation of matter, asserts that, over the long term, the mass of residuals discharged to the environment must equal the mass of materials originally extracted from the environment to make consumption goods. The environment's importance as an assimilator of residuals is equal to its importance as a source of materials.

The water sellers

One does not have to be a landowner or even a farmer to benefit from irrigation. Irrigation increases employment and provides the landless with opportunities to work on farms or in upstream or downstream activities. In Bangladesh irrigation has also opened profitable new avenues for the landless by enabling them to exploit and sell water. The "water sellers" are organized with the help of PROSHIKA, one of a number of NGOs that aim to develop an irrigation service for farmers by tapping the abundant groundwater which underlies much of Bangladesh.

Fresh groundwater is a widespread resource but is usually present in small amounts, only sufficient to service household needs. However, in the great alluvial basins such as the Nile, the Indus and the Ganges-Brahmaputra, the alluvium may be 100 m or more deep and 10 or even 20 percent of its volume may be freshwater. The vast reserve of groundwater is recharged annually by floods, canal and field seepage and rainfall infiltration.

Groundwater is particularly valuable because it is available consistently and, unlike surface reservoirs, evaporation losses are minimal. Where surface canal supplies are also available, and provide a more or less constant base supply, groundwater can be used conjunctively to satisfy the peak demands of crops. In addition, groundwater is usually available close to farms and is more under the control of farmers.

In rural Bangladesh more than 50 percent of the population is landless or has less than 1.2 ha of land. Providing the poor access to productive resources such as water is clearly important. The PROSHIKA experience was based on organizing landless groups, using credit effectively to purchase mobile pumping equipment and providing a reliable service to farmers and share-tenants.

The water sellers targeted their service in areas where farmers had very small scattered plots of land and irrigated their fields from shallow low-cost boreholes, using portable diesel pump sets. The farmers pay the sellers in crop share, cash or, occasionally, a fixed amount in kind.

The success of the PROSHIKA mission depended primarily on access to credit (which PROSHIKA helped to organize) as well as skills training and technical support relating to agriculture, management, literacy, health and group solidarity.

The water sellers: improved water-use efficiency and equity by improving the direct access of small farmers who are usually tail-enders in other systems of irrigation; benefited from the more equitable distribution of productive assets between those with and those without landholdings; created additional employment within and outside the group as a consequence of more productive agriculture; obtained cash to buy more food and promote commercial agriculture; participated in the developing water market, which has prevented richer peasants or landlords becoming monopoly "waterlords"; and showed that the poor can be creditworthy without land as collateral.

The PROSHIKA experience is being replicated throughout Bangladesh and has many lessons that may serve for other developing countries.

Source: G.E. Wood, R. Palmer-Jones, Q.F. Ahmed, M.A.S. Mandal and S.C. Dutta. 1990. The water sellers: a cooperative venture by the rural poor. West Hartford, Connecticut, Kumarian Press.

One important policy implication of the materials balance principle is that residuals must end up somewhere, either as mass or energy. The management of discharges into watercourses must be integrated with waste disposal into the atmosphere and landfills. Reducing the amount of waste discharged into water may not solve society's overall problem if the waste is sent elsewhere, such as into the atmosphere by burning or to a land site by dumping.

There are two types of water pollution: point source and non-point source. Point source pollution refers to cases where a readily identifiable source, such as a pipe or ditch, transports the pollutant to a water body. Regulation and monitoring focus on the point of discharge. In non-point source pollution, no single source of pollutant discharge is easily identifiable but the collective effect of numerous sources results in a significant impact. Non-point pollution problems pose a difficult and costly management challenge.

NON-POINT POLLUTION CONTROL OPTIONS

Policy options to control non-point water pollution present special difficulties because of the great variety of sources and pollutants. The primary source of non-point pollutants is the agricultural sector. Fertilizers and pesticides are carried off the soil surface into lakes and streams or percolate into groundwater deposits. Aquifers become polluted by nitrates from fertilizer application and livestock wastes. Timber harvesting, land clearing for urban development and mining also originate non-point pollution of waters. Urban storm drainage, leakage from buried fuel tanks and subsurface and surface mining are other contributors.

Runoff from farms and forests may carry suspended solids and sediments, dissolved solids and chemicals (mineral fertilizers, particularly nitrogen and phosphorous, and pesticides). Other substances that often occur in diffuse source runoff are oxygen-demanding organic matter, petroleum products, heavy metals and faecal bacteria. Non-point source pollution is also characterized by its episodic nature. Occasional heavy rainfall or snowmelt is typically the trigger, in contrast to the more even flows of discharge from point sources. These characteristics of source type and timing imply that a variety of control technologies may be required for effective abatement.

Non-point pollution control may also be determined by the nature of human activities causing the problem. For example, the pollution resulting from a farmer's land depends not only on the rainfall patterns and the land characteristics (slope and soil texture), but on numerous prior land-use and production decisions, including choice of crops, tillage practices and pesticide and fertilizer use. The farmers' production choices are, in turn, influenced by market prices for inputs and products as well as by government price and income support programmes. In fact, pollution from the farm sector is exacerbated by government policies that make certain crops overly attractive. Successful policy interventions must change those aspects of farmers' decisions that are the source of pollutants.

Policy options for non-point pollution control are classed as cognitive, regulatory and incentive-based. Cognitive (voluntary) approaches use education, moral persuasion and technical assistance to influence the behaviour of polluters. Cognitive approaches are attractive because of their low economic and political costs. They have been tried in some countries but have had limited success. Several factors account for this; for example, private costs incurred to change land-use practices can be substantial while private gains may not be obvious. Because of the uncertain linkage between changing production decisions and improving water quality (often at distant locations), individuals have little incentive to try new approaches.

Regulatory policies call for specific actions or prohibitions against those responsible for water quality degradation. One approach is to use "design standards" that specify actions to be taken (such as a management plan for sediment control) or actions prohibited (such as certain cropping practices on highly erodible lands). "Performance standards", in contrast, place limits on the rate of pollution discharge to a water body. In this case, interference with land-use practices is only in response to observed violations. Neither technique is without limitations. Design standard regulations are easier to enforce; however, they may be unnecessarily costly because their general application may impose costs on those who contribute little to the problem. Performance standards, in principle at least, focus more directly on the pollutant source but are difficult to monitor and enforce. Because an accurate measurement of discharges (particularly from small farms) is nearly impossible, disputes over actual sources of pollutants are unending.

The alternatives to regulatory policies include various incentive methods such as taxes, subsidies and emission trading policies.54 Taxes or fees can be levied on either inputs or pollution outputs. For example, extra charges have been imposed on agricultural fertilizers in Sweden, with proceeds used to fund water quality monitoring. Higher costs are expected to reduce fertilizer application rates and, therefore, water pollution. However, taxes are unlikely to be set high enough to affect land use significantly because of the adverse effects on income.

Alternatively, charges may be levied for pollution by imposing an "effluent charge". However, the technical and administrative complexity of setting fees and linking numerous farmers precisely to the damages caused by their effluent is mind-boggling. No successful example of this type of taxation of non-point source pollution is presented in the literature.

Subsidies could encourage farmers to reduce pollution, adopt more appropriate land-use practices or make environment-friendly investments. Subsidies to prevent soil erosion (and the associated productivity losses) have a long history in many countries and are the most politically attractive of the available options. In contrast to other approaches, which impose costs on the emitting source and spread benefits over the entire society, subsidy costs are spread over the general population and gains are offered to the land user. Nonetheless, paying polluters to avoid polluting activities remains objectionable to some groups. Moreover, payments may be made to individuals who would adopt proper practices anyway.

Finally, the outright purchase of water rights and/or land-use rights is another approach. For instance, a public agency could acquire rights to part or all of the polluting lands and manage them to safeguard water quality. The purchase of tropical forest lands by either public or private agencies has been undertaken to preserve first-growth forests, with water quality improvements as a side-benefit. Again, costs are borne primarily by beneficiaries rather than by the land users whose practices are actually responsible for the pollution.

POLICY ISSUES IN IRRIGATED AGRICULTURE

Irrigation is an essential component of sustainable agricultural development but it is not a unique sector, since it faces challenges similar to those confronting other public and private sector economic activities. The previous two sections (II and III) of this chapter examine how various demand-side policy measures can help shape decisions that encourage water-use efficiency. However, while appropriate policies and regulations are necessary for improved water productivity, a variety of additional water-saving measures are required in the irrigation sector.

Some water-saving measures involve taking more advantage of the scientific, engineering and technological advances in soils, plants and irrigation. Other measures focus on administrative and managerial reforms to improve efficiency, including the decentralization of public irrigation agencies and a greater reliance on farmer-owned and farmer-operated irrigation.

This final section highlights three key irrigation issues: declining growth and investment trends in irrigation; the difficulties imposed by irrigation-induced environmental degradation; and efforts to reform managerial and administrative systems. Many of today's irrigation-related problems appear imposing and even overwhelming. The purpose of this section is not to present a discouraging overview of irrigation's future but to focus on important issues that will shape its future. When scarce water is under human control in irrigation systems, there are many opportunities to use it optimally. Understanding the problems associated with improper irrigation as well as the potential for efficient irrigation is a first step in the search for these opportunities.

Irrigation in the 1990s and Beyond

Many pressing irrigation issues reflect the various economic, social and political influences affecting society in this period of changing economic conditions and environmental concerns. At times, irrigation-related problems are the result of a distorted macroeconomy which, despite providing operating subsidies, renders farming unprofitable and results in repeated underinvestments on farms over long periods. If the macroeconomy is performing poorly and if prices in the economy are markedly distorted from their real value to society, then it is inevitable that irrigation will suffer.

In other cases, irrigation itself is the problem. The overall performance of many irrigation projects is disappointing. Evaluations document a wide range of problems, including: cost and time overruns; poor management; the non-realization of full, planned benefits; adverse environmental and health impacts; and the exacerbation of inequities in the existing social and economic distribution of assets among farmers.

Trends in Irrigated Area

In 1800, approximately 8 million ha of farmland were irrigated around the world. By the end of the nineteenth century, the irrigated area had expanded to 48 million ha, mostly as a result of large water projects in India and what is now Pakistan. By 1990, net irrigated area reached 237 million ha, of which nearly three-fourths were in the developing countries. China, India and Pakistan alone now account for about 45 percent of the world's irrigated area and 60 percent of the developing country total.

On a global basis, irrigated area expanded by an average of 1 percent per year during the early 1960s, reaching a maximum annual rate of 2.3 percent from 1972 to 1975. The rate of expansion began decreasing after 1975 and is now less than 1 percent per year. At current levels of population growth, the slower expansion in irrigated areas is resulting in an unprecedented decline in the per caput amount of irrigated land. Among the reasons for the decrease are increased construction costs, falling real prices for wheat and rice, a growing awareness of environmental and social costs and poor irrigation performance at the farm and project levels.

Crop Prices and Construction Costs

Construction and operation costs for irrigation projects have risen steadily over the past four decades as the world's best land and most of the readily available water supplies have been developed. Over the same time period, world cereal prices fell sharply.

For example, the real price of rice fell by 40 percent between the mid-1960s and the late 1980s.

In Indonesia and India, the real costs of irrigation have doubled since the early 1970s. In the Philippines and Thailand, irrigation construction costs have increased by 50 percent and in Sri Lanka, costs have tripled. After reviewing various recent reports and evaluations, including many from the World Bank and FAO, Postel reports that: "Today, capital costs for new irrigation capacity run between $1 500 and $4 000 per ha for large projects in China, India, Indonesia, Pakistan, the Philippines and Thailand. They climb toward $6 000 per ha in Mexico.

In Africa, where roads and other infrastructure are often lacking and parcels that can be irrigated are relatively small, per hectare costs have climbed to $10 000-$20 000, and sometimes even higher. Not even double-cropping of higher-valued crops can make irrigation systems at the top end of this spectrum economical." It is not just large-scale projects that have become so expensive; FAO estimates that even medium-sized irrigation construction costs range from $2 400 per ha in Asia to $7 200 in Africa.

Likewise, the modernization of existing irrigation projects is becoming increasingly expensive. Many old projects designed for monocropping have produced gradually declining yields. These systems need to be redesigned to permit crop diversity, increase yields, conserve water and reduce environmental hazards. Modernization involves canal lining, improved hydraulic control structures, better land development and appropriate irrigation techniques.

FAO and sustainable water use

The International Action Programme on Water and Sustainable Agricultural Development (IAP-WASAD) was created by FAO with the cooperation of other UN organizations as part of a strategy to implement the Mar del Plata Action Plan for the 1990s.

IAP-WASAD identified five priority areas of action and some common measures requiring concerted action to realize Sustainable agricultural development. It pointed out that scarcity of water is a major constraint for the further agricultural development of arid and semi-arid countries. Without renewable water supplies and appropriate and reliable water control and management, sustainable agricultural development is simply not possible.

The five priority areas of action identified by IAP-WASAD include: efficient water use at the farm level; waterlogging, salinity and drainage; water quality management; small-scale water programmes; and scarce water resources management.

Efficient water use at the farm level

The current and potential roles of rain-fed and irrigated agriculture need to be quantified, taking into account the probabilities of rainfall, the available irrigation water supplies and their cost. Small-scale irrigation, including supplementary water for rain-fed agriculture, and a variety of water harvesting and water spreading techniques have considerable potential and should be developed further.

The proposed priority action plan points out that increases in developing country production in the 1990s must come first from increases on existing irrigated lands and second from increases on rain-fed lands. In order to improve performance and control groundwater levels in irrigated agriculture, it is necessary to establish monitoring, evaluation and feedback systems. Appropriate irrigation management training must be available and irrigation extension services must be strengthened and developed further. Information must be shared among farmers, extension workers, design engineers and researchers for a better understanding of various approaches and techniques. Measures should also be taken to review, develop and implement water pricing policies, establish effective demand and supply management procedures as well as cost recovery mechanisms for the operation and maintenance of irrigation projects.

In order to increase production on rain-fed lands, it will be necessary to employ existing soil and water management knowledge to help increase the efficient use of agricultural water. Additional research in the areas of rain-fed water and soil management is also necessary and examples of successful and effective rain-fed practices must be collected and disseminated.

Waterlogging, salinity and drainage

Waterlogging and salinity are among the principal causes of decreasing production on many irrigated projects. Waterlogging is due to an excessive input of water into systems that have finite natural drainage capacities. After waterlogging has occurred, soil salinity increases because the irrigation water leaves dissolved solids in the soil. It is essential to monitor the water table levels from the beginning of a project in order to implement corrective measures before soil damage has occurred.

The action plan notes that, in rain-fed agriculture, surface drainage is required to prevent any temporary waterlogging and flooding of lowlands. In irrigated agriculture, artificial drainage is essential under most conditions. It is vital to minimize drainage requirements and costs by reducing the sources of excess water through improved system design and on-farm water practices. The implementation of groundwater monitoring and water balance studies will help predict drainage requirements. Soil salinity monitoring in problem areas should also be started in order to adopt practices to overcome the problems. In addition, pilot drainage projects should be established in waterlogged and salinized areas to verify the design and effectiveness of materials.

Water quality management

In sustainable agricultural development, there are two significant aspects of water quality: the quality of water used in irrigated agriculture should not cause crop damage; and agricultural activities should not adversely affect the quality of surface or groundwater in such a way that their subsequent use is limited. The action plan suggests that groundwater quality monitoring programmes to assess agricultural water quality and its impact be developed and that strategies be implemented to minimize the extent of water pollution inflicted by agricultural activities. In addition, national strategies and plans should be prepared, outlining the rational use of treated waste water and drainage water for agriculture.

Small-scale water programmes

Small-scale projects are normally undertaken by communities or individuals who develop and operate most activities of the projects themselves, although some technical assistance is often necessary. Small-scale programmes include a diversity of technologies such as water harvesting, well development, river offtakes and use of wetlands.

The action plan submits that small-scale water programmes can assist sustainable agricultural development. However, further expansion must be founded on adequate technical advice and support, improved institutional collaboration and greater involvement of the local communities. National policies and programmes should be developed for implementing small-scale water projects for rural development. Accordingly, it will be necessary to enhance the capability of farmers to implement, operate and maintain small-scale water programmes.

The monitoring and evaluation of the small-scale water project will help identify the failures as well as the successes.

Scarce water resources management

Many countries face constraints to their development, as available water resources are insufficient to meet demand. The action plan notes that water scarcity conditions require long-term strategies and practical implementation programmes in order to ensure that agricultural water is used in ways consistent with limited water resources.

A strategy must be formulated for the management of land and water for sustainable agricultural development under water-scarce conditions.

At the same time, these policies must remain compatible with the prevailing socio-economic conditions as well as the environment. In addition, measures should be implemented to deal with drought situations and to improve community resilience during such times.

Supporting action

The five areas outlined above require common supporting actions, i.e. the development of adequate databases, adaptive research, institutional strengthening, human resource development, improvements in socio-economic analysis, environmental protection, technology transfer and infrastructure development.

Increasing real investment costs (including recognition of environmental costs) and falling crop prices have resulted in a substantial reduction in new irrigation projects. Aggregate lending for irrigation by both international donors and the major cereal-producing countries in the 1980s was only half what it was in the 1970s. This reduced investment has, in turn, resulted in falling growth rates in irrigated area.

Irrigation and Land Degradation

Escalating demand pressure on water resources during the past decade is only one of the concerns for policy-makers. Both watersheds supporting water resources and the land base supporting irrigated agriculture are becoming degraded. Industrial and domestic pollution are affecting irrigated agriculture, while sedimentation washed from denuded hillsides is filling up irrigation reservoirs and small tanks. At the same time, improper irrigation practices are causing waterlogging, salinization, soil erosion and water pollution which directly affects other irrigators.

FAO estimates that of the 237 million ha currently irrigated, about 30 million ha are severely affected by salinity and an additional 60 million to 80 million ha are affected to some extent. UNEP recently reported that the rate of loss of irrigated land from waterlogging and salinity is 1.5 million ha per year.62 Millions of hectares of irrigated land, from Morocco to Bangladesh and from northwestern China to central Asia, suffer from this progressive condition. Salinity-affected areas as a percentage of total irrigated area is estimated to be 10 percent in Mexico, 11 percent in India, 21 percent in Pakistan, 23 percent in China and 28 percent in the United States.

Salinity is caused by a combination of poor drainage and high evaporation rates which concentrate salts on irrigated land; it mainly occurs in arid and semi-arid regions. Even good-quality irrigation water contains some dissolved salt and can leave behind tonnes of salt per hectare each year. Unless this salt is washed down below the root level, soil salinity will result. A number of factors influence salinity, including the water table depth, the capillary characteristics of the soil and management practices regarding the amount of water applied in excess of plant evapotranspiration to leach the salts.

A related concern is the rapid rise in groundwater levels, leading to waterlogging and depressed crop yields. Waterlogging is not an inevitable result of irrigation. It occurs when excessive water is used in systems with finite natural drainage capacities. Seepage occurs if: soils are very light; canals and watercourses are not lined or maintained; farmers near the head of a system withdraw or apply excessive amounts of water; fields are not levelled; and/or the delivery system cannot respond to rainfall by closing inflows.

Irrigation can raise groundwater levels to within a metre or so of the surface, which results in secondary salinization when the groundwater brings to the surface dissolved salts from the aquifer, subsoil and root zone. If seepage and horizontal recharge exceed evaporation and natural drainage, then groundwater levels rise, eventually causing waterlogging. In arid areas where the upward movement of water and evaporation exceeds downward percolation and where the groundwater, soil or irrigation water contains some salt, the buildup of salt in the soil surface layers will eventually reach toxic levels.

Countries suffering from waterlogging and salinity face a dilemma. They cannot force abandonment of affected lands because of the growing populations that depend on them, but neither can they afford to drain the lands. The cure for rising water tables is drainage and improved water management to reduce percolation, but drainage is expensive and improved water management requires both on-farm investment and the training of extension personnel and farmers.

At the end of the 1950s, Pakistan began to sink wells to pump out salt-laden water. The initial capital costs were high and operating costs have been increasing constantly. Between 1971 and 1985 the cost of managing the wells and drains rose fivefold. Today, Pakistan spends more on reclaiming land than on irrigation. The cost of maintaining drains is five times the recurrent costs of supplying water and most farmers pay only half the costs of delivering irrigation. Some policy-makers argue that, as the value of water rises, management will improve and much of the wastage (which creates unhealthy conditions as well as increased drainage requirements) will be reduced. Farmers may then be willing to pay for a drainage service that makes their investments sustainable.

Irrigation: Good Government and Good Management

Political pressures often prevent the implementation of apparently sensible and fair reforms for water services. Where water is regarded as a special commodity or has emotional or religious importance, governments are reluctant to charge farmers for irrigation. Policy-makers often find it extremely difficult to raise sufficient revenue to match even their priority needs. The practical effects on traditional public service activities may be harsh. Water has been one of the first sectors to feel the effects of budget-saving efforts and changing resource availability. However, it is unlikely to be treated more austerely than other areas. Box 19 discusses the relationship between good government and irrigation performance.

A prime opportunity for irrigation advancement-and indeed for development in general-lies in the enormous potential of the 237 million ha already operating. While the total value of irrigation investment in the developing world today is about $1 000 billion, the returns are well below the known potential. Many irrigation schemes need substantial investment to be completed, modernized or expanded. Although it is increasingly expensive, rehabilitation can yield high returns.

Good government and irrigation performance

Improvement in irrigation performance depends on good government, or governance. This may be an obvious assertion, but what exactly does the term mean for irrigation? There are four main elements of governance which can be considered at the national or the local level: the legitimacy of government; its accountability, its competence; and its respect for human rights and the rule of law.1

Legitimacy refers to the way in which a population gives consent to be governed, how they are consulted and whether the consent can be withdrawn. Accountability of politicians and officials is tested by how they explain their role and decisions, provide information and can be held responsible for their behaviour. A government demonstrates competence in formulating policies and translating them into action in a timely and effective way. Governments who respect human rights establish a framework of known laws, applicable to all, without bias or corruption, with limits on and protection against the exercise of arbitrary power. We can illustrate how these four elements of governance might affect irrigation with simple examples.

Legitimacy. When a new project is planned, are those living in the area consulted about the design of the scheme? Are there recognized representative groups of farmers, including women? Are the office holders elected and accountable to the members? Do these groups participate in decisions that affect them? For example, if a groundwater irrigation project threatens the availability of drinking-water from hand pumps, are self-help groups informed and invited to make representations?

Accountability. Are the financial plans of the irrigation scheme made public and arrangements made to explain them to farmers? Are there performance criteria with audit arrangements to ensure that officials adhere to the rules and, if they fail to perform satisfactorily, call them to account? Are officials responsive?

Competence. Can the professional staff prepare accurate budgets and effectively deliver services such as timely canal maintenance? Are there arrangements for training them or replacing them with competent officers if they fall short of their duties?

Rule of law. Is there a clear legal framework to regulate groundwater abstraction to prevent overpumping of the aquifers? Is it enforced? Can pollution by industry or by saline water from upstream drainage projects be regulated? Are illegal extractions by farmers at the head of canals monitored and offenders charged by legal processes that are fair, timely, objective and without discrimination on grounds of race, gender or minority status?

Beyond capital investment, investment in human resources is needed to improve economy, efficiency and effectiveness in management.

Investment in irrigation management can be an integral component of a productive rural employment policy and resource management can be improved to match developments in engineering and science. Those concerned with irrigation development and the welfare of farmers and their families are beginning to take a broader view of their responsibilities, paying as much attention to management and development as to engineering.

A review of recent literature on public sector policy and management suggests the need for transforming the typical irrigation authority from a technical, engineering and construction culture to an organization that is focused more on people (farmers) and that is more autonomous and more responsive to customers, i.e. a strategic management service agency.

In the developing world, many water subsector groups recognize their role in the management of valuable water and other complementary resources for economic growth and poverty alleviation.

Irrigation management does not generally have a good record, but the full extent of the problems has been obscured by a lack of performance assessment criteria and a variety of hidden subsidies. It has often been assumed that, if farmers are not complaining, then management must be good. A lack of complaints in a highly subsidized system is not a good indicator of efficiency. Similarly, managers with obvious problems have sometimes had to cope as best they could with a range of exogenous factors that limit their effectiveness, for instance overvalued exchange rates.

One example of a remarkably successful administrative reform is found in the Philippines, where irrigation operating expenses have been reduced, revenue has matched operating costs and operational performance has improved in the process.

Water user Associations and NGOs

An increasing number of private sector groups, including water user associations and other NGOs, are taking over some public sector irrigation responsibilities. The inclusion of water users in irrigation planning, management and ownership is proving to be an effective method for increasing irrigation system efficiency in many cases. Studies throughout the world demonstrate that user participation in irrigation services improves access to information, reduces monitoring costs, establishes a sense of ownership among farmers and increases transparency as well as accountability in decision-making.

Water user associations are expected to increase in number and importance over the next decade as the stress on self-reliance increases. Already, governments are turning many aspects of public irrigation systems over to water user associations. Well-documented examples can be seen in Argentina, Colombia, Indonesia, Mexico, Nepal, the Philippines, Sri Lanka and Tunisia. In Indonesia, for example, the government had transferred more than 400 irrigation systems, covering 34000 ha, to water user associations by 1992. In the future, as farmer financing becomes more commonplace, user groups will become even more powerful.

Other NGOs undertake a wide range of water-related functions, from developing projects for rural water supplies and minor irrigation to fostering water user associations for water management purposes. Some NGOs encourage farmers to try new technologies, for example the catchment protection and sprinkler irrigation techniques introduced by the Aga Khan Rural Support Programme in Gujarat, India.

Many NGOs stem from local initiatives and operate as independently funded and self-managed groups. These organizations bring fresh views, new ideas and participatory working methods to other areas of development policy and practice. Much of their success is attributed to their local knowledge as well as their interest in and experience of regional conditions. They have been particularly active in promoting the interests of poor and disadvantaged groups through articulate and forceful advocacy and service provision. In addition, the local base of NGOs may allow them to reach vulnerable or remote groups which are exceptionally difficult to reach with conventional public schemes.

Water is not an easy sector in which to promote cooperation, but the potential gains are high, which makes renewed efforts worthwhile. Resolution of many water allocation and development problems requires a common willingness to forego personal benefit for the social good. Government efforts to promote personal sacrifice through economic policies, laws and regulations that require self-restraint, such as water rationing or optimum groundwater pumping regimes, have seldom proved effective. On the other hand, with their close local contacts and skills in group mobilization and cohesion, NGOs can provide the institutional leadership required to bring about socially optimum solutions.

Self-financed operations: The philippines' bureaucratic reform

The National Irrigation Administration (NIA) of the Philippines is a good example of how a bureaucracy can, over time, transform its strategy and operating style. Since the mid-1970s, the NIA has evolved from an agency that focused primarily on the design and construction of irrigation systems and told farmers about its key decisions into an agency that gives priority to the management and maintenance of irrigation systems, and that gives farmers, through their membership in irrigators' associations, the opportunity to participate in irrigation system management and to make key decisions about maintenance. How did this transformation come about and what have been its effects?

Commitment from the top. In the early 1970s, the NIA's top management diagnosed correctly that farmer organizations were crucial to effective irrigation management and, therefore, committed the NIA to developing and extending the responsibilities of irrigators' associations. The NIA's willingness to renounce its traditional authority was a key factor in this process.

Legal and financial status of the NIA. In 1974, the NIA was established as a public corporation and ceased to be part of a government ministry. It was given a five-year lead-in period in which to become financially self-sufficient in terms of its operating budget. The NIA's semi-independent status set the scene for farmer-financed irrigation and the devolvement of management tasks to farmers.

A gradual approach. The NIA did not transform itself overnight. The participative approach was first tried in the mid-1970s with smaller-scale "communal" irrigation systems that were traditionally managed by farmers. The end of the 1970s saw the development of a methodology to maximize farmer participation based on two pilot projects. Lessons learned were then incorporated into plans to manage the large-scale "national" irrigation systems jointly. Almost 20 years on, the transformation of the NIA from a top-down bureaucracy continues.

Understanding farmers. How has the NIA motivated farmers to participate in and pay for irrigation, to commit time to maintenance, to liaise with the NIA and to plan for the future? The NIA experience illustrates some important preconditions for farmer participation: teaming community organizers and engineers in order to integrate social and technical activities into one process; involving farmers in all project activities from the very beginning, thereby building up their organizational skills; modifying NIA policies and procedures that obstruct farmer participation; allowing enough time for farmers to mobilize and organize themselves before new construction activity.

The quality of the irrigation service provided by and for farmers has undoubtedly improved, system operating expenses have been reduced and the recurrent cost burden of the scheme on the national budget has been eliminated. But what about the impact on irrigation performance? Recent research suggests that the reforms have made water supply more equitable.

On five schemes surveyed five years following the cessation of subsidies, the main impact was the increased equitability of supply. For reasons unconnected with the management reforms, water supplies fell by 13 percent but crop area held constant and yields remained the same. This confirmed the connection between equity of supply and financial viability. To appreciate the value of the reform we need to consider what would have happened to the deteriorating service if the impoverished state bureaucracy had continued to run the schemes.

FUTURE DIRECTIONS IN WATER MANAGEMENT POLICY

Sustainable agricultural development depends on sustainable water use. Governments today recognize that the search for sustainable economic growth requires, in part, both economy-wide and sector-specific policy reforms. Economy-wide policies attempt to create a favourable macroeconomic environment while water sector policies, for example, seek to encourage resource efficiency among water users.

The current emphasis on macro-economic policy reforms and economic liberalization has several important implications for irrigation. One of the most important is that the era of large direct and indirect subsidies is nearly over. Moreover, recognition of the value of water (and the high cost of turning a water source into a service delivered to a farm) makes the water sector a prime target for further policy reforms. Nonetheless, irrigation remains a resource-hungry sector in this transitional period. Even successful irrigation consumes large quantities of capital and foreign exchange and ties up scarce skilled personnel.

Like many public sector personnel, irrigation managers must walk a fine line between a tighter control of finance, the need for more positive active leadership and better planning of resource allocations, on the one side, and the contradictory need for more ideas from below (farmer customers), on the other. Financial pressures are likely to be the dominant influence. Irrigation as a public sector agency still relies on budget allocations to obtain financing. Many argue that this gives little incentive to save money and may, in fact, have the reverse effect.

As private sector disciplines are applied in irrigation, policy-makers are finding that: agencies become more supportive of farmers' own efforts and less inclined to make all key decisions before informing farmers accordingly; management seeks more consensus on priorities, more information about the basis of decisions and a common view of external factors affecting management; irrigation schemes seek and receive more autonomy; the financial responsibilities and accountability of managers increases; and managers shift focus from their ministries and governments, depending on the amount of finance generated by service fees. At present, water engineering feeds off mathematics, physics, chemistry and biology; management feeds off economics, psychology, political science, history and philosophy and also has a high requirement for personal skills in communication, negotiation and teamwork. However, as changes occur in irrigation in many countries, managers find they must acquire new knowledge and a new set of skills.

Following are some of the issues emerging:

- National water politics are shifting from projects to policies-this trend is likely to continue and even accelerate.
- Water may become a test-bed for economic reform, liberalization and accountability.
- Given water's scarcity and its value to cities and industry, the water subsector will be less dominated by irrigation and its multipurpose uses will be more widely acknowledged.
- Irrigation is a service with customers and users; it is not a production industry.
- At the level of the irrigation scheme, the process of water policy formulation, assessment and appraisal needs to include more open groups that are representative of political, technical, managerial and (most important) water user associations.
- These policy groups would be consulted before policy selection and then provide feedback and adjustment in the light of experience.
- The policy groups would identify options consistent with the national policy framework, as opposed to measures to protect and satisfy special irrigation interests.
- The goal is to identify a broader range of water policy options, to have less "policy by crisis" management and more resilience in the face of outside pressures.

Irrigation allows for better and more diversified choices in cropping patterns and the cultivation of high-value crops. Successful irrigation is a crucial determinant of the world's future development because of its influence on the supply and price of food. As the debate over water policies sharpens, it is increasingly important that agricultural policy-makers help shape the nature of the debate and influence policy decisions.

THE HIDDEN TREASURE

The most prominent feature of the landscape of that garden is a large river that runs through it southwards. A part of its course is however hidden under the mountains and when updrawn with kindly thirst through the veins of porous earth it issues forth as a fresh fountain.

Rivers flow like God's blessings and the beauty and the fecundity not only of the garden of Eden but also of the entire earth are their gifts. As a feature of the surface of the earth a river is so prominent and imposing that there is no possibility of its being mistaken.

It is a surface flow in full view and therefore very familiar to us. It is always in our sight and can never be out of our mind. But there is another kind of rivers, so the early man thought. They flow underground out of our sight. Without them he found it impossible to account for the sources of water in wells, springs and fountains. These 'ingulfed' flows find a place in many ancient myths and legends. In real life also early man knew how to use naturally occurring springs and water holes as sources of fresh water. In fact the history of such use of groundwater goes to prehistoric times. During droughts and times of water scarcity early man must have deepened them. The ancient Iranians developed water-collecting galleries and tunnels, called 'kanats', which were several miles long and yielded considerable quantities of water. In course of time the people of Egypt and Afghanistan also learnt this primitive technology. The ancient Chinese perfected the art of drilling deep wells. With crude and primitive materials they built drilling machineries capable of drilling to the depths of 5000 ft, a feat not duplicated until modern times.

Though man developed the skill to exploit groundwater quite early he was yet to understand its nature. The ancient Greeks and Romans, for example, speculated about it. They thought that the limestone caverns common in their countries were passages which penetrated the entire earth to form underground rivers that were fed by the oceans whose salt water was freshened by a process of earth metabolism. As their countries were located in regions of relatively low precipitation, not the rains alone but also this water could only account for the water in their wells and springs. The ancient Indians went a step further. They believed that the natural regime of a river extended far beyond the visible surface of the earth. The Ganges, their most sacred river, not only watered their land but also the skies and the underground world where she was respectively called the Akash Ganga and the Patal Ganga. They had a myth also to explain the disappearance underground of another sacred river, Saraswati, in the dry sands of Rajputana and Sindh. It would not perhaps be too much to interpret these Indian myths as an intuition or intelligent guess about the existence of what is now called the hydrological cycle.

Sir Jagadish Chandra Bose, a modern Indian scientist, told an allegorical story in his Bhagirathir Utsa Sandhane (in search of the source of the Bhagirathi), which uses these myths and is in fact the story of this cycle. Till the beginning of the 18th century it was not recognized by educated people that rivers and groundwater were only two links in the vast and complex hydrological cycle. The credit for the final acceptance of this idea in modern times goes to two Frenchmen. Pierre Perrault (1608-80) showed that the total discharge of the Seine river from 1668 to 1670 was only one-sixth of the total volume of rainfall. Edme Mariotte (1620-84) verified Perrault's work by measuring the discharge of the Seine. He also measured the infiltration of rainwater into the subsurface grounds. Another noted French engineer, Henri Darcy (1803-58), was the first man to clearly state the mathematical law governing the flow of groundwater.

The time when these Frenchmen were trying to understand and explore groundwater in good earnest is very significant. By their time the industrial revolution was about to make its appearance in the western European countries. Till that time the world population was small, predominantly agricultural and technologically backward and stagnant. Life was simple, its demands on the physical resources of the earth was not much. Everything was in plenty and seemed inexhaustible. This was particularly the case with fresh water. People were settled mainly near rivers and other surface water bodies which were easily accessible and were more than sufficient to meet their limited fresh water needs. This gave birth to an attitude of carelessness in their use of water. But now the population began to expand and settle in areas away from surface water sources.

Growing population, industrialization, urbanization, revolutionary changes in men's ways of life and their consumption pattern are now making ever increasing demands on all the physical resources of the earth. Most phenomenal has however been the growth of the demand on fresh water. Earlier it was needed mainly for agricultural and domestic purposes. Now it is needed for industries also. The traditional surface sources began to be exploited more extensively and intensively. The sources which so long seemed inexhaustible were found to be insufficient to meet the growing needs and had to be supplemented by supplies from other sources.

This is how intensive exploration and exploitation of groundwater began. Now it has become an essential part of fresh water supply, so much so that in many areas it is the only source of fresh water. Though stress on fresh water supply is being acutely felt in many areas of the world there has not been any significant change in man's attitude of carelessness. Greater human interference in the natural regimes of the surface water bodies has brought about their degradation. Similar has been the case with groundwater. Surface water is visible but groundwater is not. While we have been careless in our use of the visible resources it is no wonder that we should not be less careless in our use of this invisible resource. As it is out of our sight it stands very much in danger of being out of our mind. The degeneration of a river is apparent to everyone--the expert and the layman alike. But the threat to groundwater is not so. It needs special efforts to understand how precious is this hidden treasure and how criminally we have been squandering that treasure.

The importance of groundwater can hardly be overestimated. 97.5% of the total quantity of water contained in the hydrosphere is in the oceans and cannot be readily used because it is saline. The remaining 2.5% is fresh water and is essential for life. About 70% of this fresh water is in a frozen state in the Arctic, the

Antarctic and the mountains, about 30% is under the ground and less than 1% is in lakes, reservoirs and rivers and streams. Thus in volume the position of groundwater is second only after the permanently frozen water and is about 30 times larger than all the water of rivers, lakes and other surface water bodies taken together. In arid and semi-arid countries it is the main, if not the only, source of fresh water, while in many water-rich countries it accounts for as much as 50% of the total supplies.

According to a European Environment Agency report, Groundwater Quality and Quantity in Europe, the share of groundwater needed by different countries of the continent to meet their total demand for fresh water ranges from 9% to 100%. About 80% of the rural water supplies in the USA and Canada comes from this source. In India, among other things, the intensive use of groundwater made the 'green revolution' possible. In highly industrialized countries about 50% of the water used for industrial purposes comes from groundwater sources. In some countries groundwater has begun to be used for unconventional purposes. In Canada, for example, it is being used as a source of energy. In that country the City of Moose Jaw has developed a geothermal heating system for a public swimming pool and recreational facility, the Carleton University of Ottawa uses groundwater to heat and cool its buildings and the health centre complex in Sussex, New Brunswick, has been utilizing an aquifer for thermal energy storage since 1995. More importantly, groundwater supplies about 30% of the water in rivers and streams. In developed countries about 70% to 80% of the population live in cities which depend mostly on groundwater for their water supplies. The same trend has overtaken the rest of the world. Today we have become so much dependent on groundwater that without it our survival is impossible. Therefore it has become very imperative for us to understand this precious treasure which nature has kept hidden underground.

WHAT IS THIS GROUNDWATER?

It is water that is found underground. But is it in some rivers or lakes as primitive man thought? Or is it, as Milton imagined, a river which passes a part of its course 'underneath ingulfed' in 'porous' earth and issues forth on the surface of the earth in the form of wells and springs 'with kindly thirst updrwan' i.e., by capillary action? Many such springs and wells have in fact given birth to rivers and streams, as it did in the garden of Eden. In certain respects Milton seems to anticipate what the scientists have found out, but his basic concept that it is a river is not correct.

According to the scientists it is neither a river nor is it collected in some underground lakes. It is not confined to only a few channels or depressions in the same way that surface water is concentrated in streams and lakes. Rather, it exists almost everywhere underground in the spaces between particles of rocks, gravels, sand and soil, or in crevices and cracks in rocks. Most of it comes from precipitation which infiltrates below the ground into the subsurface soil. Precipitation that falls on the surface of the earth is distributed in four main ways: some is returned to the atmosphere by evaporation, some is intercepted by vegetation and then evaporated from the surface of leaves, some percolates into the soil by infiltration and the rest flows on the surface of the earth as runoff giving rise to rivers, streams and lakes. Thus groundwater is an essential part of the hydrological cycle that involves the continuous circulation of water in the earth-atmosphere system.

In the upper layers of the ground this percolated water exists along with air and is called the aerated or unsaturated zone where the interstices or empty spaces are occupied partially by water and partially by air. The water found in this zone is called soil moisture. Below this zone occurs the saturated zone where all the interstices are filled with water. The topmost level of this zone is called the water table which rises or falls according as the quantity of water in the saturated zone increases or decreases as a result of heavy precipitation or drought or over-abstraction. The water table may be deep or shallow, it may be only a foot below the ground's surface or it may be hundreds of feet down. Some parts of the saturated zone contain more water than others because of their peculiar geological formation of permeable rocks or porous and loose materials like gravels, sand, limestone etc. These are called aquifers. They are like sponges which can absorb liquids that ooze out under pressure. They come in all sizes. They may be small, only a few hectares in area, or very large, underlying thousands of square kilometres of the earth's surface and extending across political boundaries. They may be only a few metres thick, or they may measure hundreds of metres from top to bottom.

Groundwater is not static but mobile, it is always in motion. But the rate of its movement varies according to the variable geological formation of the aquifers. As permeable or porous and loose or unconsolidated materials contain interconnected cracks or spaces that are numerous enough and large enough to allow water to move freely, in aquifers formed of such materials groundwater may move several metres in a day, whereas in aquifers formed of relatively impermeable or consolidated materials the rate of movement may be very slow, only a few centimetres in a century.

There are materials which are very porous yet impermeable. Clay, for instance, has many spaces between its grains, but the spaces are not large enough to permit free movement of water. Groundwater continues to descend beyond the saturated zone until at some depth it merges into a zone of dense rocks. Water is contained in the pores of these rocks, but the pores are not connected and water cannot migrate. Such water may be thousands of years old. Some aquifers are called fractured aquifers because they are rocks in which groundwater moves through cracks, joints or fractures in otherwise solid rocks. Examples of such aquifers include granite and basalt.

Limestones are often fractured aquifers, but here the cracks and fractures may be enlarged by solution, forming large channels or even caverns. Limestone terrain where solution has been very active is called karst. Sandstone is a porous media, but by solution it may become so highly cemented or re-crystallized that all its original spaces are filled and as a result it no longer remains porous. If however it contains cracks it can still act as a fractured aquifer. Aquifers may again be either unconfined-those that are bounded by the water table-or confined-those that lie beneath layers of impermeable materials. The aquifers of the latter kind are sometimes called artesian wells. The water in these wells rises higher than the top of the aquifer because of confining pressure. If the water level rises above the ground surface a flowing artesian well will occur. Groundwater usually flows downhill with the slope of the water table. Like surface water it flows toward, and eventually drains into streams, rivers, lakes and the oceans. In aquifers underlying surface drainage basins this flow does not always mirror the surface flow. Groundwater may move below the ground in directions different from those of the water flowing overland.

Groundwater moves mainly because of the operation of the hydrological cycle. The aquifers receive their supplies from the percolation of water from precipitation. This is called their charging. Eventually this water reappears above the ground by flowing into rivers, streams, lakes and the oceans. This is called discharge. The extent of charging of the aquifers depends on precipitation, the slope, soil type and the vegetable cover of the surface ground above them and the geological formation of the aquifers themselves and their consequent capability to absorb water. This also determines the quantum of the surface flow called runoff. If for any reason the underground aquifers are less capable to absorb enough water from precipitation the surface flow will be more and may cause floods. In course of time nature establishes a kind of balance among the various links in the hydrological cycle. As an integral part of this cycle groundwater also develops a regime of its own. At times this balance and the regime may get disturbed by geological and cosmic extreme events like earthquakes, droughts, heavy rains and abrupt shifts in the climatic cycle. But nature, when left to itself, has the capacity to restore them or to re-establish a new balance and regime.

Since the industrial revolution men are exploiting groundwater at an ever increasing rate to meet their ever increasing fresh water needs and thereby interfering too much in its natural regime. Now in many areas of the world the rate of withdrawal of groundwater from aquifers is much in excess of the rate of their recharging. Such over-exploitation of groundwater has serious consequences. Continued over-extraction of groundwater will cause the water table to fall resulting in the ultimate depletion of aquifers. Renewal of water in rivers, for example, takes only a few days whereas in case of groundwater it takes 1400 years. Thus if an aquifer gets depleted due to overdrawl of its water in excess of the rate of its recharging it will need these many years to get replenished. And what will happen in the mean time to the vast population which depends on this source for its survival and the material civilization it has built upon it? That civilization will come crashing like a house of cards and that population will be extinct in a matter of days.

Other adverse effects of such over exploitation of groundwater are deprivation of rivers, streams and lakes of an important source of their supplies, subsidence or caving in of land above the aquifers, drying up of wetlands and other small water bodies disastrously affecting the ecosystems they support and salt water intrusion in coastal regions rendering them unusable. Many areas of the world are already experiencing these adverse effects and in days to come many more areas will follow suit. Due to over-drafting of groundwater parts of Mexico City, for instance, have subsided as much as 10 metres in the past 70 years, resulting in a host of problems in its water supply and sewerage systems. According to the US Geological Survey in the United States more than 17,000 square miles have been directly affected by subsidence.

Over-abstraction may give rise to another danger. An aquifer which is used by more than one country or region may become a bone of contention amongst those countries or regions. Excessive irrigation on the other hand may cause water table to rise and lead to water logging making the land saline. We often ignore the geological aspect of groundwater and the adverse effects that its over-abstraction may have on the underground geological structure of an area. Engineers must consider groundwater when planning almost any kind of structure, either below or above the ground. Ignoring the slope stability can be costly and dangerous. Groundwater is a major force in geological changes. The fluid pressure exerted by groundwater, for example, play an important role in the occurrence of earthquakes. Geologists also know that the movement of water through underground geologic formations controls the migration and the accumulation of petroleum and the formation of some ore deposits.

We are threatening groundwater not only quantitatively but also qualitatively. Water is never found in a pure state in nature and both groundwater and surface water may contain many constituents which make their use without appropriate treatment unfit for specific purposes. The suitability of water for a given use depends on many factors and considerations important for surface water are equally applicable to groundwater. But one very important difference between the two is that as groundwater flows through an aquifer it is naturally filtered. This filtering, combined with the long residence underground, makes groundwater usually free from disease-causing micro-organisms. Natural filtering also means that groundwater usually contains less suspended material and un-dissolved solids than surface water. This is the reason why it is generally assumed that it is safe and is therefore used mostly without any treatment. But it may not be so. The rain water which charged the aquifer itself might have been polluted by the polluted atmosphere. The acid rain is an example.

Again, one of the most important natural changes in groundwater chemistry occurs in the soil and in course of its journey through the aquifer it dissolves certain substances it encounters. Who knows if arsenic, the greatest menace now found in groundwater throughout the world, is due to this? Most dangerous are the innumerable ways in which we are contaminating groundwater by our various activities and making it unsafe. There is a popular misconception that as it is not exposed like surface water it is less vulnerable to pollution.

Human activities which are mainly responsible for pollution of groundwater are those related to agriculture and industry. Modern agriculture is very intensive and uses heavy doses of chemical fertilizers, pesticides and herbicides containing highly toxic compounds. Industrial processes also involve the use of many toxic materials. Through our agricultural and industrial activities we also generate huge amounts of hazardous wastes both liquid and solid. They pollute not only the soil, air and surface water but also find their way to the underground aquifers. Other factors responsible for groundwater pollution are leaking pipelines and storage tanks containing petroleum products, septic systems, municipal landfills, livestock wastes, leaky sewer lines, wells for disposal of liquid industrial wastes, toxic substances from mining sites, dumping grounds for disposal of solid and liquid wastes, fly ash from coal-fired power plants, contaminants in rain water etc.

In cold countries road salt is a major source of contamination. Groundwater pollution is a serious problem and is very costly and difficult, if not impossible, to solve. That is so because of its relative inaccessibility, huge volume and slow flow rate. Once pollutants enter an aquifer, the environmental damage can be severe and long lasting because of the very long time needed to flush out the pollutants, if it is at all possible to do so. Contamination of groundwater is also very insidious, it takes many years to show up in water withdrawn from wells. By the time it is detected, it may be too late to prevent serious contamination. And as a major link in the hydrological cycle polluted groundwater pollutes surface water also.

Thus it is obvious that though the groundwater reserve is huge we cannot use it as much as and in any manner we like. Because of the threats to groundwater and its importance not only for the maintenance of the present standard of our material civilization and a sustainable development, but also for our very survival it is urgently necessary to stop its overdrawal and pollution. There should be continuous monitoring to detect and prevent them. Withdrawal of water from aquifers found polluted should be immediately stopped and appropriate steps should be taken for its early purification. It is a very difficult task for various reasons.

It is a highly technical job and there is a great shortage of groundwater experts throughout the world. Costs involved are also huge. Even in a rich country like the U.S.A. many states are unable to bear the burden of all the functions involved and some of it, like the UIC or Underground Injection Control Program, is done for them by the federal government.

Exploration of groundwater started much later than surface water and sufficient and reliable data are therefore not often available. Finally, the root cause of excessive demands not only on groundwater but also on all the physical resources of the earth is the abnormal growth of population. Unless that cause is removed it is impossible to solve the problems of groundwater. And unfortunately the rate of population growth is comparatively much higher in poorer countries. To cap it all, many of these poor countries happen to be poor in fresh water resources also. According to the UNEP Report, Global Environment Outlook-2000, India is one of those countries which are currently withdrawing 20 to 40% and will be withdrawing around 40% of their water resources by the year 2025 AD when they will face a severe fresh water crisis. According to the Report of the World Commission on Dams in India the groundwater table is falling at an alarming rate of one metre per year. It is therefore needless to say that we have a special reason to be careful in the use of our water resources. To save ourselves we have to save our groundwater too.

8

Status of Agriculture Report

ADOPTING CLIMATE CHANGE IN AGRICULTURE

- Climate change represents a serious threat to every part of the Globe, especially the developing countries facing the challenge of ensuring food and nutritional security to the growing population. There are six gases identified in the Kyoto Protocol, the cumulative emissions of which have led to the threat of climate change. Of these, CO_2 is the largest, the major source of which is the combustion of fossil fuels. Mitigation of emissions of CO_2 would require not only increased efficiency in the use of fossil fuels but a major shift to low carbon or non-carbon fuels such as solar, wind and sustainable use of bio-mass.
- The Intergovernmental Panel on Climate Change (IPCC) in its Third Assessment Report finalized in 2001 predicts that the global temperature will rise by about 1.4-5.8°C by the year 2100. This change would be much larger than any climate change experienced over at least the last 10,000 years. The mean sea level is expected to rise 9-88cms by the year 2100 causing flooding of low-lying areas. Other effects could include an increase in global precipitation and changes in the severity or frequency of extreme events. Food security is unlikely to be threatened at the global level, but some regions are expected to experience food shortages and hunger. Water resources will be affected as precipitation and evaporation patterns change around the world.

- The third assessment report of the IPCC specifically considers agriculture as highly vulnerable to impacts of climate change in the South Asian region. This is a critical issue as countries of the South Asia generated between 24% to 40% of their GDP from agriculture in 1997 facing a larger exposure to climate change than OECD countries, which generated only about 2-3%.
- In South Asia food security therefore becomes a primary concern. Crop production and aquaculture would be threatened by thermal and water stresses, sea-level rise, increased flooding, and strong winds associated with intense tropical cyclones. Acute water shortages combined with thermal stress should adversely affect wheat, and more severely, rice productivity in India given even a positive 'fertilisation' effect through an elevated atmospheric CO_2-level in the future.
- Recognizing the increasing population in the region and limited availability of land, agricultural productivity needs to continuously increase to meet the growing demand despite the adverse impacts of climate expected in the future.
- In order to increase awareness in the region and to identify vulnerable areas as well as deliberate on adaptation strategy and mitigation options, Government of India, United Nations Environment Programme (UNEP) and Consultative Group for International Agriculture Research (CGIAGR) jointly organized a three days "South Asia Expert Workshop-Adaptation to Climate Change for Agricultural Productivity" at Vigyan Bhavan, New Delhi on May 1-3, 2002. It is for the first time that a Workshop of this kind and on this scale was organized in this country.
- The main goal of the workshop was to identify strategic actions, nationally and internationally, to strengthen the planning process and decision-making framework. The decision-making framework needs to mainstream adaptation activities-and to the extent possible mitigation options-to increase in agricultural productivity as expected

to decline due to impacts of climate change and climate variability.

WEATHER CONDITIONS

- One Western Disturbance moved across Western Himalayas during the first week of April, 2002 causing moderate rain/snow in the hilly regions and light rain in the adjoining northern plains of northwest India. Due to ongoing thunderstorm activities, moderate to heavy rainfall occurred over northeastern States and Sub-Himalayan West Bengal & Sikkim.
- A western disturbance affected the hilly regions of Northwest India from 5th to 8th April resulting in rain or snow activity at a few places over Jammu & Kashmir. The system moved away eastward on 9th April. Thunderstorm activity with light to moderate rainfall occurred in Orissa, West Bengal & Sikkim, northeastern States, Maharashtra and peninsular India on some days of the week.
- A wind discontinuity was observed at 0.9 km a.s.l from Bihar to Kerala through Chhatisgarh, Andhra Pradesh and interior Karnataka during the week ending on 17th April, 2002. Thunderstorm activity with light to moderate rainfall occurred in Orissa, West Bengal and Sikkim, northeastern states and peninsular India during the week. A western disturbance affected the hilly regions of northwest India from 13th to 16th April and caused light rain / snow over Western Himalayan region. The system moved away eastward on 17th April, 2002.
- A western disturbance affected Northwest India from 23rd to 25th April and caused light to moderate rain/snow over Jammu & Kashmir, and isolated rain in Punjab. Another Western Disturbance as an upper air system was seen on 27th over North Pakistan and adjoining areas. This system moved away eastwards. It caused light rain/snow over Western Himalayas. Heat wave conditions prevailed over many parts of Northwest India, Vidarbha, east Madhya Pradesh and Chattisgarh and abated by 24th

April. These again started in west Rajasthan from 26th onwards.

- Last week's western disturbance moved away eastward on 26th April. A fresh western disturbance affected hilly regions of Western Himalayas from 27th to 29th April causing light rain/snow. Rain / Thundershower activity continued in West Bengal and Sikkim, northeastern states, Andaman & Nicobar Islands and south Peninsula.

Rainfall

- During the week ending on 3rd April, 2002, scattered to fairly widespreadrainfall/snowfall occurred in association with the Western Disturbance over Jammu & Kashmir, Himachal Pradesh and Uttaranchal and isolated light rainfall occurred in north Rajasthan, Punjab, Haryana and West Uttar Pradesh. Fairly widespread rainfall also occurred over West Bengal & Sikkim, Arunachal Pradesh, Assam & Meghalaya, Nagaland, Manipur, Mizoram & Tripura, Orissa and scattered rainfall over Chhattisgarh, Jharkhand, Vidarbha, Andaman & Nicobar Islands and southern peninsula.
- During the week ending on 10th April, 2002, rain or snow occurred at a few places in Jammu & Kashmir and at isolated places in Himachal Pradesh and Uttaranchal. Rainfall also occurred at many places in Gangetic West Bengal; at a few places in Arunachal Pradesh, Assam & Meghalaya, Sub-Himalayan West Bengal and Sikkim, West Madhya Pradesh, Vidarbha & interior Karnataka and at isolated places in Nagaland, Manipur, Mizoram and Tripura, Haryana, Punjab, Rajasthan, Chhatisgarh, Orissa, Madhya Maharashtra, Marathwada, Andhra Pradesh, Coastal Karnataka, Tamil Nadu, Kerala and Andaman & Nicobar Islands. Weather remained mainly dry in the rest regions of the country.
- During the week ending on 17th April 2002, Rain/thunder shower occurred at a few places in West Bengal & Sikkim, Assam & Meghalaya, Arunachal Pradesh and Kerala and

at isolated places in Nagaland, Manipur, Mizoram & Tripura, Orissa, Jharkhand, Chhattisgarh, Coastal Andhra Pradesh, Karnataka, Tamil Nadu, Lakshadweep and Andaman & Nicobar islands. Weather remained mainly dry in the rest regions of the country.

- During the week ending on 24th April 2002, rain or snow occurred at a few places in Jammu & Kashmir and at isolated places in Himachal Pradesh. Rain / Thundershower also occurred at many places in Arunachal Pradesh, Assam & Meghalaya, Sub Himalayan West Bengal & Sikkim; at a few places in Gangetic West Bengal, Coastal Orissa, Madhya Maharashtra, Karnataka & Kerrala and at islolated places in Punjab, Nagaland, Manipur, Mizoram and Tripura, Chhattisgarh, Coastal Andhra Pradesh, Tamil Nadu, Lakshadweep and Andaman & Nicobar Islands. Weather remained mainly dry in the rest regions of the country.
- During the last week of April, 2002 Rain or snow occurred at a few places in Jammu & Kashmir, Himachal Pradesh and Uttaranchal. Rain/thundershower also occureed at many places in Arunachal Pradesh, Assam and Meghalaya, Nagaland, Manipur, Mizoram & Tripura, West Bengal & Sikkim and Andaman & Nicobar Islands and at isolated places in Punjab, Haryana, Karnataka, Kerala, Tamil Nadu, Lakshadweep. Weather remained mainly dry in the rest regions of the country.

Summary of Week to Week Status of Rainfall pattern from 1st March to 30th April, 2002. (pre-Monsoon)

Rainfall									
	W-1	*W-2*	*W-3*	*W-4*	*W-5*	*W-6*	*W-7*	*W-8*	*W-9*
Excess	4	3	7	2	5	6	5	3	3
Normal	2	2	1	5	8	10	10	10	8
Deficient	3	7	7	10	8	11	10	11	16
Scanty/no rain	26	24	21	19	15	9	11	12	9

- The table below gives the comparison of rainfall for the past five years for the period from 1st March to 1st May. (Pre-monsoon)

No. of Sub-divisions with rainfall	For the period from 1st March to				
	29 April 1998	28 April 1999	3rd May 2000	2nd May 2001	1st May 2002
Excess	19	1	4	19	3
Normal	23	5	12	25	11
	4	4	8	6	8
Deficient	3	3	12	6	16
Scanty	6	21	9		9
	12	30	23	10	25
No Rain	3	6	2	4	0
Data Inadequate	0	0	0	0	0
Total	35	35	35	35	35

The cumulative rainfall during the period 1st March to 1st May, 2002 was normal to excess in 11 out of 36 meteorological sub-divisions of the country. About 30% of districts had excess to normal rainfall against 61% last year in the corresponding period.

- At all-India level, 5.94 cms of rainfall occurred so far in Pre-monsoon season-2002 against the average rainfall of 6.83 cms.
- The cumulative area weighted rainfall in Pre-monsoon season-2002 so far was below normal, being 13% less than LPA (Long Period Average).
- Out of the three broad homogenous regions of the country, two regions of North-West India and Peninsular India received deficient / scanty rainfall during the Pre-Monsoon season so far while North-East India received normal rainfall. North-west India received 5.3 cm rainfall against 6.9 cm of average rainfall. Peninsular India received 1.6 cm rainfall against 2.8 cm of average rainfall. North-east India received 16.85 cm rainfall against 16.10 cm of average rainfall.

- All India % Rainfall Departure in this year Pre-Monsoon Season-2002 verses last five years is giver in the table below.

Category ALL INDIA % R/F Dep.	01.05.2002	02.05.2001	03.05.2000	28.04.99	29.04.98	30.04.97
	-13%	-6%	-18%	-62%	-15%	13%

TEMPERATURE

Night Temperature

- Week 1 : Above normal by 5° to 6° C in parts of Rajasthan & West Madhya Pradesh on a few days of the week. Above normal by 5° C in Coastal regions of Saurastra & Kutch and Tamil Nadu on one or two days of the week.
- Week 2 : Heat wave conditions prevailed in parts of Haryana, Rajasthan and Northern parts of Madhya Pradesh during the first half of the week. Maximum temperatures were nearly normal in the rest of the country. The highest temperature was 43.4° C at Dholpur in Rajasthan on 7th April, 2002.
- Week 3 : Heat wave conditions prevailed in parts of Northwest India during 12th to 14th April and extended towards Vidarbha, East Madhya pradesh and chhattisgarh by the end of the week. Highest temperature, was 45.8° at Pusad in Maharashtra on 17th April 2002.
- Week 4 : Heat wave conditions continued over parts of Vidarbha, East Madhya Pradesh and Chhattisgarh till 22nd April. Heat wave conditions also started from 20th April onwards over many parts of northwest India.
- Week 5 : Maximum temperature was above normal by 3° to 4° C in Central India and adjoining peninsula and below normal in Bihar, Sub-Himalayan West Bengal and Sikkim and northeastern States. Highest temp was 47° C in Rajasthan on 30th April & 1st May.

RESERVOIR POSITION (70 MAJOR RESERVOIRS)

Reservoir Storage Status – April, 2002

Period	Current Year's Storage as a % of FRL *	Current Year's storage as % of last year	Current year as a % of 10 years average level
Beginning of the month	24	108	73.01
End of the month	16	94	69%
* Live storage as % to Full Reservoir Level (FRL) of 130.55 Th. Million cub. Mts.(TMC)			

- In the first week of April, 2002, against the FRL of 130.55 TMC, water availability in 70 major reservoirs was 30.78 TMC which was more than the last year's position by 2.37 T. M. Cum. but less than the average of last 10 years storage by 11.38 T.M. Cum. In the last week of the month, water stock decreased to 21.39 TMC which was less than the last year's position by 1.31 T. M. Cum. and less than the average of last 10 years storage by 9.58 T.M. Cum.

Storage Status in Select States

- Himachal Pradesh : There are two major reservoirs in Himachal Pradesh, namely, Gobind Sagar (Bhakra) and Pong Dam (Beas). Total water available in these major reservoirs during the first week of the month was 1.38 TMC against the designed storage of 13.77 TMC which was 96.57% of last year's storage level and 39.82% of ten year's average level. In the last week of the month, the water level of major reservoirs in Himachal Pradesh decreased to 1.34TMC which was about 110.50% of last year's level and 45.94% of ten years' average.
- Gujarat : There are seven major reservoirs, namely, Ukai, Sabarmati (Dharoi), Kadana, Shetrunji, Bhadar, Damanganga and Dantiwada in the State. Total water available in these major reservoirs during the first week of the month was 2.22 TMC against the designed storage of 10.35TMC which was 202% of last year's storage level and 58.26% of ten year's average level. In the last week

of the month, total water in major reservoirs of the state decreased to 1.59 TMC which was about 225.78% of last year's level and 57.75% of average of ten years' level.

- Rajasthan : There are three major reservoirs, namely Mahi Bajaj Sagar, Jhakam and Ranapratap Sagar in the state. Total water available in these major reservoirs during the first week of month was 0.37 TMC against the storage of 3.538 TMC which was 153.50% of last year's level and 45.16% of ten year's average level. In the last week of the month, total water in major reservoirs decreased to 0.32 TMC which was 165.80% of last year level and 39.51% of average of ten years' level.
- Madhya Pradesh: There are three major reservoirs in the state, namely, Gandhi Sagar, Tawa and Bargi. Total water available in these reservoirs during the first week of the month was 1.012 TMC against the storage of 11.873 TMC which was 154.74% of last year's level and 29.89% of ten year's average level. In the last week of the month, water level in major reservoirs of the states decreased to 0.772 TMC which was 151.67% of last year's level and 32.70% of average of ten years level.
- Maharashtra: There are ten major reservoirs namely, Jayakawadi (Paithan), Koyana, Bhima (Ujjaini), Isapur, Mula, Yeldari, Girna, Khadakvasla, Upper Vaitarna and Upper Tapi. Total water available in these major reservoirs during the first week of the month was 2.729 TMC against the designed storage of 9.913 TMC which was 110.49% of last year's level and 74.93% of ten year's average level. In the last week of the month, total water in major reservoirs of the state decreased to 1.662 TMC which was about 109.70% of last year's level and 67.40% of average of 10 years level.
- Orissa: There are six major reservoirs in the State, namely, Hirakund, Balimela, Salanadi, Rengali, Machkund and Upper Kolab. Total water available in these major reservoirs during the first week of the month was 5.270 TMC against the storage of 13.872 TMC which

was 185.11% of last year's level and 97.79% of ten year's average level. In the last week of the month, water level in these major reservoirs decreased to 2.804 TMC which was 157.79% of last year's level and 94.63% of last 10 years' average level.

- Karnataka: There are twelve major reservoirs in the state, namely, Krishnaraja Sagar, Tungabhadra, Ghataprabha (Hidkal), Bhadra, Linganamakki, Narayanpur, Malaprabha (Renuka), Kabini, Hemavathy, Harangi, Supa and Vani Villas Sagar. Total water available in these major reservoirs during the first week of the month was 2.661 TMC against the designed storage of 20.88 TMC which was 47.86% of last year's level and 49.55% of ten year's average level. In the last week of the month, total water in major reservoirs of the state decreased to 1.617 TMC, which was about 40.55% of last year's level and 41.80% of average of 10 years' level.
- Tamil Nadu : There are six major reservoirs in Tamil Nadu, namely, Lower Bhawani, Mettur (Stanley), Vaigai, Parambikulam, Aliyar and Sholayar. Total water available in these major reservoirs during the first week of the month was. 0.598 TMC against the designed storage of 4.389 TMC which was 31.77% of last year's level and 29.90% of ten year's average level. In the last week of the month, total water in major reservoirs decreased to 0.475 TMC which was 23.41% of last year's level and 22.62% of average of ten years level.
- Andhra Pradesh: There are five major reservoirs in the state namely, Srisaila, Nagarjuna Sagar, Sriram Sagar, Somasila and Lower Manair. Total water available in these major reservoirs during the first week of the month was 3.757 T.M. cum against the designed storage of 20.103 T.M. cum which was 128.97% of last year's level and 100.05% of ten years' average level. In the last week of the month, total water in major reservoirs of the state decreased to 2.360 T.M. cum which was 94.21% last years level and 103.51% of ten years' average level.

Last five weeks trend of reservoir level this year against corresponding weeks of last year as well as ten years average trend is depicted in the graph below:

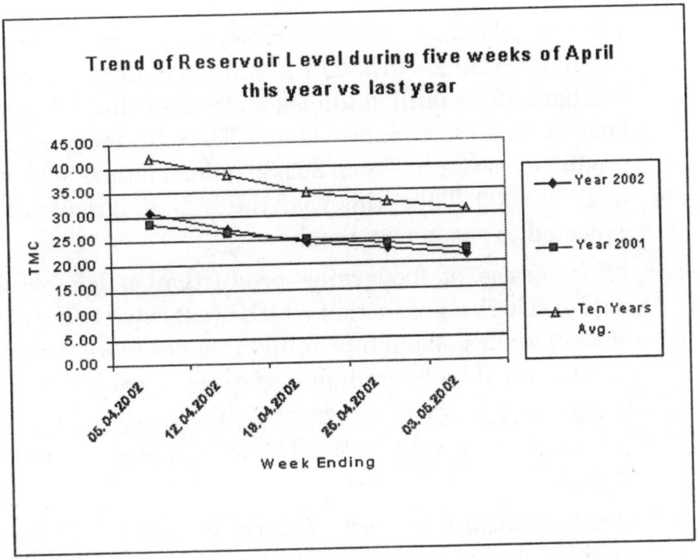

CROP PROSPECTS

Third Advance Estimates of Agriculture Production for 2001-02

The prospects of crop production for 2001-02 were updated on 05-04-02 and its chief features are as under:

- Though the level of monsoon rainfall during 2001 was at par with that of last year, its spatial and temporal distribution was favorable for the agriculture and hence the country is expected to achieve an all time record of foodgrains production.
- The paradigm shift from the schematic approach to Marco-Management mode which provided required flexibility to the States in implementation of Plan Schemes, as per their area specific requirements, has yielded the expected results.
- The inputs sector was also effectively managed ensuring

adequate availability of quality seeds, fertilizers and pesticides etc. to the farming sector.

Foodgrains

- The overall foodgrains production, as per third advance estimates, is likely to be 211.17 million tonnes which will be about 15.25 million tonnes more than the last year's production of 195.92 million tonnes. The record of foodgrains production so far has been 209.80 million tonnes achieved in 1999-2000. Thus, this year the Indian agriculture is expected to reach new heights.
- Performance of foodgrains production is led by the impressive rice production which is expected to be 90.75 million tonnes, about 5.88 million tonnes more than the production of 84.87 million tonnes achieved last year.
- The production of wheat at 73.53 million tonnes is expected to be higher by 4.77 million tonnes as compared to last year.
- One significant feature of current year's foodgrains production performance is that the targets of production of coarse cereals as a group has been accomplished. The country is expected to achieve a production of 33.10 million tonnes against the target of 33.00 million tonnes. The production of coarse cereals last year was 31.62 million tonnes.
- In this group, maize and bajra have performed particularly well. Against a target of 12.00 million tonnes, the production of maize is expected to be 13.78 million tonnes, which is about 1 million tonne more than last year's production.
- The production of bajra is expected to be 7.07 million tonnes against the target of 6.95 million tonnes.
- The overall Kharif foodgrains production at 109.5 million tonnes is also expected to be close to the target of 110.13 million tonnes set for the season
- Performance of the States in Eastern India has been particularly impressive. States of Assam, Bihar,

Jharkhand, Orissa and West Bengal are expected to contribute an additional 5.5 million tonnes of foodgrains to the total output. The Northern States of Haryana, Himachal Pradesh and Jammu & Kashmir are also expected to achieve an all time record of foodgrains. Wheat production in Haryana is expected to reach 10 million tonnes for the first time.

Commercial Crops

- The oilseeds production is expected to be around 21.16 million tonnes during the current year as against 18.40 million tonnes produced last year.
- Both groundnut and soyabean are expected to contribute about 12.91 million between themselves, which will be higher by 1.42 million tonnes compared to last year's production.
- The production of rapeseed and mustard at 5.34 million tonnes is expected to be higher by 1.13 million tonnes compared to last year.
- Among other commercial crops, the area coverage under cotton increased substantially and consequently the production prospects are expected to be significantly higher at 11.30 million bales compared to production of 9.65 million bales achieved last year. This will be approximately 17% higher than the production achieved in last year.
- The sugarcane production is expected to be 289.41million tonnes as against 299.21 million tonnes produced last year.

Report on Onion

- The Kharif and late Kharif crop of Onion account for about 18% and 22% of the total Onion production respectively. The normal annual Onion production is 4.6 million tonnes.
- This year Rabi Onion production is likely to be 8% higher than the last year production.

PEST SITUATION AND DISEASES

- The pest and disease incidences generally remained below ETL (Economic Threshold Level).
- No report of shortage of commonly used pesticides.

AGRICULTURAL PRICES AND MARKETING

Minimum Support Prices (MSP)

The wholesale prices of foodgrains ruled below the MSP in the open market during April, 2002 as detailed below:

Sl.No.	Commodity	Centres
1.	Paddy	Darbhanga (Bihar), Dohad (Gujarat) Jeypore (Orissa), Kanchipuram, kumbakonam and Tiruchirapalli (Tamilnadu) Bahraich & Varanasi (UP) and Santhia & Contai (West Bengal).
2.	Wheat	Khagaria, Sasaram (Bihar), Jaipur (Rajasthan), Bahraich, Hapur, Kanpur, Jhansi and Lucknow (UP)
3.	Jowar	Akola (Maharashtra) and Varanasi (UP)
4.	Bajra	Jaipur (Rajasthan) and Varanasi (UP).
5.	Maize	Khagaria (Bihar)
6.	Barley	Muzzafarpur (Bihar) Abohar (Punjab) Ajmer & Bhilwara (Rajasthan) Hapur & Sitapur (UP).

Price Scenario

During the month of April, 2002 the price trend of foodgrains remained comfortable with the WPI of foodgrains and cereals (week ending 27.04.2002) showing a monthly fall of 0.1% and 0.2% repectively.

Rice

The WPI of rice shows a monthly rise of 0.6% with an annual fall of 3.2%. The wholesale prices of rice at selected centers exhibited a mixed trend.

Wheat

The WPI of Wheat shows a monthly fall of 2.4% with an

annual fall of 0.7%. The wholesale prices of wheat at selected centers fluctuated marginally.

Pulses

The WPI of pulses shows a monthly rise of 0.7% and an annual fall of 1.4%.

Sugar, Gur and Khandsari

The WPI of sugar, gur and khandsari registered a monthly fall of 1.5% and an annual fall of 4.0%.

Oilseeds

The Wholesale Price Index (WPI) of nine major Oilseeds (Group) at 143.8 during April, 2002 registered an increase of 2.9% over the month. In Comparison to last year, the price index in April, 2002 was higher by 10.9%. The W.P.I. of individual oilseeds exhibited generally a mixed trend during the month under review. While the W.P.I. of Rapeseed/Mustard, Nigerseed and Safflower seed declined by 1.2%, 1.9% & 2.0%, respectively during the month; the prices of the following Oilseeds firmed up in April, 2002 viz., Groundnut (3.6%), Cottonseed (0.3%), Copra (7.7%), Gingelly seed 4.4% and Sunflowerseed (1.5%) & Soyabean (7.1%) respectively.

Fruits & Vegetables

The Wholesale Price Index (WPI) of Fruits & Vegetables (Group) at 190.1 in April, 2002 was higher by 3.0% over the month. As compared to the previous year, the price index was firmed up by 7.5%

Potato

The Wholesale Price Index (WPI) of Potato at 176.0 in April, 2002 was lower by 0.5% during the month under review. However, the index increased by 13.8% over the corresponding index of the previous year.

Onion

The Wholesale Price Index (WPI) of Onion at 98.9 in April, 2002 was lower by 0.2% over the month and by 0.1% as compared to the corresponding index of the previous year.

Raw Cotton

The Wholesale Price Index (WPI) of Raw Cotton at 127.2 in April, 2002 stood higher by 3.2% over the month. However, over the year the index declined by 20.2%.

Raw Jute

The Wholesale Price Index (WPI) of Raw Jute at 187.1 in April, 2002 was higher by 1.1% during the month and by 4.8% over the corresponding index of the previous year.

Procurement and Stocks of Foodgrains

During the month of April, 2002 a total quantity of 139.03 lakh tonnes of wheat has been procured as against 98.30 lakh tonnes during April, 2002.

The cumulative progressive procurement in the current rabi marketing season 2002-03 upto (01.05.2002) at 139.03 lakh tonnes was 40.73 lakh tonnes more than that of last year.

The cumulative progressive procurement of rice in the current marketing season 2001-02 (up to 29.04.2002) at 18.08 million tonnes was more by 0.28 million tonnes than that of last year.

The stock position of rice and wheat with the Government agencies is quite comfortable. The stocks of rice and wheat as on 01.04.2002 were 24.91 million tonnes and 26.04 million tonnes respectively.

Nafed

Under the ongoing Price Support Scheme (PSS) for oilseeds and pulses, a quantity of 224719 MTs of mustard seed was procured in the States of Rajasthan, Madhya Pradesh, Uttar Pradesh, Gujarat, and Haryana as on 27.4.2002.

A quantity of 276 MTs of Safflower seed was procured in the States of Maharashtra and Andhra Pradesh, a quantity of 50081 Mts of copra was procured in the States of A & N, Goa, Tamil Nadu, Andhra Pradesh and Karnataka and a quantity of 2838 MTs of Arhar was procured in the States of Delhi, Andhra Pradesh and Karnataka upto 24.04.2002.

RESEARCH AND TECHNOLOGY DEVELOPMENT

Integrated Nutrient Management in Banana For More Yield

In farmer's practice a ratoon in banana cv. Ney Poovan (premium table variety) is allowed only at 9th month (after bunch emergence in mother plant) after planting and farmer has to wait for 10-12 months for the next bunch. But by following Integrated Nutrient Management practices through soil (40% nutrients) and by foliar application (60% nutrients), the ratoons have been allowed at 4th month of planting of mother plant at the Indian Institute of Horticultural Research, Bangalore. By supplying 60% nutrients through foliar, expenses on fertilizer have been reduced by Rs. 5/-per plant (Rs. 20000/-per ha) and deficiencies have been corrected fast. Foliar spray has been standardized with indigenously available fertilizers like urea, SOP, $ZnSO_4$ and Borax and lime fruits and shampoo sachets as spray adjuvant. Average bunch yields of 15 kg have been recorded in mother plants and the ratoon (daughter plants) are already 7 months old and well grown and in another 4-5 months, one more bunch can be harvested. Banana yield can be doubled in cv. Ney Poovan from 12000 kg/acre/year to 23000 kg/acre/year which is very beneficial to small farmers.

Handmade Paper From Jute Waste

In the handmade paper industry various textile wastes, viz., hosiery cuttings, tailor's cuttings are traditionally used as cellulosic raw material. But due to rising price of such material and burgeoning demand of raw material in paper industry, Jute wastes have been considered as suitable raw material due to its abundant availability in eastern India.

National Institute of Research on Jute & Allied Fibre Technology, Barrack pore has standardized the technology for making handmade paper using jute wastes as raw material and a large quantity of paper and paperboard were produced through trials. Such paper and paperboards have been found to possess good strength and quality. Some useful products like paper dish, paper folder etc. have also been prepared from the sold paper sheets and boards.

Moulded Products From Jute Based Composite

Jute fibre has been found to be suitable raw material in making jute based composite and moulded products.

In order to utilize jute, an agro-fibre in developing an environment friendly and cost effective technique, the National Institute of Research on Jute & Allied Fibres Technolgy, Barrackpore has developed composites by dyeing with reactive dyes and some of the moulded products have been developed from jute non-wovens using polyester resin which include moulded tool box (size : 46.5 x 31 x 26 cm, Weight : 5 kg), moulded traffic signal light case (size : 28 x 28 x 49 cm, weight : 3 kg), moulded boat (size 13 x 4 ft, weight : 150 kg., capacity : 8 persons).

Vegetable Planter Attachment For Power Weeder

Tamil Nadu Agricultural University, Coimbatore Centre of the All India Coordinated Research Project on Farm Implements and Machinery has developed a vegetable planter attachment to the self-propelled portion of the power weeder.

It can be used for sowing different vegetables like small onion, tomato, chillies, lady's finger etc. Spoon/cup feed type mechanism is provided to facilitate metering of small onion bulbs/ seeds without breakage.

The performance of the vegetable planter attachment was tested for sowing small onion and lady's finger in comparison with manual dibbling method. The effective field capacity was found to be 0.09 and 0.11 ha/h in case of small onion bulbs and lady's finger, respectively. There was net saving of Rs.350 460 per ha in cost of seeding by the vegetable planter as compared to manual sowing.

Germplasm Exchange

Import

A total of 544 samples of various crops were introduced from eight different countries viz., Australia, Canada, Italy, The Phillippines, Peru, Syria, USA and UK. Promising accessions were : grapes (Vitis vinifera) improved Sirius, Bianca, Regent,

Hibernal (EC No.493999-4003) from Canada; dry bean (Phaseolus vulgaris) variety "Jaguar"-upright mid season and resistant to certain diseases (EC No. 493713) from USA.

Export

Twenty-two samples of different crops viz., safflower, berseem, soybean, groundnut and Lucerne were exported to two countries viz., Uzbekistan and Germany.

INTERNATIONAL AGRICULTURAL TRADE

Export

The total value of agricultural exports during the period April, 2001 to January, 2002 was Rs. 23666.38 crores which is higher by to 859.88 crores or 3.77 % as compared to the value of exports during the corresponding period of last year.

The increase in value of agricultural exports during the period under review has been primarily because of higher exports of Sugar by Rs. 1174.92 crores or 367.42%, Wheat by Rs. 901.15 crores or 709.06%, Rice (other than Basmati) be Rs.364.44 crores or 58.63%, Miscellaneous Processed items by Rs.165.79 crores or 43.97%, Paper/Wood Products by Rs.137.17 crores or 12.41%, and Fresh Vegetables by Rs.104.28 crores or 29.91%.

In contrast there was declines in the export of Marine Products by Rs.453.93 crores or 8.31%, Rice Basmati by Rs.281.72 crores or 16.74%, Castor oil by Rs.223.20 crores or 30.06%, Pulses by Rs.175.4 crores or 36.82%, Cotton Raw including waste by Rs.175.07 crores or 87.79%, and Meat and Preparation by Rs.149.24 crores or 13.30%, cashew by Rs.546.54 crores or 31.73% respectively.

The percentage share of agricultural exports in the total value of national exports during the period under review had declined marginally to 13.84 from 13.90 during the corresponding period of last year.

Import

The total value of agricultural imports during the period of April, 2001 to January, 2002 was Rs.13833.52 crores which is higher by Rs.3460.66 crores or 33.36% as compared to the value of import during the corresponding period of last year.

The increase in value of agricultural imports during the period under review has been primarily because of higher imports of Pulses by Rs.2299.58 crores or 685.11%, Cotton Raw and Waste by Rs.711.46 crores or 65.85%, Vegetable oils Fixed (edible) by Rs.451.51 crores or 8.95%, Wood and Wood Products by Rs.384.13 crores or 20.62%, and spices by Rs.162.43 crores or 77.23%.

On the other hand there was decline in the imports of Cashew nuts by Rs. 511.25 crores or 56.46%.

The percentage share of agricultural imports in the total value of national imports during the period under review has been higher at 6.82, compared with 5.40% during the corresponding period of last year.

MISCELLANEOUS DEVELOPMENTS

National Conference on Agriculture For Kharif Campaign 2002-03

- National Conference on Agriculture for Kharif Campaign 2002-03 was organized on 4th and 5th April, 2002 in New Delhi. The main objectives of the Conference were to review the performance of Rabi Crop season, preparation and fixation of crop-wise targets for the ensuing Kharif season in consultation with the State representatives of concerned Central Ministries and National Level Institutions.

International Cooperation

Indian delegation led by Agriculture Minister attended the 6th Cooperative Minister's Conference in Kathmandu, Nepal from 2-7 April, 2002

The Australian High Commissioner called on the Hon'ble Agriculture Minister on 16th April, 2002 to discuss measures for better cooperation between the two countries in the field of agricultural research.

NCDC

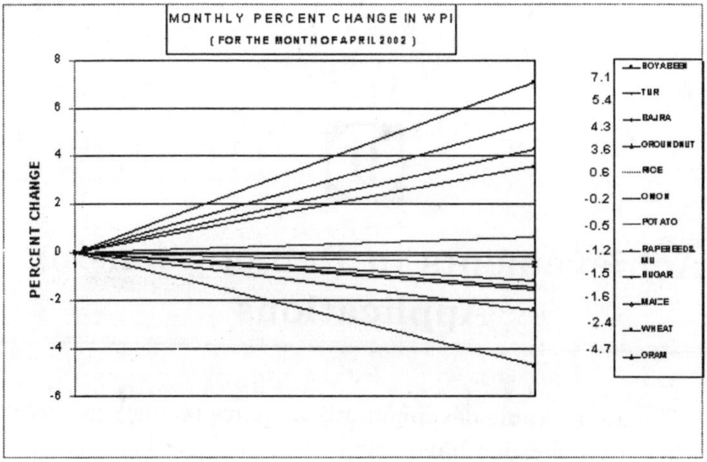

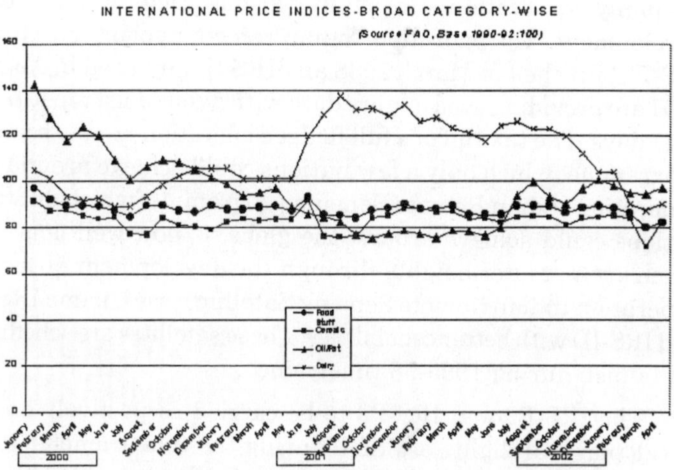

During the current financial year, 2002-2003, NCDC has approved financial assistance for the various post harvest agricultural an allied cooperative sector activities to the tune of Rs.969.49 lakhs and has released an amount totaling Rs.781.00 lakhs during the month of April, 2002.

9

Achievements in Remote Sensing Applications

The remarkable developments in space technology during the last two decades have firmly established their immense potential for the optimum utilization of this technology for taking up many application project in various sectors of national development. The operation Indian remote Sensing Satellites, IRS-IA launched in March 1988 an dIRS IB launched in August 1991 are providing good quality data with a combined repetitivity of 11 days. The take off of a full fledged operation remote sensing programme, which only a few nations could achieve around the generation Indian Remote Sensing programme, which only few nations could achieve around the globe, is now well poised to reach even greater heights through the development of second generation Indian Remote Sensing Satellite series, name IRS-IC and IRS-ID with better capabilities. These satellites are scheduled for launch during 1995-98 timeframe.

The IRS-P2 and IRS-P3 to be carried respectively on the developmental flights of PSLV during the time frame of 1994-96 are progressing well. Efforts are underway to realize an indigenously developed Ocean Satellite. Under the umbrella of National Natural Resources Management System (NNRMS), operationalisation of remote sensing in several new application areas was achieved with the active involvement of user agencies. IRS data is being used on an operational basis for several applications such as agriculture crop acreage and yield estimation, draught monitoring and assessment flood mapping, landuse and land cover mapping, wasteland management, urban planning, mineral prospecting, forest resources survey and management, soil mapping, water resources management, fisheries potential forecasting, coastal zone management environment impact assessment etc. a unique programme on integrated Mission of Sustainable Development aimed at generation of locale specific action plans for development at microlevel using integrated approach has been taken up covering one watershed/blocklevel using integrated approach has been taken up covering one in 7 districts have already been generated and they are being implemented. Further, Ministry of Rural Development has selected 92 blocks among the IMSD districts for implementation of Information system is progression satisfactorily. Department of Space (DOS) is providing adequate support for carrying out various national level projects. Facilities available at the state remote sensing centres and Central user departments also provide support for these projects. Towards human resources development, regular training programmes are being offered besides introduction of remote sensing in the curricula of many universities and institutions.

INTRODUCTION

The pressure of growing population, increased demand for food, fodder and fuelwood combined with rapid industrialization and urbanization have caused tremendous pressure on natural resources and environment. The consequent impact of these activities have given rise to crisis in agreoecosystems like land degradation, accelerated erosion, shifting cultivation, degradation of forests, increase in frequency of floods, pollution, urban sprawl etc. The challenge before us, therefore, is to reverse the process of degradation and undesirable changes in the environment in order to conserve and sustain the resource base of the country to meet the present demand as well as the future needs of the people.

In this context, the direct benefits from space technology and the applications driven approach adopted by the Indian Space Remote Sensing Programme have firmly established its immense potential to cater to the needs of national development. The evolution of National Natural Resource Management System (NNRMS) towards fully harnessing the potentials of space remote sensing and the development of the series of Indian Remote Sensing Satellites, besides establishment of necessary ground based data establishment of necessary ground based data reception processing and dissemination systems as well as remote sensing facilities at National Remote Sensing Agency (NRSA), Space Applications Centre (SAC) and Regional Remote Sensing (Service Centres (RRSSCs) for efficient and effective analysis of remotely sensed data are the major steps accomplished in pursuit of this goal. With the establishment of Remote Sensing Applications Centres in several States under many Governmental organizations, remote sensing today has come to stay as an integral part of the national development efforts in the vital sectors of agriculture, hydrology, geology, forestry, oceanography, mineral resources and distaster management like drought, flood, cyclone, earthquake, landslides crop pests, forest fires etc., thus touching every facet of national development. Today, India has acquired a strong self reliant base to harness the full potential of this technology and as a result, the national objective of achieving sustainable development at microlevel is being addressed through the integration of remotely sensed data with other relevant collateral information to arrive at locale specific, environment friendly, economically viable and culturally acceptable treatment packages.

Space and Ground Segments

The Indian Remote Sensing Satellite (IRS-A), the first in the operational series of Indian Remote Sensing Satellites launched in March 1988, has been functioning satisfactorily for the past 6 ½ year but still continues tpo provide quality data. The second satellite in the IRS series, IRS-IB, launched in August 1991, is performing very well. These two satellites have become the mainstay of the National Natural Resources Management System (NNRMS) IRS-1A/1B provides imagery from the two cameras, linear Imaging Self Scanners, LISS-I with both the resolution 72.5m and LISS-IIA and LISS-IIB both with a resolution of 36.25m. IRS-1A and 1B together provide imagery with a combined repetivity of 11 days. While IRS-IA has so far provided more than 5,00,000 scenes, IRS-1B has provided more than 2,00,000 scenes. The successful implementation of the operational IRS-IA 1B system in the country and the need to cater tot eh enhanced user demands in the 1990's has given rise to configuring the second generation remote sensing satellitesm IRS-IC and ID taking in to account the technology development scenario and user requirements during the nineties.

Future Satellite Programmes

The second generation of IRS Satellites namely IRs-1C and 1D which are now under development for launch in 1995 and 1998 respectively have made very good progress during the year. These satellites will have better spectral and spatial resolutions, more frequent revisits, stereo-viewing and onboard data recording facility.

The imaging sensors planned for IRS-IC and ID are a multi-spectral Linear Imaging Self Scanner (LISS-3) in visible and near Ir bands, a short Wave infrared (SWIR) band, a panchromatic camera with stereo viewing capability and a Wide Field Sensor (WIFS) in visible and near IR(Jayaraman et. al 1992). It is also planned to have onboard data recording capabilities to record the pay load data for wider data coverage/distribution. IRS-ID identical to IRS-IC will be in-orbit to ensure data continuity beyond the mid nineties.

The development flights of PSLV during the timeframe of 1994-96 are progressing well. The IRS-P2 will carry the payload flown onboard IRS-IA and IB in order to provide continuity of data services to the remote sensing user community in the country.

The IRS-P3 will carry a payload mix of sensors for application related to oceanography and vegetation dynamics. besides a scientific payload is planned to be included of experimental studies in X-ray astronomy. Thus IRS-P3 will carry a Modular Optoelectronic canner (MOS), a Wide field Sensor (WiFS) ad an X-ray astronomy payload.

Table 1 Orbital Characteristics of IRS-1C/1D

Orbit	:	Polar sun-synchronous
Altitude	:	817 km
Repetitivity	:	24 days
Local time of Equator Crossing	:	10.30 AM
Mission Life (planned)	:	3 years

Table 2 Characteristics of IRS-1C/1D Payloads

Characteristics	Payloads Linear Imaging Self Scanning Sensor (LISS-3)	Wide Field Sensor (WiFS)	Panchromatic Camera (PAN)
No. of Spectral Bands	4	2	1
Spectral Bands (microns)	B2 0.52 - 0.59 B3 0.62 - 0.68 B4 0.77 - 0.86 B5 1.55 - 1.70	B3 0.62 - 0.68 B4 0.77 - 0.86	0.50 - 0.75
Spatial Resolution (m)	23.5 for B2, B3, B4, and 70.5 for B5	188	Better than 10m
Swath (Km)	142 km	774	70 km with steering Range +26°

The capability for microwave remote sensing has also been achieved in the India through development of airborne C-band SAR, multifrequency micro-wave radiometer and multifrequency scatterometer. Based on the encouraging results obtained from several pilot scale studies on ocean applications and considering the serious interest in monitoring and forecasting of a sea state from meteorological point of view, efforts are underway to realize and indigenously developed Oceansat.

DATA RECEPTION, PROCESSING AND DISSEMINATION

The National Remote Sensing Agency (NRSA), Hyderabad continued to acquire and archive data from Indian Remote Sensing Satellites, IRS-IA and IRS-IB. In addition, data from other contemporary satellites, viz, Landsat NOAA and ERS-1 SAR are also being received. Augmention of ground segment elements for IRS-1C/1D data reception and processing is nearing completion. It is proposed to received SeaWiFS data after the launch SEASTAR satellite. Satellite data products are being disseminated to the users in the form of photographic films, paper prints, CCT's floppy and cartridge products. About 705 of the user demands in the country is met by IRs-1A/1B data.

As part of aerial remote sensing programme, about 759 ours of aerial flying were undertake during the year mainly for aeromagnetic survey, town and country planning, sea level rise, oil exploration and metropolitan developments.

Remote Sensing Applications

With concerted efforts by Department of Space jointly with user departments, several applications, agriculture water, geology, forestry, oceanography and marine resources. Extensive organizational and institutional support services have been established with active involvement of use agencies both at Central State levels. The scenario of operation applications and the projections for immediate future application in the country is given in Figure 1.. Highlights of major operation application mission projects carried out in the country consists of :

- Preharvest crop acreage and production estimates (CAPE) for wheat, rapeseed and mustard, Sorghum, rice, cotton and sunflower for large part of the country.
- Monitoring of seasonal drought conditions over the country based on satellite derived vegetation index.
- Near real time flood damage assessment in al the major flood prove river basins using optical and microwave data.
- Current landuse/landcover mapping for entire country towards agro-climatic zonal planning.
- Forest cover monitoring on a biennial basis to assess and detect changes
- Mapping of saline/alkaline soils for the entire country.
- Coastal landuse mapping for all maritime states of the country.
- Sea surface temperature (SST) retrieval and its applications including fisheries.
- Methodology development for retrieval of winds, waves, bathymetry, sea mounts, internál waves, ocean circulation etc., from ERS-1 microwave data.
- Applications of microwave SAR data for soil moisture assessment and crop identification.
- Geosphere Biospehre studies on carbon cycle in oceans, macro vegetation dynamics, forest biodiversity, forest eco dynamics etc.

Integrated Mission for Sustainable Development

Sustainable development of natural resources relies on maintaining the fragile balance between productivity functions and conservation practices through precise identification and systematic monitoring of problem area in various resources and developmental sectors. It also calls for application of alternate agricultural practices, crop rotations use bio-fertilisers, energy-efficient farming methods and reclamation of under utilised and wastelands, planned exploitation of mineral and ground water resources etc. There fore optimal and exploitation of the resources (both renewable and non-renewable resources) calls for an holistic approach. The synoptic view provide by satellite remote sensing offers technologically the appropriate method for studying land and water resources, characterizing the coherent agricultural zones and identifying the constraints/ecological problems at microlevel.

Effective use of space based remote sensing data suitably merged with collateral, socio economic and meteorological data through the use of geographic information system helps arriving at locale specific prescriptions to achieve sustainable development of natural resources of the region. The process of sustainable development packages evolving from such an integrated effort will be economically acceptable and environmentally friendly. Towards this, Department of space in 1988had initiated pilot studies in 21 perennially drought affected districts of the country to generate locale specific action plans. These pilot studies carried out has demonstrated the efficacy of using remote sensing based approach for optimal utilization of land and water resources towards combating drought on a long term basis. Based on the results obtained form these pilot studies, Department of Space has launched a major, unique programme on Integrated Mission for Sustainable Development. This mission, as of now, covers a total of 157 problem districts of the country, covering nearly 45% of India's geographical area which are perennially affected and tribal areas.

The methodology of study involves generation of thematic maps showing current landuse/landcover, types of wasteland, forest cover/types, surface water resources. Drainage pattern, potential ground water zones, land forms (geomorphology, geology (rock types, structural features, mineral occurence0, soil types etc using data from Indian Remote Sensing Satellite. The map showing slope/aspect is prepared using topographic contour information and the meteorological data (rainfall intensity distribution etc0. are collected form existing database. The integration of the various thematic maps and attributes data, and further analysis for identified alternatives for development are carried out using geographic information system to identify set of coherent micro-level land units which are unique in terms of their resources potential and problems.

Specific developmental plans for these units are arrived at in consultation with and close coordination between space scientists, experts from various central/state developmental departments, agricultural universities/research institutions, district level officials and local farmers, so as to ensure the technical feasibility and cultural acceptability of such action plans. Further, methodology has been developed to overlay the land capability map over the cadastral maps to provide information at the field levels.

Various elements of such action plans are prioritized and categorised as those relating to land and water resources and others. Sensitivity of each element of the action plan would also be studied to see visible regress over the coming years, once they are implemented. The parameters such as, vegetation index, forest cover, land use, agricultural production, ground water table, soil erosion, etc., would be identified for bench marking the impact of such an implementation.

So far, action plans have been generated for one watershed each in 7 districts. The action plans are being implemented by the district authorities for these watersheds. The initial feedback on the implementation of action plans in the watersheds of Anantapur has been encouraging as shown by increased ground water levels through water harvesting structures and consequem agncumetna activities.

The supports for implementation is derived from ongoing developmental programmes such as Drought Prone Area Development Programme (DPAP), Desert Development

Programme (DDP), Integrated Wasteland Development Programme (IWDP), National Watersheds Development Project for Rain-fed Areas (NWDPRA), Hill Area Development Programme (HADP), etc. It is also proposed to use satellite data for monitoring of the impact of these action plans. Further, in view of the advantages of the integrated approach wherein local specific action plans will be generated with cadastral overlays, Ministry of Rural Development has suggested taking up of 92 selected blocks from among the IMSD districts, on an urgent basis in a timeframe of 18 months. Ministry of Rural Development will provide funds for implementation of these action plans through pooling of resources from the various ongoing schemes for rural development.

National (Natural) Resources Information System (NRIS)

A National (Natural Resources Information System (NRIS) for the country has been evolved to aid decision makers at national/regiona/state/district/taluk levels.

A numbe of pilot scale studies on various themes viz., wasteland development, land capability classes, district level planning, regional mineral targeting, etc., were carried out towards implementation of NRIS. Several geographic information packages have also been developed indigenously to cater to computer based decision support systems.

Infrastructure/Facilities Development

Fuller utilisation of this technology by uses has been ensured through establishing appropriate remote sensing facilities at central and state level user departments/agencies. As many as 22 States have established Remote Sensing Application Centres, which are carrying out several application projects of relevance to their region, besides participating in national level projects. They have established a strong interaction with all the concerned users. The DOS Centres such as NRSA, Hyderabad; SAC, Ahmedabad and RRSSCs located at Bangalore, Dehradun, Jodhpur, Kharagpur and Nagpur continued to execute various national level missions/projects, user projects, application validation projects, technology and software development activities and conduct of regular training programmes for users.

Training and Education in Remote Sensing

With the increased awareness and utilisation of remote sensing in India, need for adequate number of trained manpower for harnessing the benefits of remote sensing technology has steeply gone up. Adequate efforts are being made to increase the present throughput of trained manpower (of about 800) in various themes in collaboration with central/state/academic institution by way of augmenting the existing training infrastructure.

Regular training courses are being conducted by several training institutions such as Indian Institute of Remote Sensing (IIRS, Dehradun), Centre of Studies for Resources Engineering (IIT, Bombay), Institute of Remote Sensing (Anna University, Madras), Survey of India, ecological Survey of India Training Institute, Forest Survey of India and Indian Agricultural Research Institute (IARI, Delhi).

Besides these regular courses, on the job training is being provided by National Remote Sensing Agency (NRSA, Hyderabad) and Space Applications Centre (SAC, Ahmedabad) for specific themes and training in digital analysis and GIS by RRSSCs. So far as many as 6300 scientists have been trained in remote sensing. Efforts are also on to introduce remote sensing evening school and college curriculum. Many universities have introduced remote sensing in their post-graduate courses as a full-fledged degree course or a part of a core subject.

International Collaboration

India has many collaborative programmes with several countries in promoting active cooperation in remote sensing. For example, the ESCAP/UNDP Regional Remote Sensing Programme (RRSP), under the execution of the ESCAP, is playing a crucial rle in promoting active cooperation in remote sensing among member counties of Asia-Pacific region, by bringing together experts from different areas who can share their experiences, disseminating information on available expertise, disseminating information on available expertise, disseminating information on available experts where needed.

The SHARES (Sharing of Experience) program initiated by India is also continuing to provide assistance to candidates from developing countries for participation in remote sensing training courses in India. The data reception/processing courses in India.

The data reception/processing facility at Norman, USA has been recently established, to receive data from India Remote Sensing Satellite (IRS) as part of arrangements between EOSAT, USA and Department of Space/Antrix/NRSA, India, IRS-IC data is also planned to be acquired at this station once the satellite is launched. The DLR of Germany is providing a payload called Modular Opto-electronic Scanner (MOS) proposed to be flown in IRS-P3.

CONCLUSION

India was achieved a viable, self-reliant remote sensing programme with the establishment of expertise and self sufficiency in operationalisation of the Indian Remote Sensing Satellite series, establishment of a well kuit infrastructure for reception, processing, dissemination, analysis and interpretation of remote sensing data, operatonalisation of remote sensing data, operationalation of remote sensing applications in a wide range of resource sensing applications in a wide range of resource themes and developmental sectors and development of a resource information system using Geographic Information techniques. With the launching of a unique planning system of intergrated mission for sustainable development using space remote sensing inputs coupled with GIS to provide a holistic approach and to meet the growing demand of the increasing population, the remote sensing is pinsed to play a key role in the overall development of the nation. The availability of data from second generation satellites will further enhance the effectiveness of the mission for national development at microleved.

10

Horticulture Research in India

INFRASTRUCTURE, ACHIEVEMENTS, IMPACT, NEEDS AND EXPECTATIONS

India has a wide variety of climate and soil on which a large range of horticultural crops such as, fruits; vegetables, potato and other tropical tuber crops; ornamental, medicinal and aromatic plants; plantation crops; spices, cashew and cocoa are grown. After attaining independence in 1947, major emphasis was laid on achieving self sufficiency in food production. Development of high yielding wheat varieties and high production technologies and their adoption in areas of assured irrigation paved the way towards food security ushering in green revolution in the sixties.It, however, gradually became clear that horticultural crops for which the Indian topography and agro climates are well suited is an ideal method of achieving sustainability of small holdings, increasing employment, improving environment, providing an enormous export potential and above all achieving nutritional security. As a result, due emphasis on diversification to horticultural crops was given only during the last one decade.

Research Infrastructure

The Indian Council of Agricultural Research is the premier agency which pioneered systematic research on agricultural crops in the country. Horticulture research in India received very little attention till the 3Rd fiva received very little attention till the 3Rd five year plan. The establishment of the Indian Institute of Horticultural Research at Bangalore and starting of eight All India Coordinated Crop Improvement Projects to cover different horticultural crops was a landmark in the history of horticulture in 4TH five year Plan (1969-74). Rapid expansion of infrastructure took place in 7^{Th} and 8^{Th} Plans. To-day, the horticultural research in the country is being carried out at eight ICAR institutes (with 26 regional stations),10 National Research centres (on major crops) and a Project Directorate on Vegetable crops.

Area specific, multi-disciplinary research is also being conducted under 14-All India Co-ordinated Research Projects each on Tropical, Sub-Tropical Arid Fruits; Vegetables, Potato, Tuber Crops, Mushrooms; Ornamental Crops, Medicinal and Aromatic crops; Palms, Cashew, Spices and Betel vine; and Post Harvest Technology at 215 centres located at various research Institutes, and State Agricultural Universities. In addition, four net work projects each on 'Hybrid research in vegetable crops', 'Drip irrigation in perennial horticultural crops', 'protected cultivation of ornamental crops' and 'Phytophthora disease of horticulture crops' are now in operation. Research on horticulture is also being undertaken at several multi-crop, multi-disciplinary Institutes.

Departments of Horticulture in 24 Agricultural Universof Horticulture in 24 Agricultural Universities, one deemed to be University and one full fledged University of Horticulture and Forestry are also engaged in horticultural research. Besides 280 adhoc schemes supported from Agriculture Produce Cess Fund and a number of foreign-aided projects have also been in operation on specific problems of different horticulture crops. As a result, the country now has a sound research infrastructure in horticulture to meet the growing needs and expectations of the fast developing horticulture industry.

Budgetary Support

The investment in horticulture research by the ICAR in the Central sector has increased significantly in the last two plans. The Plan allocation for horticultural crops started in 4TH Plan (1969-74) with a modest allocation of Rs. 34.78 million and was enhanced to Rs. 319.56 million in the 7th Plan (1985-90) and to Rs.1047 millions in the 8^{Th} Plan (1992-97). Non-Plan expenditure also increased from Rs. 73.55 million in the 5TH Plan to Rs. 768

million in 8^{Th} Plan. Overall increase in Plan investment in 25 years has been of the order of 2775.21 per cent. The per cent budget allocation for horticulture research out of the total budget for agriculture research rose from 6.1 in 5^{Th} to 6.5, 6.67and 7.7 in $6^{Th,}$ 7^{Th} and 8^{Th} five year plans respectivelySUP> and 8^{Th} five year plans respectively. Similarly, expenditure for Central Sector Schemes of the Department of Agriculture & Cooperation for horticulture crop development also rose tremendously from Rs. 20.5 million (4^{Th} Plan) to Rs. 76.18 million (5TH Plan), Rs. 146.37 million (6^{Th} Plan), Rs. 250 million (7^{Th} Plan) and Rs 10,000 million (8^{Th} Five Years Plan).

Manpower

Nearly one sixth of the total strength of 5906 scientists working in ICAR in different disciplines is allocated for horticulture research in ICAR Institutes. Besides, 560 scientists are working in State Agricultural Universities in ICAR funded All India Coordinated Projects. In addition, a large number of scientists are working in horticultural crops in State Agricultural Universities.

RESEARCH ACHIEVEMENTS

Introduction and Cultivation of New Crops

Several new crops have been introduced for commercial cultivation, eg. :

- Kiwi fruit in sub-mountain areas of North India.
- Olive in mid hills of North Western Himalayas.
- Low chilling stone fruits in the North Western plains.
- Oilpalm in some coastal states.
- Gherkin in south and west India.
- Baby corn and sweet corn in certain specific pockets.
- Broccoli, Brussels' Sprouts, Asparagus, Celery, Parsley near the cities.

Crop Improvement

- A large number of high yielding varieties developed in several horticultural crops e.g. fruits (76), vegetables

(160), potato (29), other tuber crops (24) ornamental crops (>300) palms (20), spices (51), cashew (33) and betel vine (1).

- First seedless variety of mango developed.
- 40 F1 hybrids developed in brinjal, tomato, chillies, cauliflower, carrot, capsicum and muskmelon.
- Self incompatible lines in cauliflower, gynodioecious lines in cucumber and muskmelon and genetic male sterile lines in tomato developed. Temperature tolerant strains of button mushroom developed.

Propagation of Quality Planting Material

- Standardised Propagation technique for many fruits hitherto propagated by seed.eg., *Aonla*, *bael*, *ber*, black pepper. cardamom, cashew, cassia, cinnamon, clove, custard apple, jack fruit, *jamun*, nutmeg, sapota and walnut.
- Standardisation of Seed Plot Technique resulting in successful disease free potato seed production in the tropics and sub tropics of the country. Standardised method of micro-propagation and in vitro micro-tuber production in potato.
- Identification of suitable parental lines for production of True Potato Seed (TPS)and standardised technology for raising commercial crops.
- Micropropagation protocols developed in bananaal crops.
- Micropropagation protocols developed in banana, black pepper, betel vine, cardamom, ginger and turmeric.
- P roduction of cococnut hybrids through establishment of Seed gardens of Tall (T) x Dwarf (D) and D x T hybrids.
- Standardised rootstocks in citrus, grape and apple.

Agrotechniques

- standardised high density plantations in banana, citrus, mango, and pineapple and high production technology in several crops eg., pineapple, black pepper and cardamom.

- Year round production technology in tomato and "off season" cultivation of onion and cauliflower developed.
- Arecanut, coconut and Potato, based cropping systems developed to maximise productivity under high management conditions.
- Standard used commercial use of several plant growth regulators and chemicals now commercially employed in production and quality improvement of horticultural crops eg., paclobutrazol for induction of flowering in mango; gibberellic acid for improving berry size and quality in grape, Maleic hydrazide for preventing sprouting in onion and potato, Dormex for hastening bud burst in grapes and; boron and calcium for changing flower cycle in some cucurbits.

Crop Protection

- Developed improved disease detection techniques such as ELISA and ISEM for improving seed quality and tissue culture technique for rapid multiplication of potato.
- Develolture technique for rapid multiplication of potato.
- Developed IPM for fruit borer in brinjal, diamond back moth in cabbage, thrips in chillies, phytophthora foot rot in black pepper, "Katte", rhizome rot in cardamom, rhizome rot in ginger, late blight and bacterial wilt of potato.
- Developed biological control measures for mealy bug in grape, fruit borer in tomato and okra.

Post Harvest Management

- Preharvest treatments to control post harvest losses in citrus, mango and grape standardised.
- Maturity standards for mango, guava, grape, litchi, *ber* standardised.
- Chemical treatment for regulation of ripening in mango, sapota, banana standardised.
- Optimum storage temperatures worked out for several fruits, vegetables and tuber crops.

- A mango harvester and fruit peeler; hand and pedal operator cassava chipping machine, harvesting tools(5-14 times efficient); Implements for mechanization of potato cultivation eg., oscillating tray type potato grader, fertilizer application cum line marker, potato culti ridger, soil crust breakers, potato digger and automatic potato planter diggers.
- Low cost environment friendly storage system for fruits, vegetables, potato and onion developed.

IMPACT OF RESEARCH

Fruits

Area under fruits increased from 1.22 million hectares to 3.35 million hectares in 1995-96.India wit 1.22 million hectares to 3.35 million hectares in 1995-96.India with a production of 41.50 million tonnes (1996-97) is the second largest fruit producer (next to China 45.46 million tonnes) with a share of 8% in world fruit production.

India produces 65% of world's mango, 11% of world's banana, ranking first in the production of both the crops. It has the highest productivity of grapes in the world. Significant expansion has taken up in *aonla*, *ber*, pomegranate and sapota cultivation.

Vegetables

India ranks second in the world vegetable production (71.59 million tonnes) after China. Vegetable production has increased three times during the last 50 years.

A large area is now covered with F1 hybrids in vegetable crops resulting in increased yield and better socio-economic status of farmers. Vegetables like tomato, cabbage, cauliflower, radish and onion are now produced almost round the year and India has attained self sufficiency in seed production of temperate vegetables.

Mushroom production has increased from 100 tonnes in 1970 to 30,000 tonnes in 1996-97. The productivity has increased from 10-12 Kg/m^2 in 1985 to 18-22 Kg/m^2 in 1995. Mushroom cultivation has spread to almost all parts of the country.

Potato

In potato, area, production and productivity has increased from 0.234 million hectares, 154 million tonnes and 6.59 t/ha in 1949-5million hectares, 154 million tonnes and 6.59 t/ha in 1949-50 to 1.14 million hectares, 1924 million tonnes and 16.9 t/ha respectively.

This increase is 12,4.9 and 2.6 times respectively. The annual compound growth rate for potato during this period was 6.07 compared to 5.6% for wheat, 2.7% for rice and 2.74 for total food grains. India is the only country in south east Asia having a national disease free seed production programme producing 2600 tonnes of breeder's seed annually.

Cassava

In cassava, productivity increased from 7t/ha in 1960-61 to 22t/ha during 1992 which is more than double the world average (9.81t/ha). Sago and starch industry based on cassava developed.

Floriculture

Protected cultivation of cut flowers started a decade back and India has already entered the world cut flower market. Micro propagated ornamental foliage plants are being exported in millions internationally. Export of dried flowers from India is increasing.

Coconut

In coconut, area has increased from 1 million hectares in 1980 to 1.793 million hectares in 1996-97. India has become one of the largest coconut producing country of the world. Production of coconut has gone up from 5677 million nuts to 13968 million nuts.

The productivity in coconut has increased from 5249 nuts/ha to 7808 nuts/ha. Coconut contributes 700 billion rupees to the GDP of the country. The contributes 700 billion rupees to the GDP of the country. The contribution of the crop to the total edible oil pool in India is around 6 per cent. India also exports coir and coir products derived from coconut husk to the tune of 2260 million Rupees.

Arecanut

India continues to dominate the world in area, production and productivity of arecanut and has achieved self sufficiency in arecanut production (0.27 million tonnes). Most of the production is domestically consumed.

Oilpalm

Area in oil palm has gone up from 200 ha in 1965 to 40,700 ha in 1996-97. Average productivity in oil palm plantations is now from 4-5 tonnes/ha which compares favourably with other countries.

Spices

India is the largest producer (2.48 million tonnes), exporter (0.20 million tonnes) and consumer of spices. Indian spices flavour foods in over 134 countries. Spice exports touched Rs. 11800 million during the last year.

Cashewnut

In cashewnut, area has increased from 0.176 million hectares in 1961 to 0.659 million hectares in 1996-97. The production in cashew has gone up from 0.079 million tonnes to 0.430 million tonnes in 1996-97. India exported cashew kernels worth Rs.13000 moillion (362 million $U.S during 1996-97).Export of cashew rising @ 27% per annum. These export earnings are exceeded only by coffee and rice among agri-exports.

Needs and Expectations

In spite of significant achievements in horticulture R&D, a number of challenges still need to be met. These are:

- Inadequate supply of quality planting material.
- Heavy losses caused by several biotic and abiotic stresses.
- Several unresolved chronic disorders.

As a result, the productivity per unit area is low resulting in high cost of production. Further, the quality of produce in many cases is far from satisfactory. The post harvest losses continue to be high. Full advantage has yet to be taken of several frontier areas eg., biotechnology, protected cultivation, computer aided management of inputs, integrated nutrient management, leaf nutrient standards, biofertilizers, integrated pest management and mycorrhiza.

There is also need for change both in the content and approach of research which can be taken up in partnership with private sector on aspects like production of hybrids, green house production of flowers, biotechnology, value addition and export. The future growth of horticulture industry will largely depend on new and globally competitive technologies. As such ambitious research programme is called for in horticultural crop in the following thrust areas.

Genetic Resources

- Introduction of some fruits eg. mangosteen, durian, rambutan, longan, macadamia an fruits eg. mangosteen, durian, rambutan, longan, macadamia and berries not yet commercially exploited in India.
- Widening genetic base in mango (*Mangifera* species of South East Asia), Citrus (newly developed rootstocks), apple (scab resistant cultivars), guava (coloured varieties), papaya (species and varieties) and litchi (varieties from South East Asia). Also, widening genetic base for improvement of medicinal and aromatic plants required by pharmaceutical industries.
- Enrichment of various germplasm collections with species/ cultivars which are high yielding and resistant/tolerant to different biotic and abiotic stresses.
- Exploitation of full potential for cultivation of avocado, kiwi and olive.
- Standardize long term techniques for cryopreservation of propagating materials and pollen grains.
- In situ conservation of endangered genetic wealth.

Crop Improvement

- Development of dwarf rootstocks/ scion varieties for high density planting and export in mango, litchi, sapota, citrus, *ber*, coconut, arecanut, oilpalm and cashewnut.

- To induce and exploit useful genetic changes through mutations in commercial cultivars.
- Development of rootstocks and scion varieties in fruits resistant/tolerant to major biotic and abiotic stresses, e.g. malformation in mango, guava rootstocks for wilt, citrus rootstocks against phytophthora, root wilt resistance in coconut, frost and PRophthora, root wilt resistance in coconut, frost and PRV resistance in papaya, weevil in sweet potato, cassava mosaic and stress tolerance in arecanut and spices.
- To develop F_1 hybrids in vegetable crops for yield, nutritional quality and export.
- Development of virus resistant potato varieties having high tuber dry matter and low accumulation of sugars during low temperature storage and varieties with high temperature tolerance.
- Evolving varieties with bolder nuts and higher shelling percentage in cashew.
- Domestication of indigenous medicinal plants with bulk demand both in the modern and traditional system of medicine.
- Studies on quality control, seed health, packing and storage of seeds of annual crops.

Crop Production

- Standardise rootstocks for all important fruit crops e.g. mango, guava, litchi, sapota, *ber* and walnut.
- To develop horticultural crop based cropping systems for different agro-ecological regions.
- To develop integrated nutrient management system i.e. efficient utilization of chemical fertilizers, use of bio-fertilizers and addition of organic material using leaf nutrient standards.
- Standardize water management practices in major crops including micro-irrigation and fertigation.
- Develop techniques of organic farming for export oriented horticultural crop.

- Standardize practices for production of horticulture crops partidardize practices for production of horticulture crops particularly flowers and vegetables under protected cultivation involving computer aided supply of inputs.
- Standardize production technology for quality crops for export e.g. mango, grape, litchi, cashew, potato and spices.

Crop Protection

- Develop IPM strategies for important pests of commercial crops.
- Develop biological control for important diseases and insects affecting commercial crop production.

Post Harvest Management

- To reduce losses occurring during harvesting, storage and transport and improve shelf life of perishable horticultural commodities.
- To conduct basic and applied research in CA/ modified atmospheric storage of high value perishable crops.
- Improve indigenous low cost storage systems developed for onion, potato, fruits and vegetable crops.
- Develop techniques for bulk preservation of fruit pulps. Improve drying systems for raisins, mushroom and different vegetables. Standardize technique for frozen vegetables.
- Initiate post harvest research on ornamentals with special emphasis on export market.
- Utilization of wastes for development of economically viable products.
- Development / fabrication of low energy requiring machinery for horticultural crop cultivation.

Biotechology

- To standardise in vitro culture techniq
    * To standardise in vitro culture techniques for mass multiplication of rootstock/scion of difficult to micro propagate plants like mango, guava, sapota, litchi, walnut, date palm, coconut and oil palm.

* Development of protocols for rapid propagation of seedless water melon, vegetable crops with male sterlity and self incompatibility barriers eg., tomato, capsicum and selected ornamental crops.
* Use of anther culture system for production of di-haploids for integration with breeding programmes.
* To identify molecular markers based on RAPD and RFLP in important horticultural crop varieties.
* Develop transgenic plants with endogenous resistance to insect pests eg. bacterial canker in kagzi lime, salt and drought tolerance in tomato and capsicum.

National Problems

Intensify interdisciplinary research to find solution to nationally important problems eg., malformation and irregular bearing in mango, wilt in guava, die back in citrus and root wilt in coconut.

CONCLUSIONS

India has a good natural resource base an adequate R&D infrastructure and excellence in several areas. As a result, the horticultural scenario of the country has been changing fast. Both production and productivity of several crops has increased manifold and India can boast itself as a leading horticultural country of the world. Many new crops have been introduced aral country of the world. Many new crops have been introduced and many others have adapted to non conventional areas. Some other crops are under adaptive trials. A number of turn key projects in mushroom and flower production have been established.Near self sufficiency has been achieved in many crops. Export of fresh as well as processed fruits has been increasing. The demand of horticulture produce is on the rise due to increasing population, changing food habits, realisation of high nutritional value of horticultural crops and greater emphasis on value addition and export. However, several challenges are yet to be met. These are, fast eroding gene pool, fast population build up, shrinking land and other natural resources, serious production constraints, biotic and abiotic constraints and huge post harvest losses. Further, in the era of globalisation,our produce has to be of international quality and globally competitive. Our future expansion of horticulture has also to be in arid and semi arid areas and on under utilized horticultural crops.

While the impact of green revolution in India was felt mainly in assured irrigation areas, horticultural crop production has brought prosperity even in arid and semi arid areas. Horticulture is no longer a leisurely avocation and is fast assuming position of a vibrant commercial venture. Nature has placed India in a state of advantage and it is now on us horticulturists to work towards ushering in a GOLDEN REVOLUTION in years to come in India.

INFRASTRUCTURE, ACHIEVEMENTS, IMPACT, NEEDS AND EXPECTATIONS

India has a wide variety of climate and soil on which a large range of horticultural crops such as, fruits; vegetables, potato and other tropical tuber crops; ornamental, medicinal and aromatic plants; plantation crops; spices, cashew and cocoa are grown. After attaining independence in 1947, major emphasis was laid on achieving self sufficiency in food production. Development of high yielding wheat varieties and high production technologies and their adoption in areas of assured irrigation paved the way towards food security ushering in green revolution in the sixties. It, however, gradually became clear that horticultural crops for which the Indian topography and agro climates are well suited is an ideal method of achieving sustainability of small holdings, increasing employment, improving environment, providing an enormous export potential and above all achieving nutritional security. As a result, due emphasis on diversification to horticultural crops was given only during the last one decade.

RESEARCH INFRASTRUCTURE

The Indian Council of Agricultural Research is the premier agency which pioneered systematic research on agricultural crops in the country. Horticulture research in India received very little attention till the 3rd Five Year Plan. The establishment of the Indian Institute of Horticultural Research at Bangalore and starting of eight All India Coordinated Crop Improvement Projects to cover different horticultural crops was a landmark in the history of horticulture in 4th Five Year Plan (1969-74). Rapid expansion of infrastructure took place in 7th and 8th Plans. Today, the horticultural research in the country is being carried out at eight ICAR institutes (with 26 regional stations), 10 National Research Centres (on major crops) and a Project Directorate on Vegetable crops.

Area specific, multi-disciplinary research is also being conducted under 14 All India Coordinated Research Projects each on Tropical, Subtropical and Arid Fruits; Vegetables, Potato, Tuber Crops and Mushrooms; Ornamental Crops, Medicinal and Aromatic crops; Palms, Cashew, Spices and Betel vine; and Post Harvest Technology at 215 centres located at various research Institutes, and State Agricultural Universities.

In addition, four net work projects each on hybrid research in vegetable crops, drip, irrigation in perennial horticultural crops, protected cultivation of ornamental crops and *Phytophthora* diseases of horticulture crops are now in operation. Research on horticulture is also being undertaken at several multi-crop, multi-disciplinary Institutes. Departments of Horticulture in 24 Agricultural Universities, one deemed to be University and one full fledged University of Horticulture and Forestry are also engaged in horticultural research. Besides 280 adhoc schemes supported from Agriculture Produce Cess Fund and a number of foreign-aided projects have also been in operation on specific problems of different horticulture crops. As a result, the country now has a sound research infrastructure in horticulture to meet the growing needs and expectations of the fast developing horticulture industry.

BUDGETARY SUPPORT

The investment in horticulture research by the ICAR in the Central sector has increased significantly in the last two Plans. The Plan allocation for horticultural crops started in 4th Plan (1969-74) with a modest allocation of Rs. 34.78 million and was enhanced to Rs. 319.56 million in the 7th Plan (1985-90) and to Rs. 1047 million in the 8th Plan (1992-97). Non-Plan expenditure also increased from Rs. 73.55 million in the 5th Plan to Rs. 768 million in 8th Plan.

Overall increase in Plan investment in 25 years has been of the order of 2775.21 per cent. The per cent budget allocation for horticulture research out of the total budget for agriculture research rose from 6.1 in 5th to 6.5, 6.67 and 7.7 in 6th, 7th and 8th five year plans, respectively.

Similarly, expenditure for Central Sector Schemes of the Department of Agriculture & Cooperation for horticulture crop development also rose tremendously from Rs. 20.5 million (4th Plan) to Rs. 76.18 million (5th Plan), Rs. 146.37 million (6th Plan), Rs. 250 million (7th Plan) and Rs 10,000 million (8th Five Years Plan).

Budgetary Support (Million Rupees)

Five year plans	Total for Agriculture Research	Share of Horticulture (%)	Total Development Support
IV 1969-74	6105	N.A	20.50
V 1974-78	7292	6.10	76.18
VI 1980-85	10684	6.50	146.37
VII 1985-90	8445	6.67	250.00
VIII 1992-97	15165	7.70	10,000.00

Manpower

Nearly one sixth of the total strength of 5906 scientists working in ICAR is allocated for horticulture research in ICAR Institutes. Besides, approximately, 560 scientists are working in State Agricultural Universities in ICAR funded All India Coordinated Projects. In addition, a large number of scientists are working on horticultural crops in State Agricultural Universities.

Total Scientists in ICAR	5906
Scientists working in the Division of Horticulture	832
Scientists working in other ICAR Institutes	150
% of Total	15
Scientists working in SAUs in ICAR funded projects	560

Research Achievements

Introduction and Cultivation of New Crops

Several new crops have been introduced for commercial cultivation, *e.g.*:

- Kiwi fruit in sub-mountain areas of North India
- Olive in mid hills of North Western Himalayas
- Low chilling stone fruits in the North Western plains
- Oilpalm in coastal states of Karnataka, Andhra Pradesh, *etc.*
- Gherkin in south and west India
- Baby corn and sweet corn in certain specific pockets, and
- Broccoli, Brussels' sprouts, asparagus, celery, parsley near the cities.

Crop Improvement

- A large number of high yielding varieties developed in several horticultural crops *e.g.* fruits (76), vegetables (160), potato (29), other tuber crops (24), ornamental crops (300), palms (20), spices (51), cashew (33) and betel vine (1).
- First seedless variety of mango developed.
- 40 F_1 hybrids developed in brinjal, tomato, chillies, cauliflower, carrot, capsicum and muskmelon.
- Self incompatible lines in cauliflower, gynodioecious lines in cucumber and muskmelon, genetic male sterile lines in tomato and temperature tolerant strains of button mushroom developed.

Propagation of Quality Planting Material

- Standardized propagation technique for many fruits hitherto propagated by seed. *e.g., aonla, bael, ber,* black pepper, cardamom, cashew, cassia, cinnamon, clove, custard apple, jack fruit, *jamun,* nutmeg, sapota and walnut.
- Standardized Seed Plot Technique resulting in successful disease free potato seed production in the tropics and sub

tropics of the country. Standardized method of micro-propagation and *in vitro* micro-tuber production in potato.

- Identification of suitable parental lines for production of True Potato Seed (TPS) and Standardized technology for raising commercial crops.
- Micropropagation protocols developed in banana, black pepper, betel vine, cardamom, ginger and turmeric.
- Production of coconut hybrids through establishment of Seed gardens of Tall (T) x Dwarf (D) and D x T hybrids.
- Standardized rootstocks in citrus, grape and apple.

Agrotechniques

- Standardized high density plantations in banana, citrus, mango and pineapple and high production technology in several crops *e.g.*, pineapple, black pepper and cardamom.
- Year round production technology in tomato and "off season" cultivation of onion and cauliflower developed.
- Arecanut, coconut and potato based cropping systems developed to maximize productivity under high management conditions.
- Standardized use of several plant growth regulators and chemicals now commercially employed in production and quality improvement of horticultural crops *e.g.*, paclobutrazol for induction of flowering in mango; gibberellic acid for improving berry size and quality in grape; Maleic hydrazide for preventing sprouting in onion and potato; Dormex for hastening bud burst in grapes; and Boron and Calcium for changing flower cycle in some cucurbits.

Crop Protection

- Developed improved disease detection techniques such as ELISA and ISEM for improving seed quality and tissue culture technique for rapid multiplication of potato.
- Developed IPM for fruit borer in brinjal, diamond back moth in cabbage, thrips in chillies, phytophthora foot rot

in black pepper, "Katte", rhizome rot in cardamom, rhizome rot in ginger, late blight and bacterial wilt in potato.

- Developed biological control measures for mealy bug in grape, fruit borer in tomato and okra.

Post Harvest Management

- Preharvest treatments to control post harvest losses in citrus, mango and grape standardized.
- Maturity standards for mango, guava, grape, litchi and ber standardized.
- Chemical treatment for regulation of ripening in mango, sapota and banana standardized.
- Optimum storage temperatures worked out for several fruits, vegetables and tuber crops.
- A mango harvester, fruit peeler, hand and pedal operator cassava chipping machine, harvesting tools (5-14 times efficient); Implements for mechanization of potato cultivation *e.g.*, oscillating tray type potato grader, fertilizer application cum line marker, potato culti-ridger, soil crust breakers, potato digger and automatic potato planter/diggers developed.
- Low cost environment friendly storage system for fruits, vegetables, potato and onion developed.

Impact of Research

Fruits

Area under fruits increased from 1.22 million hectares to 3.35 million hectares in 1995-96. India with a production of 41.50 million tonnes (1996-97) is the second largest fruit producer next to China (45.46 million tonnes) with a share of 8% in world fruit production.

India produces 65% and 11% of worlds mango and banana, respectively, ranking first in the production of both the crops. It has the highest productivity in grape in the world. Significant expansion has taken up in apple, *aonla, ber,* pomegranate and sapota cultivation.

Vegetables

India ranks second in the world vegetable production after China (71.59 million tonnes). Vegetable production has increased three times during the last 50 years.

A large area is now covered with F_1 hybrids in vegetable crops resulting in increased yield and better socio-economic status of farmers. Vegetables like tomato, cabbage, cauliflower, radish and onion are now produced almost round the year. India has attained self sufficiency in seed production of temperate vegetables.

Mushroom

Mushroom cultivation has spread to almost all parts of the country. Its production has increased from 100 tonnes in 1970 to 30,000 tonnes in 1996-97. The productivity has increased from 10-12 kg m^{-2} in 1985 to 18-22 kg m^{-2} in 1995.

Potato

In potato, area, production and productivity has increased from 0.234 million hectares, 154 million tonnes and 6.59 t/ha in 1949-50 to 1.14 million hectares, 1924 million tonnes and 16.9 t/ha respectively. This increase is 12, 4.9 and 2.6 times, respectively.

The annual compound growth rate for potato during this period was 6.07 compared to 5.6% for wheat, 2.7% for rice and 2.74 % for total food grains. India is the only country in South East Asia having a national disease free seed production programme producing 2600 tonnes of breeder's seed annually.

Production, Demand and Projections of Horticultural Crops

	1996-97		Demand		Target 2002	
	Area*	Production**	Area	Production	Area	Production
Fruits	4.54	46.97	5.24	59.47	4.93	56.00
Vegetables	5.12	80.80	6.96	131.2	5.73	108.00
Spices	2.54	2.78	2.94	4.43	2.60	3.90
Coconut	2.00	9.75	2.67	15.60	2.57	15.00
Cashew	0.63	6.45	0.69	0.80	0.60	0.70
Arecanut	0.24	0.31	0.24	0.39	0.25	0.39
Total	15.07	141.06	18.74	211.89	16.68	183.99

*Area in million hectares; **Production in million tonnes

Cassava

In cassava, productivity has increased from 7t/ha in 1960-61 to 22t/ha during 1992 which is more than double the world average (9.81t/ha). Sago and starch industry based on cassava has been developed.

Floriculture

Protected cultivation of cut flowers started a decade back and India has already entered the world cut flower market. Micro propagated ornamental foliage plants are being exported in millions internationally. Export of dried flowers from India is increasing.

Coconut

In coconut, area has increased from 1 million hectares in 1980 to 1.793 million hectares in 1996-97. India has become one of the largest coconut producing country of the world.

Production of coconut has gone up from 5677 million nuts to 13968 million nuts.

The productivity in coconut has increased from 5249 nuts/ha to 7808 nuts/ha. Coconut contributes 700 billion rupees to the GDP of the country. The contribution of the crop to the total edible oil pool in India is around 6 per cent. India also exports coir and coir products derived from coconut husk to the tune of 2260 million Rupees.

Export of Horticultural Produce

Arecanut

India continues to dominate the world in area, production and productivity of arecanut and has achieved self sufficiency in arecanut production (0.27 million tonnes). Most of the production is domestically consumed.

Oilpalm

Area under oil palm has gone up from 200 ha in 1965 to 40,700 ha in 1996-97. Average productivity in oil palm plantations is now 4-5 tonnes/ha which compares favourably with other countries.

Spices

India is the largest producer (2.48 million tonnes), exporter (0.20 million tonnes) and consumer of spices. Indian spices flavour foods in over 134 countries. Spice exports touched Rs. 11800 million during the last year.

Cashewnut

In cashewnut, area has increased from 0.176 million hectares in 1961 to 0.659 million hectares in 1996-97. The production in cashew has gone up from 0.079 million tonnes to 0.430 million tonnes in 1996-97. India exported cashew kernels worth Rs. 13000 million (362 million $US during 1996-97). Export of cashew rising @ 27% per annum. These export earnings are exceeded only by coffee and rice among agri-exports.

Needs and Expectations

In spite of significant achievements in horticulture R&D, a number of challenges still need to be met. These are:

- Inadequate supply of quality planting material,
- Heavy losses caused by several biotic and abiotic stresses, and
- Several unresolved chronic disorders.

As a result, the productivity per unit area is low, resulting in high cost of production. Further, the quality of produce in many cases is far from satisfactory. The post harvest losses continue to be high. Full advantage has yet to be taken of several frontier areas *e.g.*, biotechnology, protected cultivation, computer aided management of inputs, integrated nutrient management, leaf nutrient standards, biofertilizers, integrated pest management and mycorrhiza. There is also need for change both in the content and approach of research which can be taken up in partnership with private sector on aspects like production of hybrids, green house production of flowers, biotechnology, value addition and export. The future growth of horticulture industry will largely depend on new and globally competitive technologies. As such, ambitious research programme is called for in horticultural crops in the following thrust areas.

Genetic Resources

- Introduce fruits like mangosteen, durian, rambutan, longan, macadamia and berries not yet commercially exploited in India.
- Widen genetic base in mango (*Mangifera* species of South East Asia), Citrus (newly developed rootstocks), apple (scab resistant cultivars), guava (coloured varieties), papaya (species and varieties) and litchi (varieties from South East Asia and China). Also, widen genetic base for improvement of medicinal and aromatic plants required by pharmaceutical industries.
- Enrich germplasm collections with species/ cultivars which are high yielding and resistant/tolerant to different biotic and abiotic stresses.
- Exploit full potential for cultivation of avocado, kiwi and olive.
- Standardize long term techniques for cryopreservation of propagating materials and pollen grains.
- *In situ* conservation of endangered genetic wealth.

Crop Improvement

- Develop dwarf rootstocks/ scion varieties for high density planting and export in mango, litchi, sapota, citrus, *ber*, coconut, arecanut, oilpalm and cashewnut.
- Induce and exploit useful genetic changes through mutations in commercial cultivars.
- Develop rootstocks and scion varieties in fruits resistant/ tolerant to major biotic and abiotic stresses, *e.g.* malformation in mango, guava rootstocks for wilt, citrus rootstocks against phytophthora, root wilt resistance in coconut, frost and PRV resistance in papaya, weevil in sweet potato, cassava mosaic and stress tolerance in arecanut and spices.
- Develop F_1 hybrids in vegetable crops for yield, nutritional quality and export.

- Development of virus resistant potato varieties having high tuber dry matter and low accumulation of sugars during low temperature storage and varieties with high temperature tolerance.
- Evolving varieties with bold nuts and higher shelling percentage in cashew.
- Domestication of indigenous medicinal plants with bulk demand both in the modern and traditional systems of medicine.
- Studies on the quality control, seed health, packing and storage of seeds of annual crops.

Crop Production

- Standardise rootstocks for all important fruit crops *e.g.* mango, guava, litchi, sapota, *ber* and walnut.
- Develop horticultural crop based cropping systems for different agroecological regions.
- Develop integrated nutrient management system *i.e.* efficient utilization of chemical fertilizers, use of bio-fertilizers and organic material using leaf nutrient standards.
- Standardize water management practices in major crops including microirrigation and fertigation.
- Develop techniques of organic farming for export oriented horticultural crops.
- Standardize practices for production of horticulture crops particularly flowers and vegetables under protected cultivation involving computer aided supply of inputs.
- Standardize production technology for quality crops for export *e.g.* mango, grape, litchi, cashew, potato and spices.

Crop Protection

- Develop IPM strategies for important pests of commercial crops.
- Develop biological control for important diseases and insects affecting commercial crop production.

Post Harvest Management

- Reduce losses occurring during harvesting, storage and transport and improve shelf life of perishable horticultural commodities.
- Conduct basic and applied research in CA/ modified atmospheric storage of high value perishable crops.
- Improve indigenous low cost storage systems developed for onion, potato, fruits and vegetable crops.
- Develop techniques for bulk preservation of fruit pulps, improve drying systems for raisins, mushroom and different vegetables, and standardize technique for frozen vegetables.
- Initiate post harvest research on ornamentals with special emphasis on export market.
- Utilize wastes for development of economically viable products.
- Develop/fabricate low energy requiring machinery for horticultural crop production.

Biotechnology

- To standardise *in vitro* culture techniques for mass multiplication of rootstock/scion of difficult to micro propagate plants like mango, guava, sapota, litchi, walnut, date palm, coconut and oil palm.
- Development of protocols for rapid propagation of seedless water melon; vegetable crops with male sterility and self incompatibility barriers *e.g.*, tomato and capsicum and selected ornamental crops.
- Use of anther culture system for production of di-haploids for integration with breeding programmes.
- To identify molecular markers based on RAPD and RFLP in important varieties of horticultural crops.
- Develop transgenic plants with endogenous resistance to insect pests *e.g.* bacterial canker in kagzi lime, salt and drought tolerance in tomato and capsicum.

National Problems

Intensify interdisciplinary research to find solutions to nationally important problems *e.g.*, malformation and irregular bearing in mango, wilt in guava, die back in citrus and root wilt in coconut.

CONCLUSIONS

India has a good natural resource base, an adequate R&D infrastructure and excellence in several areas. As a result, the horticultural scenario of the country has been changing fast. Both production and productivity of several crops has increased manifold and India can boast itself as a leading horticultural country of the world.

Many new crops have been introduced and many others have adapted to non conventional areas. Some other crops are under adaptive trials. A number of turn key projects in mushrooms and flower production have been established. Near self-sufficiency has been achieved in many crops.

Export of fresh as well as processed fruits has been increasing. The demand of horticulture produce is on the rise due to increasing population, changing food habits, realisation of high nutritional value of horticultural crops and greater emphasis on value addition and export. However, several challenges are yet to be met. These are, fast eroding genepool, fast population build up, shrinking land and other natural resources, serious production constraints, both biotic and abiotic and huge post harvest losses. Further, in the era of globalisation, produce has to be of international quality and globally competitive. The future expansion of horticulture has to be in and semiarid areas and on under utilized crops.

While the impact of green revolution in India was felt mainly in assured irrigation areas, horticultural crop production has brought prosperity even in and semiarid areas. Horticulture is no longer a leisurely avocation and is fast assuming position of a vibrant commercial venture. Nature has placed India in a state of advantage and it is now on us horticulturists to work towards ushering in a GOLDEN REVOLUTION in years to come in India.

RESEARCH PREPAREDNESS

The horticulture scenario of the country is rapidly changing. The production and productivity of horticultural crops have increased manifold. Production of fruits and vegetables has tripled in the last 50 years. The productivity has gone up by three times in banana and by 2.5 times in potato.

Today horticultural crops cover about 25 per cent of total agricultural exports of the country. The corporate sector is also showing greater interest in horticulture. A major shift in consumption pattern of fresh and processed fruits and vegetables is expected in the coming century. There will be greater technology adoption both in traditional horticultural enterprise as well as in commercial horticulture sectors. Diversification and value addition will be the key words in the Indian horticulture in the 21st Century.

Horticulture research in India is about four decades old. Systematic research on fruit, vegetable and ornamental crops began in 1954 with the initiation of independent institutions and programmes.

The research agenda is designed relevant to national plans and priorities for the horticulture development. Today, eight ICAR institutes with 27 regional stations, 1 project directorate, 10 national research centres, 16 all India coordinated research projects (AICRPS) with 223 research stations, 1 full-fledged university of horticulture, 25 state agricultural universities and 7 multi-disciplinary institutes of the ICAR are engaged in horticulture research.

In addition, a few R&D establishments of crop/commodity boards and private sectors are providing research support to Indian horticulture. Research system in horticulture is now geared to provide necessary technological support to the expanding horticultural industry.

The research efforts in the past were mainly concentrated on crop improvement, propagation of seed/planting material, agrotechniques, crop protection and post harvest management. Some of the improved technologies developed are enumerated below.

Technology Generation

Varietal Development

Among the fruit crops, improved high yielding mango varieties, Mallika, Amrapali, Ratna, Sindhu, Arka Aruna, Arka Puneet, Dashehari-51 and hybrids namely CISH-M-1 and CISH-M-2 have been developed. Mallika is coming up in southern states like Karnataka and Amrapali is performing well in eastern India. Dashehari-51, a regular bearing cultivar with about 38 % higher productivity than the normal Dashehari, has been identified after 14 years of rigorous selection. In guava, three selections, namely Lalit, CISH-G-1 and CISH-G-2 have been developed for domestic and export markets. The fruits of Lalit are of medium size weighing about 150 g each and suitable for both table and processing purposes. In banana, high yielding hybrids like FHIA-01 and FHIA-03 are promising for replacing varieties, Panchananda and Bluggoe, respectively. Cultivar, Saba is found promising under sodic soils.

In addition, high yielding varieties like Col, Hl and H_2 have been developed. In grape, superior and high yielding varieties have been developed *e.g.* Beauty Seedless and Pusa Seedless and early ripening variety, Perlette for cultivation under North Indian conditions and Anab-e-Shahi, Dilkhush, Thompson Seedless, Tas-A-Ganesh, Sonaka, Bangalore Blue and Pachadraksha for south Indian conditions. In citrus, high yielding and cluster bearing varieties of acid lime have been developed. *e.g.*, Rough Lemon, Rangpur Lime, Pramaini, Vikram PKM-1. Trifoliate oranges, namely Flying Dragon and Rich 16-6 are dwarfing types. In papaya, high yielding superior varieties both for table purpose and papain production have been developed. *e.g.*, Co-1 to Co-7, Coorg Honey Dew, Pusa Delicious, Pusa Majesty, Pusa Giant and Pusa Nanha. In apple, superior hybrids have been developed. *e.g.*, Lal Ambari, Sunehari. Red Spur, Star Crimson, Golden Spur, Red Chief, Oregon Spur, Skyline Supreme and Vance Delicious have been identified. Tissue culture protocols for micro-propagation of two commercial varieties have been developed.

Among the vegetable crops, more than 130 open pollinated varieties, 36 hybrids, 3 synthetics and 29 resistant varieties of 20 vegetable crops have been developed and released for cultivation in different agro-climatic regions. These include 40 in tomato, 45 in brinjal, 13 in cauliflower, 12 in chillies, 20 in pea, 9 in musk melon, 16 in onion and 44 in other crops.

In potato, 33 high yielding varieties have been developed indigenously for large scale cultivation in different regions. Kufri Ashoka and Kufri Pukhraj mature in 75 days. Kufri Jawahar and Kufri Satluj are field resistant to late blight. Kufri Jawahar has most ideal plant type for inter-cropping. Kufri Chipsona-1 and Kufri Chipsona-2 have been developed with excellent processing attributes, comparable to exotic varieties. Kufri Swarna resistant to golden nematode is ideal for Nilgiri Hills.

In tuber crops, improved varieties of different tuber crops have been recommended/released for commercial cultivation. These includes 9 varieties of cassava, 15 varieties of sweet potato, 6 varieties of colocasia, 3 varieties each of greater yam and lesser yam, 1 each of *Amorphophallus,* taro and yambean. Cassava varieties, Sree Visakham and Sree Prakash are popular in Kerala. Triploid clone, Sree Harsha with high dry matter and starch content is suitable for industrial belt of Tamil Nadu. Two early maturing varieties Sree Jaya and Sree Vijya have been released for culinary purposes. Elephant foot yam variety, Am-15 has been released with high yield potential of 41 t/ha.

Among the plantation and spice crops, India is the first country to exploit hybrid vigour in coconut. Twelve hybrids involving tall and dwarf parents and 4 varieties have been released for commercial cultivation. These varieties yield 21 to 89 % more than the local cultivars. Some of the released varieties like Chandra Kalpa and Pratap (Banawali Green Round) are receiving wide acceptance of farmers. Chowghat Green Dwarf variety is good for tender coconut purpose. In arecanut, 4 high yielding varieties, namely, Mangala, Sumangala, Sreemangala and Mohitnagar have been developed, giving about 30 % higher yield than the local cultivars.

In oil palm, first efforts for improvement were made by producing Tenera hybrids using Pisifera pollen imported from Nigeria. Dura x Pisifera hybrids are field tested in East and West Godavari districts, Khammam and Krishna districts of Andhra Pradesh, with yield potential of 20-25 tonnes/ha of FFB from the fifth year. In cashew, 22 region specific selections and 12 hybrids with yield potential of 1.5-2 tonnes of raw nuts/ha have been produced and released for commercial cultivation. The present standards fixed for cashew varieties include export grade kernels of W-210 to W-240 and at least one tonne per ha yield with 30 per cent shelling. In black pepper, 6 varieties, namely, Sreekara, Subhakara, Palode-2, Panniyur-2, Panniyur-4, Panchami and Pournami, and 2 hybrids *viz.* Panniyur-1 and Panniyur-4 have been developed. In cardamom, a number of improved varieties have been developed and released for commercial cultivation *e.g.*, CCS-1, Mudigere-1, PV-1, ICRI-1 and ICRI-2. In ginger, varieties like Suprabha, Suruchi, Suravi and Varada have been developed. In turmeric, several varieties *viz.*, Co-1, Krishna, Sugandham, BSR-1, Suvarna, Roma, Suroma, Rajendra Sonia, Sugana, Sudarshana, Ranga, Rasmi, Prabha, Prathiba, Mega Turmeric and RCT-1 have been developed with yield potential of up to 44 tonnes of fresh rhizomes per ha. Three high yielding cinnamon lines, namely, Navashree, Nithyashree and Konkan Tej have been released for cultivation.

Seed/planting Material Propagation

In most of the fruit crops, vegetative propagation techniques have been standardized. Soft wood grafting has been standardized for mango, sapota, custard-apple and jackfruit. Other vegetative propagation techniques have been developed for *ber, aonla,* jackfruit, custard-apple and *bael*. In mango, veneer grafting and stone-grafting is practised commercially. Mango variety, Vellaikolumban is suitable semi-dwarfing rootstock for Alphonso. Old unproductive mango trees can be rejuvenated successfully by pruning the 4th order branches during December-January. Flowering and fruiting are regular in pruned trees. For mandarin orange, Rangpur lime is a drought hardy rootstock. In grapes, Dogridge and Salt Creek (Ramsey) are suitable for minimizing adverse effects of soil salinity on Thompson Seedless. A tissue culture technique for mass multiplication of Dogridge has been standardised. In banana, sword suckers of 700-1000 g are optimum. Rhizomes with active lateral buds and dead central buds are preferred for distant transportation in western India. Double paring and shade drying followed by dipping in Monocrotophos

(0.5 %) and Bavistin (0.2 %) is recommended to disinfect nematodes and soil borne fungi. Tissue cultured banana plants are now commercially adopted for their uniformity in flowering and produce. Shoot-tip grafting technique in citrus has been considerably advanced.

In vegetable crops, seed production of over 120 open pollinated high yielding varieties of different vegetables has been well established in the country. Hybrid seed production has become easier with the development of male sterile lines in tomato, self incompatible lines in cauliflower and gynoecious lines in cucumber and muskmelon. In brinjal, functional male sterility controlled by a single recessive gene has been identified. Temperature barrier in cole crops (cabbage and cauliflower) has been overcome by developing heat tolerant hybrids. It is now possible to cultivate cabbage and cauliflower in southern India. Development of tomato varieties resistant to bacterial wilt has made their cultivation successful in non-traditional areas. Onion seed production technology for cultivation in kharif season has been developed for north Indian states especially, Haryana, Punjab and western Uttar Pradesh.

Seed Plot Technique has been developed for production of disease-free potato seed in plains. It is widely adopted by farmers. A new technology for raising commercial crop of potato using 'True Potato Seed' (TPS) has been developed and standardized as supplementary technology to the traditional tuber grown crop. Two TPS populations, TPS-C-3 and HPS-113 are recommended for commercial production in Bihar, Gujarat, Tripura and West Bengal. Micropropagation protocols have been developed in banana, oil palm, cashew, black pepper, ginger, *etc*. Seed gardens of Tall (T) x Dwarf (D) and D x T hybrids have been established for production of coconut hybrids.

Agrotechniques

In fruit crops, improved agrotechniques developed have helped the farmers in improving the productivity and quality of produce. Soil application of paclobutrazol (4 g/tree) increase flowering and fruiting in mango on commercial scale in coastal Maharashtra. It also controls irregular bearing in cultivar Dashehari. Spray of NAA @ 200 ppm in October is recommended for control of malformation. Heavy fruit drop at maturity in cultivar Langra can be controlled by spraying NAA (20 ppm). In guava, double spray of 10 and 20 % urea on cultivars, Allahabad Safeda and Sardar twic at bloom eliminate poor quality rainy season crop and increases winter season yield by 3 and 4 times, respectively. Application of neem coated urea (800 g/plants) yields 98 kg fruits/ plant in variety, Sardar compared to 37 kg from untreated plants. In banana, high density planting (4550 plants/ha) yield up to 174 t/ha. Adoption of improved technology in Maharashtra has resulted in fruit yield increase up to 52 t/ha. In citrus, two grafting methods using inverted 'T' cut and apical triangle cut have been developed with overall success of around 36% using either method. For accelerating the survival of growth, shoot tip grafts, the successful grafts are double grafted (side grafted) on vigorous green-house grown Rough Lemon and Rangpur Lime seedlings. Rangpur Lime rootstock is found superior for sweet oranges and mandarins. In papaya, closer spacing of 1.4 x 1.4 m is recommended for high yield. Drip irrigation techniques have been standardized. In banana, it has resulted in production gain (60-70%) and early harvesting (40-50 days), besides improved water efficiency. Likewise, in grapes higher yields have been obtained with better water use efficiency (11 %).

In vegetable crops, improved production technology has been developed for major crops. Drip irrigation is economical in tomato and brinjal. In cucumber, replenishment of evaporation loss through irrigation resulted in maximization of yield of quality fruits. Drip irrigation in watermelon provided 33% higher yield with a water saving of 40%. Nutrient requirements and fertiliser schedules have been worked out crop-wise and recommended for different agro-climatic regions. In leguminous vegetables, high N depresses nodulation. The VAM fungi increases P availability to plants. In all leguminous vegetables, inoculation of the VAM fungi along with *Rhizobium* culture is beneficial. Production technologies for *kharif* onion in northern India and long day type onions for high altitudes have been standardized. Pendimethalin (Stomp) has been found effective in controlling weeds in tomato, brinjal, chilli, bell pepper and okra. In potato, a number of potato-based multiple and inter cropping systems have been developed for different potato growing regions. Intercrop combinations with sugarcane in Maharashtra, wheat in Chhota Nagpur area and linseed in central Uttar Pradesh are found remunerative. A suitable method of urea application has also been worked out.

In tuber crops, short duration legumes *viz.*, groundnut and French bean and cowpea can be successfully inter-cropped with cassava. Short-duration cassava, Sree Prakash is ideal in double cropped rice fields. Studies on cassava-based multiple cropping systems involving banana, coconut, *Leucaena* and Eucalyptus, have shown banana-cassava combination to give maximum root yield. Banana and coconut combination reduces soil loss and surface run-off considerably.

Dioscorea and elephant foot yam with banana, Nendran can generate an additional income of Rs 20,000/-over the sole crop of banana. For Inter-cropping *Dioscorea* in coconut garden, the ideal planting density is 9000 plants/ha. When *Amorphophallus* is raised as an inter-crop in coconut garden, one third dose of recommended fertilizers is sufficient. Inoculation with VAM fungi in cassava give about 15-20% increase in yield.

Among the plantation and spice crops, density of 175 coconut palms/ha (7.5 m x 7.5 m spacing) is found ideal. In general, NPK application of 500:320:1200 g/palm/year is found optimum. A multi-storied cropping system involving black pepper trained on coconut trees, and cocoa in between the rows of coconut and pineapple in the ground floor has been found ideal for exploiting light, soil and air spaces.

In arecanut, application of NPK (100:40:140 g) and green leaf (14 kg) per palm per year is recommended for coastal regions of Kerala and Karnataka and for plains of West Bengal, Karnataka and Assam. In oil palm, application of NPK (1200:600:1200 g/palm) is found to give 17.1 tonne of FFB per ha. In black pepper, rapid methods for production of rooted cuttings of pepper have been developed and a commercial protocol has been standardised for micropropagation of black pepper. Ginger yield could be increased up to 33 percent by application of neem cake at the rate of two tonnes per ha and the fertiliser schedule of 75 kg each of N, P_2O_5 and K_2O. Technology for storage of ginger seed rhizome is standardised and recommended.

Protection Technologies

For major fruit crops, plant protection schedules have been developed for the control of significant insect-pests for wider adoption. In the recent years, research efforts are directed to devise eco-friendly, economical and long lasting control measures. Success has been achieved in biological control of mealy bugs in mango and guava.

The *Beauveria bassiana* has been found killing mango mealy bug and hopper. In grapes, integrated management of *Spodoptera* caterpillar involving light and pheromone traps, NPV and neem based insecticides and biological control of mealy bug by the beetle *Cryptolaemus montrouzieri* have been standardized. Studies on pesticide residues have resulted in working out of safe-waiting periods for harvesting and consumption of fruits.

In vegetable crops, about 50 improved measures for efficient management of diseases and 23 for insect-pests have been worked out and popularized in different agro-climatic regions in the country. Integrated pest management (IPM) for controlling diamond back moth on cabbage through a trap crop like mustard has been demonstrated. Fruit borer *(H. armigera)* on tomato can be controlled by the release of *Trichogramma pretiosum* alone and in combination with HaNPV.

In potato, integrated management schedules for control of bacterial wilt and tuber moth have been developed. A late blight forecasting system has been developed for the hills.

Among the tuber crops, the major diseases affecting tuber crops are cassava mosaic and brown leaf spot in cassava, *Phytophthora* leaf blight in colocasia, *Fusarium* wilt in elephant yam and virus diseases of sweet potato.

Foliar sprays of Bavistin (0.1%) combined with disodium and dipotassium phosphates (100 ppm) and calcium sulphate at 15-day interval was found to check foliar diseases in sweet potato. The major pests include spider mites, scale insects and white fly on cassava, weevil on sweet potato, defoliators, aphids and mites on colocasia, and scales and mealy bugs on yams and elephant yam. Cultural methods for weevil control include clean cultivation, destruction of alternate hosts and timely harvest. An effective IPM package using synthetic sex pheromone has been developed. Control measures involving insecticides have been evolved for the control of pests of other tuber crops.

Among the plantation and spice crops, bud rot of coconut caused by *Phytophthora palmivora* can be effectively controlled by spraying Bordeaux mixture. Calyxin root feeding and drenching of soil with 1% Bordeaux mixture along with neem cake application @ 5 kg per palm per year is recommended for controlling Thanjavur wilt disease reported in Tamil Nadu, Andhra Pradesh and Karnataka.

A package of practices has been developed for managing mycoplasma like organisms (MLOs) in root wilt affected coconut palms in Kerala and Thatipaka disease affected palms in Andhra Pradesh. Eradication of all root wilt affected palms is recommended.

In cashew, tea mosquito bug (TMB) can be effectively controlled through a schedule of spray coinciding with flushing, flowering and fruiting. For effective control of stem and root borer infestation, constant monitoring and adoption of strict sanitation in the plantations coupled with prophylactic application of coal tar and kerosene in the ratio of 1:2 on trunks are recommended. In black pepper, spraying Bordeaux mixture (1 %) and drenching the soil with copper oxychloride (0.2 %) is found effective in managing *Phytophthora* foot rot.

Post Harvest Management Technologies

The post harvest handling of fruits and vegetables accounts for 20-30% of losses at different stages of storage, grading, packing, transport and finally at marketing as a fresh produce or in processed form. A number of improved technologies have been developed for commercial exploitation.

An on-farm, low cost, environment friendly cool chamber, Zero Energy Cool Chamber has been developed using locally available material. The principle of evaporative cooling reduces the inside temperature by as much as 17-18 °C and keeps the relative humidity above 90% during peak summer. The chamber increases the shelf life and reduces PLW of banana, mango, orange lime, grape fruit, tomato and potato in different situations in India. Maturity standards for mango, guava, grape, litchi and *ber* and chemical treatments for regulation of ripening in mango, sapota and banana have been standardised. Optimum storage temperatures worked out for several fruits, vegetables and tuber crops.

A mango harvester, fruit peeler, hand and pedal operator cassava chipping machines, harvesting tools (5-14 times efficient), coconut dehusking machine, implements for mechanization of potato cultivation and other crops have been developed.

A number of improved technologies have been developed for commercial exploitation *viz.*, tent type foldable solar dryer, packaging boxes for distant transportation of apple, mango, citrus and plum, production of value added products-pectin from peel and flour from mango fruit kernel, production of fruit post carbonated beverages *etc.*

Production Constraints

In spite of great strides made, the productivity of horticultural crops, in general, is still quite low and the post harvest losses particularly of perishable commodities, are considerable. Improvement in quality standards of the produce and their marketing are essential to increase our share in the global market.

The research agenda in horticulture is by design relevant to national plans and priorities and research programmes are normally formulated keeping in view the thrust areas in development. The major technology related constraints contributing to low productivity of horticultural crops and inferior quality of produce are:

- Vast majority of holdings are small and un-irrigated.
- Large tracts of low and unproductive plantations needing replacement/rejuvenation.

- Low productivity of crops due to inferior genetic stocks and poor management.
- Inadequate supply of quality planting materials of improved varieties.
- High incidence of pests and diseases.
- Heavy post harvest losses and low utilization in processing sector.

For addressing the above constraints, research institutions are engaged in both basic and applied research. While formulating research strategies some of the inherent weaknesses associated with perennial tree crops and certain perpetual problems in Indian horticulture must be kept in mind. They are:

- Long period required for development of improved genotypes. Application of biotechnological tools/methods in horticultural crops is still in its early stage of development in the country.
- Chronic production problems due to major disorders like alternate bearing, malformation and spongy tissue in mango, guava wilt, citrus decline, root wilt in coconut, viral disease in vegetables, *Phytophthora* diseases in large number of crops *etc*. remained largely unresolved.
- Lack of advanced technologies for post harvest handling, processing and marketing of produce.

Losses caused by biotic stresses are very high and due to pesticide residue problems development of eco-friendly IPM strategy is more relevant in horticulture. There is a threat for loss of valuable genetic resources, if measures are not taken for their conservation.

Wastelands and hilly terrains being the potential future expansion areas, matching technologies for dry land and hill horticulture need to be developed.

Counter seasonal advantages from diverse agro-climatic situations provide strength for extended availability of horticultural crops round the year and such potentials can be harnessed only with relevant research support.

RESEARCH STRATEGIES AND PROGRAMMES

Keeping in view of the strength and weaknesses of the research system and priority areas of horticulture development the following strategies and programmes are suggested for horticultural research:

Rationalization of Research

There is a need to shift from commodity/discipline oriented research to system based research and to establish stronger Inter-institutional linkages with SAUs, CSIR, DBT and BARC. Greater private sector partnership for diversification, value addition and export promotional research and seed production programmes will be required to modernize horticulture industry.

Introduction of project based budgeting in the Institutes/ NRCs will bring better accountability and one time catch up grant to modernize old Institutes will be essential.

Development of database on technologies evolved, market intelligence, export projections/removal of quantitative restrictions, R&D scenario in horticulture should receive priority attention.

Safeguard for Intellectual Property Rights (IPR)

A fool proof description of varieties and their registration and finalisation of material transfer agreement and channelization of germplasm exchange need to be institutionalized. Similarly, specification of quality/codex standard for export of indigenous fruits and vegetables need to be developed. Phytosanitary regulations for importing vegetatively propagated materials need a relook/revision and rigorous enforcement.

Genetic Resource Management

Greater emphasis need to be given on (a) *in situ* conservation of endangered species, *ex situ* conservation of base collections and *in vitro* storage and cryopreservation of important germplasm. Clonal repository of vegetatively propagated crops and germplasm screening for processing and diversified use will be certain other areas of priority research.

Horticultural Biotechnology

Biotechnology as a tool for rapid multiplication of quality planting material, virus cleaning, genetic transformation *etc.*, will be of very great importance. The priority research programmes are:

- Development of micropropagation protocols in selected crops
- Genetic engineering for integration of desirable traits
- Molecular characterization of germplasm and development of molecular linkage maps
- Value addition to products
- Preservation of post harvest losses through control of metabolic process

Integrated Production System

Production related technologies can bring quick improvement in production and productivity on different regions.

Short or medium range programme on horticulture based cropping systems; water management including microirrigation and fertigation, greenhouse cultivation of vegetables and flowers, integrated nutrient and pest managements, environment pollution and pesticide residue problems have already received research attention.

Further refinement of the technologies and their transfer will bring perceptible change/improvement in production of different crop commodities.

Export Promotional Research

There is a need for development of bulk handling system of tropical fruits, including pre-cooling and CA/MA storage and post harvest protocols for sea transport of major fruits like banana, mango, litchi, sapota, Kinnow and pomegranate.

Disinfestation technology including vapour heat treatment (VHT) for export of fresh fruits and extension of shelf life by preventing desiccation of vegetables should help in further export promotion.

Organic farming for vegetable and spice crops and residue free IPM technology are other important areas of research.

Quality Planting Material Production

For resolving the long standing problems of supply of good quality planting materials of different horticultural crops, following research areas are flagged:

- System of certification and standardisation of planting materials;
- Micropropagation protocols for mango, litchi, coconut, walnut, date palm, oil palm and apple rootstocks;
- Refinement of TPS and micro-tuber production technology in potato;
- Improvement in STG techniques and cross-protection in citrus for virus elimination and control; and
- Seed production system for hybrid vegetables and commercialization of micropropagation in floriculture.

Post Harvest Management

In order to reduce post harvest losses at production centres low cost ecofriendly on-farm storage structures can play a crucial role. Significant advancement has been made in that direction and some small and medium sized cool chambers on the principles of evaporative cooling have been devised. Further refinement of the technology will go on a long way. Also, standardisation of packing line operations and proper packaging of different commodities are of urgent need. Pesticide residue management and newer product developments will add values to the produce.

Human Resource Development

Advanced training in research methodologies and instrumentation, biotechnology, micro-irrigation, fertigation, IPM, INM, biofertilizer, biopesticide, pesticide residue, PHT and product development need priority attention for increasing research capabilities of the scientists.

Skill development for state level development functionaries through in-service training at different R&D institutions will enhance capabilities of extension staff. Post Graduate programmes in fruit, vegetable, floriculture, plantation crops and post harvest management of horticultural crops will help in providing trained manpower in specialized areas.

Technology adoption pattern can not bc uniform throughout the country and will vary from crop to crop and even from region to region. Certain degree of flexibility in research planning and research strategy is therefore obvious. Also, with the opening of global markets and removal of quantitative restrictions under the WTO export-import scenario is likely to change at much faster pace.

Market forces will play a more dominant role and demands for modern technologies will increase. Research system in horticulture will have to be very alert and should be able to adjust with the changes. Development of both short term and long term strategies for modernising Indian horticulture will depend largely on the research support and strength of research system.

Bibliography

Angel, Bradley: *Toxic Threat to Indian Lands: A Greenpeace Report*, San Francisco, Greenpeace, 1991.

Barnum, Susan R.: *Biotechnology: An Introduction*, Belmont, Thomson/Brooks/Cole, 2005.

Burch, William R. Jr.: *Human Ecology: An Environmental Approach*, Belmont, Duxbury Press, 1994.

Campbell, R. R., and Wade, J. L.: *Society and Environment: The Coming Collision*, Boston, Allyn and Bacon, 1972.

Chrispeels, Maarten : *Plants, Genes and Crop Biotechnology*, Sudbury MA, Jones and Barlett Publishers, 2003.

Cox, Earl D. : *Beyond Humanity: Cyber Evolution and Future Minds*, Roackland, Charles River Media, 1996.

Daubenmire, R. F.: *Plants and Environment*, New York, Wiley, 1947.

Dixon, Dougal: *After Man-A Zoology of the Future*, New York, St. Martin's Press, 1981.

Dodds, John H.: *Plant Genetic Engineering*, New York, Cambridge University Press, 1985.

Edwards-Rees, D.: *The Service of Youth Book*, Wallington, Religious Education Press, 1943.

Erickson, Kai: *A New Species of Trouble: Explorations in Disaster, Trauma, and Community*, New York, W.W. Norton, 1994.

Gelobter, Michael: *The Distribution of Air Pollution by Income and Race*, Berkeley, University of California, 1989.

Gitman, Lawrence J.: *Principles of Managerial Finance*, MA: Addison Wesley Longman, 2000.

Johnson, Hazel: *Financial Institutions and Markets: A Global Perspective*, NY, McGraw Hill, 1993.

King, R.B., Mihony, G., and Sheldon, J.K.: *Practical Environmental Bioremediation*, Lewis Publishers, Boca Raton, 1992.

Kruvant, W.J.: *People, Energy, and Pollution*, Cambridge, Ballinger Publishing, 1975.

Martin, Justin: *The Man Behind Money*, Perseus Book Group, 2000.

Matthews, J. E.: *Working with Youth Groups*, London, University of London Press, 1966.

Milson, F.: *Growing With the Job*, London, National Assocation of Youth Clubs, 1968.

Murray, David: *Seeds of Concern: The Genetic Manipulation of Plants*, Sydney, University of New South Wales, 2003.

Petty, Keown, Scott, and Martin: *Basic Financial Management*, Prentice Hall, 1993.

Primrose, S.B.: *Principles of Gene Manipulation*, London, Blackwell Scientific Publications, 1989.

Retzer, W.J.: *Biotechnology Workbook*, Englewood Cliffs, Prentice Hall, 1991.

Schall and Haley: *Introduction to Financial Management*, McGraw-hill, 1988.

Shetty, Kalidas: *Food Biotechnology*, New York, Dekker/CRC Press, 2005.

Sontheimer, Sally: *Women and the Environment: Crisis and Development in the Third World*, New York, Monthly Review Press, 1991.

Vallette, J.: *The International Trade in Wastes: A Greenpeace Inventory*, Washington, Greenpeace, 1989.

Walden, Richard: *Genetic Transformation in Plants*, England, Open University Press, 1988.

Zupan, J.M.: *The Distribution of Air Quality in the New York Region*, Baltimore, Johns Hopkins University Press, 1973.

Index